Failing the future

A Dean Looks at Higher Education

in the Twenty-first Century

ANNETTE KOLODNY

Duke University Press   Durham and London 1998

©1998 Duke University Press
All rights reserved
Printed in the United States of America on acid-free paper ⊗
Typeset by Tseng Information Systems, Inc.
Library of Congress Cataloging-in-Publication Data
appear on the last printed page of this book.

With the exception of those identified by name, throughout
this book persons referred to as members of the University
of Arizona community have been substantially altered in
identity or redrawn as composites so as to protect the
privacy of individuals.

Sections of several chapters originally appeared in the
following:

"Colleges Must Recognize Students' Cognitive Styles and
Cultural Backgrounds," *Chronicle of Higher Education,*
6 February 1991, A44.

"Creating the 'Family-Friendly Campus,'" *The Family Track:
Keeping Your Faculties While You Mentor, Nurture, Teach,
and Serve,* ed. Constance Coiner and Diana Hume George
(Champaign: University of Illinois Press, 1998).

"Paying the Price of Antifeminist Intellectual Harassment,"
Antifeminism in the Academy, ed. Veve Clark, Shirley
Nelson Garner, Margaret Higonnet, and Ketu H. Katrak
(New York and London: Routledge, 1996), pp. 3–33.

"Raising Standards While Lowering Anxieties: Rethinking
the Promotion and Tenure Process," *Concerns* 23, no. 2
(Spring 1993): 16–40.

"Setting an Agenda for Change: Meeting the Challenges and
Exploring the Opportunities in Higher Education,"
Transformations 4, no. 2 (Fall 1993): 5–30.

"'60 Minutes' at the University of Arizona: The Polemic
against Tenure," *New Literary History* 27, no. 4 (Autumn
1996): 679–704.

"Why Feminists Need Tenure: Combatting the Right's
Agenda," *Women's Review of Books* 13, no. 5 (February
1996): 23–24.

With gratitude and affection, this book
is dedicated to my graduate students,
who keep teaching me new tricks.

For us, the hope of intellectual independence is to resist, and the necessary first step in resistance is to discover how the institutional grip is laid upon our mind. -Mary Douglas, *How Institutions Think* (Syracuse, N.Y.: Syracuse University Press, 1986), p. 92.

Contents

Acknowledgments

As this project moved from handwritten journal entries, scattered articles, and miscellaneous notes, I incurred many debts of gratitude. A number of friends and colleagues listened with patience as I groped for clarity, recommending useful readings to help me along; others read early drafts of several chapters, offering helpful advice and raising pertinent questions. It is a pleasure to thank Cathy Davidson, Bonnie M. Davis, Alex Dunkel, Gary Fenstermacher, Rita R. Foy, Elissa Gelfand, Anne Hutchins-Tatum, Fred Kiefer, Susan Koppelman, Barbara Kosta, Lola Mapes, Naomi Miller, Angie Moreno, Debra Olson, Robert Pack, Susan Pack, Virginia Richardson, Roland Richter, Jeffrey Rivkind, Sheila Slaughter, Karen L. Smith, Linda Stapleton, Charles Tatum, John Taylor, Emily Toth, Tilly Warnock, and Amy Williamsen.

At an early stage of composition, the chapter on cognitive diversity benefited from review, comments, and materials provided by Richard D. Hallick, Christopher G. Johnson, and Mary Wildner-Bassett. Dennis Evans researched materials that went into a first draft of the chapter on setting an agenda for change. Keith Lehrer shared the audio cassette of his interview with Lesley Stahl and thus enabled me to compose the chapter on CBS's "60 Minutes" at the University of Arizona and the public debate over tenure; he was also warmly generous in reviewing the developing essay at different stages.

The chapter on antifeminist intellectual harassment owes a special debt to the women who shared their stories, allowed me to use those stories, but preferred anonymity. The chapter could not have been written, however, without the kindness and cooperation of Jean Jew and Jane Schaberg, who exhibited extraordinary courage and dignity in terrifying situations.

Some of my first published articles on professional issues—articles that later became the basis of several chapters—were strengthened by the research and editing skills of my former graduate research assistants, Julia Balén and Ruthe Thompson. Their unflagging intelligence, care, and good humor turned that early work into pleasure.

As an unwieldy manuscript began to take shape as a book, Ellen Messer-Davidow went beyond friendship in helping me to focus and clarify, even when it meant putting aside her own book project. Gently but firmly, she identified awkward sentences and encouraged my candor.

The final manuscript was prepared for publication by my graduate research assistant, Chadwick Allen, who also helped me finish the research and who offered acute editorial suggestions for every chapter. In the process of working with me for over two years on this book, Chad became both colleague and friend. He was never less than an honest critic and an insightful reader.

It was a joy to work with the talented and supportive team put together by Duke University Press. I owe particular thanks to Paul Betz, the freelance copyeditor hired for this assignment, for his gentle ministrations to the manuscript; to Jean Brady for smoothly managing a tight production schedule; to Mary Mendell for letting down the drawbridge and, most of all, for her exquisite sense of style; to Emily Young for her enthusiasm and her creative approach to marketing; and, finally, to my editor, Reynolds Smith, for his encouragement, his sustaining faith in this project, and his many excellent suggestions for improving the manuscript.

My most profound debt of gratitude, as always, is to my husband, Daniel Peters. The effort to complete this book coincided with a prolonged period during which my rheumatoid arthritis worsened daily, leaving me increasingly fatigued, weak, and crippled. Few relationships survive the ongoing strain of one partner's demanding dependency and the other's unending caretaking. But through it all, Dan kept us both going, no matter what burdens he had to shoulder. With his irreverent sense of humor and unfailing gentleness, he made me believe that he wanted only two things: to watch me get better and to keep loving me. His love has proven my most trustworthy medicine.

A Personal Preface: Reflections on
Five Years in a Dean's Office

"I made some studies, and reality is the leading cause
of stress amongst those in touch with it."
—Spoken by the character "Crazy Trudy," in Jane Wagner's
The Search for Signs of Intelligent Life.

i.

In the summer of 1988, I left my position as professor of literature at Rensselaer Polytechnic Institute in Troy, New York, to become dean of the College of Humanities at the University of Arizona in Tucson. With that transition, I became responsible for the smooth functioning of seven departments, five programs, and two research centers. I oversaw an annual state-funded permanent budget of $13 million and directly dispersed another $4–$5 million, allocated to me yearly by the provost and senior vice president for academic affairs, to cover everything from the stipends for graduate student teaching assistants to the purchase of computers for the dean's office. With just under 200 full-time faculty attempting to serve the needs of the 22,000 students (both graduate and undergraduate) who enrolled each semester in humanities courses, the money was always tight. I was constantly juggling dollars—while begging for more. In addition to endless committee meetings and monthly deans' council marathons, two or three times each month, I met for an hour with the provost and senior vice president for academic affairs, the administrator to whom I reported and at whose pleasure I continued in my post as dean. The person who held that position changed repeatedly, however, so that in five years as dean I reported to five different acting, interim, or permanent provosts in succession.

Meanwhile, I had no time for scholarship or research beyond stolen hours on an occasional weekend, and books and articles that I wanted to read simply collected dust in the growing piles on my study floor.

Even more troubling, I never had time to teach a course of my own, settling instead for a year of team-teaching an experimental undergraduate course and offering invited guest lectures or guest seminars in other people's classes. Friends and colleagues who knew how deeply I loved teaching and research often asked, with avid curiosity, whether I liked the move to administration. During my first year as dean, exhilarated by new challenges, I replied that I loved the job. By the end of my second year, I said I loved half the job and would happily chuck the rest. For the remainder of my five-year term, this continued to be my answer.

What had changed in those first two years was my growing alarm at the apparently intractable disjunction between the humanities faculty's sense of its educational mission and the view of the humanities disciplines among my fellow academic deans and within central administration. Gifted and talented humanities faculty members spoke of strengthening their majors with new courses and innovative curricula; they experimented with instructional technologies and taught them to the graduate students; and they developed cross- and interdisciplinary programs for both undergraduates and graduate students. For them, the humanities were vital and rigorous disciplines, the key to understanding the vast diversity of human culture over time and a tool for solving current social problems. For the scientists, engineers, and business people who controlled central administration, however, the humanities were what they had always been on this campus: a service unit, the place where engineering students were taught to compose grammatically correct sentences, the place where an international business major gained a smattering of some foreign language. Rarely did these colleagues in administration understand that classics, religious studies, English, and the like might be independent bodies of theory and knowledge, with valuable intellectual methods of their own to impart.

To be sure, the president and the provost who hired me had done so with the explicit understanding that the College of Humanities was now to take a more prominent role on campus and that, in order to accomplish this, the various humanities programs and departments needed to go through a process of both updating and upgrading. While other units on campus had benefited from years of internal and external investment, the humanities had been allowed to drift until, without adequate resources or institutional support, they had become stagnant. My job was to facilitate change. As I understood the task initially, I was to enhance the current faculty's ability to make significant contributions in teaching and research and to bring in new faculty, with fresh ideas and exciting research areas. This was the part of the job I loved. But as the first year stretched into the second, these activities occupied less than half my time.

By January 1989, the provost who had recruited me the previous April left to take up the presidency of another institution. Thus, after only six months in the dean's office, I lost my best mentor. By the end of my second year, burgeoning enrollments coincided with deep cuts in state funding so that the campus found itself running a deficit. The president who had hired me—a deeply cultured man, genuinely committed to the arts—was under pressure from the Board of Regents to resign. The humanities' turn had come—but too late. Given the financial realities and his own precarious political situation, even a supportive president was in no position to shield my college's budget from the ax.

The unending scramble to protect precious resources, the demands of an aggressive fundraising campaign, and the wearying efforts to justify the importance of the humanities to central administrators who only cared about the bottom line had now become more than half the job. It was the half I hated.

Although I still managed to fund the recruitment of new faculty, personally meeting all the finalist candidates who came to campus, and although I still met with a variety of faculty committees, in fact, I was becoming increasingly isolated from the company I most craved—my faculty colleagues. Despite my "open door" policy, most faculty saw me infrequently, and few had any idea of how I spent my time. Only rarely did I find a few free minutes to walk the halls and strike up easy conversations about books and students. Only seldom could I save an hour to sit in on a class or attend a colleague's public lecture. Instead, I was trapped in my office, mired in budget numbers, or trapped in administrative meetings called to deal with the latest threatened budget cut. When I socialized during the weekends, it was more often at fundraising events to cultivate potential donors than at dinners with faculty whose books I was hoping to read or whose archeological digs had intrigued me. Too often frantic with overwork, I missed shmoozing with friends about ideas; I missed the passionate give-and-take of a good intellectual argument.

I also missed the comfort of a job where the expectations were limited and clear. As a faculty member, I always understood how many courses I was to teach and what level of research and publication was required for advancement. I knew my obligations to mentor graduate students and to volunteer for service on university committees. But a dean, I found, is expected to be an "all purpose" administrator, performing a multitude of functions, meeting with all constituencies and responding to every individual, even with inadequate staff to support her. Faculty and administrators alike want her to continue to be visible as a distinguished scholar in her field, so that she can bring added prestige to the institution, and they want her to speak with knowledgeable authority on behalf of all of the disciplines in her college. Yet they also want her to be an accomplished administrator, articulating large visions while always on top of the smallest detail. What constitutes an accomplished administrator, however, is always in the eyes of the beholder. The faculty want a fighter who can protect their disciplinary interests, while central administration wants a team player who is sensitive to the needs of the campus as a whole. Faculty want a dean committed to collegial and shared decision-making. Central administration demands that the dean make tough independent decisions, even if that means countering faculty sentiment. Department heads want a dean who will provide all requested resources and then leave them alone to conduct department business as they see fit. Central administration wants a dean to ride herd on department heads, micromanaging them in the same manner that central administration is attempting to micromanage the dean. Donors are looking to back an articulate leader, but many of them also want to be consulted at every juncture or wooed with tickets to major athletic events. Undergraduates rightly complain that, except for ceremonial occasions like Honors Convocation or graduation, deans are invisible. Graduate students want the dean who is a distinguished scholar to teach their seminars and direct their Ph.D. dissertations. And everyone expects the dean to shape a vision for the college, especially when faculty, staff, and students are deeply divided over what that vision should encompass.

As creatures of the governors who appoint them (or, in some states, the voters who elect them), Boards of Regents shift priorities along with the prevailing political winds, and what they want in a dean changes accordingly. The board in place when I first arrived in Arizona—a board mostly appointed by proeducation Democratic governors—demanded a greater representation of women and minorities in administrative positions (pressure that surely influenced my own hiring and, four years later, the hiring of the first Hispanic to serve as president of an AAU Research-I university); and that board wanted deans to diversify the faculty and improve graduation rates for minority students. As that board was replaced by the appointees of an antieducation Republican governor, deans got the message that affirmative action programs were now suspect (see Healy A58). In league with the conservative members of the Board of Regents, fiscally conservative state legislators want deans who will keep faculty "in line" and increase their teaching but not their pay.

What seems to escape these regents and legislators is that, above all, faculty simply want a dean who gives them the resources to teach well and decent salaries that at least keep pace with inflation. By contrast, cost-conscious regents, conservative elected officials, and a financially strapped administration all want a dean who disburses as little money as possible.

Position announcements for senior academic administrators—from deans to presidents—often list "stamina" and "energy" as job requirements. They should also list the capacity to tolerate cognitive dissonance, that is, the capacity to live with simultaneous competing and mutually exclusive work demands. Each of them *urgent*.

Even during the best of times, a dean's job is fraught with conflict and contradictions. But during periods of crisis and financial uncertainty, the dean's job becomes impossible. The fact is, as the budget crunch got worse, I found myself disappointing every constituency and every individual. It was often a tightrope act to keep a significant donor on board when some pet project of his had to be set aside for more pressing priorities. In a college deeply committed to affirmative action—an atmosphere that I had worked hard to encourage—it was painful to limit the number of minority scholarships when so many students were deserving. And in a society bred on rising expectations, it was difficult to explain to faculty and staff why this would be another year without raises. To this day, I remember the palpable hurt and anger of a new acting department head who felt I hadn't given her a sufficient raise for taking on administrative duties. In fact, compared to other faculty, she was already earning well above rank; and she had no interest in hearing about the other desperate priorities that I had traded away in order to get the provost to approve her salary increase in a year when there were none for anyone else. Her friendship and her support both cooled. In ways I never anticipated, in the half of the job I was coming to detest, the professional had turned personal. To my dismay, I learned how easily academic culture divides into the "us" and "them" of faculty and administration.

ii.

So why did I go into administration? To begin with, I had become impatient with feminist studies of academe that cataloged unfair promotion and tenure practices or that analyzed how university decision-making structures continued to marginalize female and minority staff and faculty. Too often these analyses settled for the conclusion that, because power structures in the university are always contingent and provisional, they are available to change. "The way things always were," in other words, did not mean the ways things had to be in the future. Unfortunately, the potentially liberating insight of such studies seemed to me muted by the lack of concrete plans of action. Feminist academics were very smart about identifying problems, but we seemed less eager to take on the positions of power within academe that might allow us to solve those problems. In consequence, our repeated assertion of the proposition that change is both needed and possible had done little to alter the status quo. As one of those feminist academics I have just described, I felt vaguely like a hypocrite.

I also went into administration because I was losing confidence in the people willing to take on these jobs. With prominent exceptions, too many academic administrators see administration as a career ladder, and their eyes are always focused on the next rung up. This leaves some career administrators wary of creativity and shy of experimentation. Any rocking of the boat might jeopardize the next promotion. Even in a period of massive transitions in academe, rather than seeing themselves as change agents, hesitant administrators try to contain change by settling for incremental alterations and minute accommodations. Quick fixes and Band-Aids. Divorced from their prior research and teaching commitments, academic administrators are often incapable of explaining to governing boards or to the general public just what it is that faculty do—and why it's important. As a result, in the face of legislative funding cuts or calls to close academic programs, too many administrators either capitulate quietly or respond with a muddied defensiveness. Indeed, I have yet to come across any senior administrator willing to go public with the fact that quality education costs money and that anything less than the highest quality education —especially in these globally competitive times—is money wasted.

With characteristic *chutzpah*, I was sure I could do better.

I especially wanted to do better at what most administrators have nervously termed "managing diversity." As Arthur E. Levine, president of Teachers College at Columbia University, has revealed, "When talked with confidentially and asked candidly what they would like to see happen with the issue, most senior administrators use the same language. They would like to see it go away" (Levine 337). But since my own entry into the professoriate almost thirty years ago represented part of the diversification process—women professors having been few and far between during my college years—I have never been inclined to see the inevitable demographic shifts in the faculty and student body as a problem. Instead, I entered academic administration with a pragmatic agenda. Given the fact that "new entrants to the labor force [will] increasingly come from the ranks of minorities, immigrants, and women" (Callan 18), I saw an opportunity for defining at least one clear and pressing role for public universities: they needed to work with primary and secondary schools on developing innovative programs that could ensure this cohort's eventual entry into higher education. After all, as a 1987 Hudson Institute report made clear, "the capacity of states to compete for high-wage industries and jobs depend[s] in no small part on the skill and competence of these emerging workers" (Callan 18). If only for self-serving economic interests, therefore, states will need to fund the programs that can educate the new workers of the twenty-first century.

Especially in a state like Arizona—with its large Native American and Mexican American populations and its continuing immigration from Mexico and Latin America—this was an argument I was eager to make.

Because the academic dean functions at the juncture where faculty and student needs, aggregated into programs and departments, intersect with collective transinstitutional imperatives like resource allocation and public relations, that position struck me as the critical administrative point at which meaningful change might be effected. So I accepted a deanship at a large research university where both faculty and central administration claimed they wanted substantive change (even if they did not entirely agree on what needed to be changed or how). In facilitating that stated desire for change, I hoped to test my hypothesis that, once given a position of recognized decision-making authority, a feminist committed to both equity and educational excellence could prove an instrument for progressive evolution.

I made myself comfortable with what appeared to be a sudden career swerve by announcing, soon after the job had been offered, that I intended to remain a dean for only a single five-year term (which I did). Because I had never before been an administrator—not even a department chair—and because I had no aspirations to remain an administrator, I hoped I might function with greater boldness and creativity than career administrators who trimmed their sails to the safest course. My lack of prior administrative experience, I hoped, would push me to rely on the considerable expertise of a seasoned and hardworking staff; and it would, as well, I hoped, prompt me to work collaboratively with faculty, just as I had done when I was one of them. Collaborative relationships with faculty and staff might even help me to experiment with innovative problem-solving mechanisms.

I was, of course, extremely naive as I went into the job. None of my four campus visits and the many meetings with students, staff, faculty, and other administrators had prepared me for the severity of the looming budget crisis. I never anticipated the killing hours that my activist agenda would require of me. And I significantly overestimated the capacity for change in a college that, for too long, had practiced the strategies of complaint and resistance. After years of underfunding and neglect from central administration, most humanities faculty members were distrustful of any administrator, while ancient personality clashes within some departments had festered into ongoing feuds and hardened factions. Even if I was naive, however, entries from my personal journal, composed during the on-campus interviews, indicate that I was not wholly ignorant of what lay ahead.

iii.

Room 23, The Lodge on the Desert,
Tucson, Arizona
11 P.M., February –, 1988

I am being interviewed for a job that can't be done. This is my second visit to the campus, and the search committee has made it clear that I'm their top candidate. The provost is even more straightforward: "What do we need to do to get you here?" I like him enormously. But, as I see it, the job just isn't doable. The Board of Regents is putting pressure on the three state universities to hire more women and minorities on the faculty and in the administration. I'm sure that's part of the reason they pursued me so eagerly at the outset, and it certainly creates a helpful atmosphere in which to develop affirmative action strategies. But the very fact that there are so few senior women on the faculty, and even fewer minority members across the faculty ranks; and the fact that, given the culturally diverse population of Arizona, women and minorities are so few in number within the administration suggests there's solid resistance, not just inaction.

Do I really want to take on this battle? Because it will be a battle. The president says all the right things to me about affirmative action—he's determined to see the school's statistics change in that area—but the policies aren't in place to make it happen.

The killer, though, is going to be the budget. Since I'm still only a candidate, very little budget data has been shared with me. But this much is clear: the College of Humanities has been chronically underfunded, meaning it would take a huge commitment of resources to alleviate the growing problem of salary compression[1] and hire the requisite number of new faculty needed to accommodate what looks like a 35 percent increase in student enrollments—with even greater student numbers predicted for the future. The Humanities are housed in old-fashioned, poorly designed buildings, with insufficient office space and just the scant beginning of a modern language learning laboratory, with interactive computers. Two and three faculty members share offices sized for a single occupant, and the new language laboratory can handle only a fraction of the students enrolled in the introductory foreign languages courses. So it's clear they need to renovate the present building and probably build a new one, as well. But I'm already told that state revenue bonding will take years—and no one has ever considered putting the Humanities on the capital plan for any kind of new facilities. At one of my meetings with a group of faculty, someone complained that there isn't even chalk in the classrooms. Several of his colleagues concurred. These people are angry.

I'm picking up a lot of anger and suspicion. Faculty in the smaller-sized departments feel that the huge English Department has received the lion's share of the resources, to the detriment of the smaller units, and there's fear that, as an American literature specialist, I'll continue to favor that department as dean. The English Department, in turn, has been burdened with the sole responsibility for all composition instruction, but its funding levels for graduate teaching assistants have remained inadequate, even in the face of increasing freshman enrollments. As a result, their underpaid graduate students burn out from a two-thirds-time teaching load and don't complete their degrees. Someone whispered that the attrition rate among the Ph.D. candidates is 99 percent in some years.

I checked the enrollment figures and discovered what look like gross disparities between departments. In some units, all faculty teach two courses each semester, regardless of the numbers of students enrolled. In other departments, faculty teach three or even four courses in a semester, some heavily enrolled. And none of this appears to correlate to research activity or to publication productivity. At first glance, it looks like these patterns developed over many years and then just calcified. I don't think differences in fields or disciplinary distinctions explain all the disparities.

Then there's the faculty. What they really want is a dean who can bring in substantial new resources and walk on water. Make needed changes but offend no one. There are factions, deep divisions, animosities that surface briefly in every open meeting—but nothing I can really define or get a handle on.

But what keeps surprising me is how few people know anyone outside their own department or program. There seems to be no shared sense of participation in a larger College of Humanities; instead, I see only departmental loyalties and interdepartmental rivalries.

Something else divides this faculty: the period in which they were hired and the expectations that were set for them. Some came when only good teaching was required for tenure, and few of these individuals were given the incentive or the opportunity to develop any kind of research or publication agenda. They are tenured, most trapped in the associate rank; they know they will never be recruited by any other institution; they teach with continued devotion despite all, and volunteer for committees. But they are suffering from salary compression and know there's nothing they can do about it. They are not going to attract outside offers to use as bargaining levers for increasing their salaries here. And they are becoming frustrated and alienated. For them, the rules changed when the University of Arizona aspired to become an AAU Research-I institution. At that point, another kind of faculty member was sought: someone who both taught and published. The school wanted prestige beyond its championship basketball and football teams. But because the university's initial emphasis was on upgrading the sciences and professional schools, the publication requirements for this new group in the humanities were never strict. Some published energetically, others only enough to get tenure. In more recent years, as the University of Arizona's humanities graduate programs grew and the job opportunities in the humanities declined, a few senior, well-published "stars" were hired. And the departments were also able to attract junior faculty with promising research credentials from first-rate institutions. In addition to teaching well, new faculty were now expected to publish actively and win research fellowships from prestigious foundations. The stakes had been raised and, as a result, the newest junior hires have almost nothing in common with some of the most senior people in their departments, the very people who should be their mentors and who will, eventually, decide on these younger colleagues' tenure and promotion. The fissures between these very different groups of faculty do not bode well for building any sense of community here.

If I take this job, this is where I'll have to learn to walk on water. If

I aggressively go after outstanding women and minority faculty hires at prevailing market rates, some of them will come in as untenured assistant professors earning salaries comparable to tenured associate professors who have been here fifteen or twenty years. If I don't persuade central administration to provide me the salary levels necessary to compete, then affirmative action hiring is a dead issue. But, at the same time, if I don't get equity money for those suffering from salary compression, then the new hires are going to come into an environment of resentment and jealousy. Salaries here are public information—and lots of angry faculty will examine the big book at the front desk of the main library.

As I'm beginning to understand it now, the problem is this: it's really not a lot of faculty on any campus who, on principle or because of ingrained prejudice, oppose affirmative action hiring. But that minority can be vocal. The more dangerous group is that large mix of angry and alienated faculty who have no particular objection to affirmative action but who suffer year after year from salary compression and now watch some newly minted woman or minority Ph.D. come in at a salary near (or even higher) than the tenured associate professor's. The associate professor sees himself as exploited and unrewarded, despite his years of good teaching and active campus citizenship. And this same associate professor then finds himself falling in with those who oppose affirmative action, even if he doesn't agree with their arguments. It's a dangerous mix, and it's potentially volatile not because diversifying the faculty, by itself, causes problems. In fact, where it's begun, the personal relationships appear friendly. The situation is volatile because older underpaid faculty suspect that the higher salaries paid to women and minorities are coming at their expense. For this group of faculty, the manifest benefit of bringing to campus talented young teachers and scholars from divergent cultural and intellectual traditions is overshadowed by what now seems to them an issue of fairness in salary distribution. And if not addressed, this will be the unraveling of affirmative action.

I ask myself, Is this a battle I want to take on at the University of Arizona, where the central administration keeps making contradictory sounds about the Humanities? Yes, they want me to pursue affirmative action hiring policies—that's one of the reasons they're inter-

ested in me as a candidate for the deanship; they think I might actually get the job done. And yes, they also want to see the humanities departments and programs attain the stature and national visibility of some of the science programs. But resources are getting tighter, everyone tells me. I can't expect significant budgetary increases any time soon, even the provost warns.

Everybody wants everything, but nobody wants to pay for it. And the faculty are harboring impossible expectations for this new dean.

iv.

Room 25, The Lodge on the Desert,
Tucson, Arizona
10:30 P.M., March –, 1988

When I called home last night, I told Dan I wouldn't touch this job with a ten-foot pole. Tonight, however, I am tempted; and as I packed for the flight back to Albany a while ago, I admitted to myself that, impossible though the job is, I want to give it a try. Two things changed my mind. The director of the University of Arizona's well-established Women's Studies Program gave a dinner for me tonight at her home and invited not only faculty women but a few women from the community, as well. I liked them all, and their considerable numbers gave me the sense that I wouldn't be alone here. There seems to be a strong women's community, friends I could turn to, and they're all urging me to come. But what really changed my mind was the women's studies director's comment as I was leaving. I was telling her how demanding the job seemed, how many things needed to be done. "But you don't have to do them all at once," she replied. And suddenly it didn't seem quite so impossible.

v.

After only a few months as dean, one realization brought me up short: by joining the middle management of academic administration, I came to know the functioning of a large research university in a way that had never been available to me previously. Not even as a faculty member who served on myriad committees at a variety of institutions and not even as someone who had held elected executive positions in national professional and scholarly organizations. However engaged I was in campus life, as a faculty member I had had only a limited understanding of how any institution functioned, from its budget to its relationships with different political constituencies. What I realized with a shock as dean, in other words, was how abysmally ignorant most faculty—including myself—really are about the workplace in which they function.

The price we pay for such ignorance is the faculty's inability to respond effectively during periods of crisis. By not understanding how a public university is financed in any given state, faculty fail to grasp why there may be money to erect a new building but none for correcting salary compression.[2] By not knowing about the multiple and often conflicting constituencies that compete to shape the president's agenda, faculty are at a loss to assess accurately the rationale behind some new policy move or public speech. Such ignorance makes a sham out of the concept of shared governance, and it leaves faculty focusing their frustration on the dean, the provost, or the president as the closest cause for the problems they're suffering. Even more dangerous, such ignorance also leaves faculty views vulnerable to dismissal by governing boards and state legislators. In their eyes, faculty appear both uninformed and naive. As one member of a Board of Regents in the southwest put it recently, "For some reason, the faculty hasn't quite got it. There are some tough times ahead" (Lamplot 8).

But the fact is, what the faculty lacks is not an apprehension that there are "tough times ahead." Budget cuts have wracked every campus in this country, and most of the professoriate is bracing for more to come. What faculty at most schools do not have is a comprehensive grasp of the budget details and the ways in which different kinds of monies are allocated on a campus. Without this kind of information and without clear signals about future financing possibilities, how are faculty—as this regent asks—to "work with the institutions to come up with additional budget-cutting ideas" (Lamplot 8)? Given the predictions of substantially increased student enrollments in the next decade, perhaps the more apt question might be how faculty can work with administrators, university development officers, and governing boards to secure the funding needed to sustain quality education into the next century. Unfortunately, the kind of cooperation implied by the second question is one in which most of the professoriate cannot yet meaningfully engage, however much they may want to.

During my years as dean, the situation began to reach a crisis point for faculty as legislative calls for disciplining university budgets targeted faculty salaries and tenure protections. The increasing costs of college and university tuition since the 1980s were attributed to rising faculty salaries in the popular press; and, in a wild leap of logic, some called for limiting tenured positions as a response. But as I learned from scrutinizing the salaries of faculty in the College of Humanities at the University of Arizona and at other peer institutions, faculty salary averages had not even kept pace with inflation. The more important sources of rising costs were the institution's investments in improving educational quality, equipping state-of-the-art computer laboratories for undergraduates, and purchasing new technologies to make the library user-friendly. As the student body became more diverse, a new range of student support services was required, and this too cost money. Retrofitting old buildings to make them handicapped-accessible—mandated both by the Americans with Disabilities Act and by schools' genuine commitments in this area—drained capital improvement budgets. And the desire to ensure access for talented low-income students proved increasingly expensive as federal supports dwindled while the student need for financial aid increased. To make up the difference, most colleges and universities reached deep into their own pockets. All these—and not overblown faculty salaries —accounted for the escalating costs of a college education, I learned. But most faculty in the College of Humanities—like me a year earlier —did not possess sufficient information to make those arguments.

Shaken by the recognition of what had been my own level of ignorance, in the dean's office I found myself eager to share every bit of information with faculty, department heads, program directors, and staff. I wanted them to become informed and active partners with me in devising budget strategy and determining policy. My openness cost me the resignation of one of my associate deans, who resisted the inclusion of support staff in policy and personnel discussions and warned against sharing confidential material with secretaries. His leaving was a real loss to the office, but I stubbornly persisted. I used dean's office staff meetings for information-sharing and strategy sessions; I briefed department heads and program directors on all agenda items from deans' council meetings; and I developed a large, inclusive faculty advisory group charged with making recommendations on everything from faculty workload policy to promotion and tenure procedures to budget allocations. All groups also met with one another and with the rest of the faculty, my aim being to involve everyone in collective problem-solving.

In every instance, I distributed all the information and hard data that were available to me, and I discovered, in turn, that I received equivalently useful information from those with whom I was meeting. Everyone—staff and faculty alike—had their own unique observations and thoughtful analyses. Together, as we pooled resources and data, we defined problems more clearly, and solutions emerged that had both logic and persuasiveness.

When I complained to a staff member one day that I missed the classroom, she replied that I was still a teacher. "You're using the dean's office as your classroom now," she continued, "and you're teaching everyone how the university runs." I was deeply comforted by her analogy, and it has remained with me, prompting me nowadays to plead—wherever I have a public forum—for the restructuring of graduate education. As institutions of higher learning experiment with new forms of organization, governance, budgeting, and decision-making, it is incumbent on us to prepare the next generation of professors for meaningful participation in those changes. We simply cannot continue training prospective faculty for their roles as teachers and researchers while altogether ignoring their responsibilities as citizens in a profession. The literature Ph.D. whom we train today will not simply spend her professional life sitting in a library and teaching small classes of freshman composition students. Even in graduate school, we need to provide advanced Ph.D. candidates with data and with an informed understanding of national educational issues. Only then can we empower faculty to silence those who would like to continue claiming, "For some reason, the faculty hasn't quite got it" (Lamplot 8).

vi.

The memory that most vividly persists from my five years as dean is of recalculating the budget figures, yet again, to accommodate still another 3 percent cut in state funding. In addition to the state cuts, in some years there were newly discovered deficits in other areas of the university's finances, thus leaving central administration desperate to figure out how much money we actually had to work with. At the worst interval, the college deans had to feverishly recalculate our operating budgets halfway into the academic year, wondering in December if we could meet our spring semester instructional obligations. Whatever the calendar for cuts, however, the deans were called upon to provide endless budget projections to cover endless eventualities. Consolidation, internal reallocation, and returning money to a nervous central administration—always under impossible deadlines—became the order of the day. Semester after semester, year after year.

What no one ever even attempted to quantify in this process was the enormous waste of human time and energy. In some semesters, fully half of my associate dean's activity was given over to preparing budget recommendations. Joining the associate dean in that effort were the department heads, program directors, and various faculty oversight committees. And because the numbers provided by central administration never coincided with our own, an already overburdened support staff—in the departments and within the dean's office—worked overtime to assemble the requisite data or double-check the latest enrollment figures. For months at a time, in consequence, everything else that was important to us—curriculum renewal, designing mentorship programs for undergraduate and graduate students, recruiting new faculty—got put on hold. For me, with an energetic agenda that I kept refusing to abandon, the university's chronic budget difficulties played out like agonizing bouts of paralysis.

By my third year as dean, I understood why large public universities seemed so stodgy, so resistant to change. It wasn't ossified bureaucracies, administrative ineptitude, or faculty sloth—as legislators and media so often charged. Rather, it was the endless preoccupation with one budget crisis after another that was threatening my own college's ability to direct our attention to the goals we had set for ourselves. Repeatedly, the faculty advisory committee charged with developing policy on faculty workloads had to divert its attention to a review of complicated budget proposals. Faculty preparing to train graduate students in the latest technologies for computer-assisted instruction found themselves without the promised equipment when the university suddenly froze capital purchases. Support staff who had volunteered significant energy and creativity to reconfiguring office assignments so that departments and the dean's office might work more efficiently together were stopped dead in their tracks when central administration announced a moratorium on filling vacant secretarial lines.

Ironically, many of the activities thwarted by these repeated budget crises were designed to pare costs and consolidate assignments. The College of Humanities' efforts to reconfigure job descriptions and develop better teamwork represented current investments of time for the sake of long-term permanent future savings in personnel and equipment. But the crisis management demanded by midyear state rescissions and local budget deficits made this kind of reasoned planning impossible.

What frustrated me most, however, was the duplicity of it all. Predictably, the provost would demand that cuts be made in such a way as "to protect academic quality," or some similar wording. Even in the face of constantly rising enrollments, the president and the provost were quick to reassure the public that the university would absorb year after year of substantial funding cuts without jeopardizing the quality of education. The assurances were patently absurd, of course, and they were especially absurd in the College of Humanities, a unit with a long history of inadequate funding. When departments could not even purchase annual service contracts for antiquated copiers, and when part-time student workers were being employed to replace full-time secretaries whom we could no longer afford, the only place left to make cuts was the instructional budget. Class sizes increased, and faculty began to burn out from the overload.

My frustration finally erupted in two recurring bad dreams. In one, I am reminding the provost that we have renegotiated the contracts of the graduate teaching assistants from two-thirds-time to half-time or twenty hours per week. If we now add twelve more students to each freshman composition section, as he is demanding, then the graduate teaching assistants, who teach two sections each semester, will have their workload increased by a third or more. They will no longer be able to prepare and teach their courses, grade the weekly papers, and hold sufficient office hours all within twenty hours. And if, in order to compensate for the higher numbers of students, we substantially reduce the number and complexity of writing assignments in freshman composition courses, then we vitiate the very purpose of those courses. But the provost doesn't want to hear any of this. He orders me to cut the graduate programs, increase enrollments in freshman composition, and *make* the numbers "add up."

In the second bad dream, I am meeting with yet another provost, boasting to him of the success of one of our larger departments which has worked for two years to completely redesign its graduate program in order to shift more tenure-track faculty into woefully understaffed undergraduate courses. As a reward for the department's considerable efforts—which will require some faculty to retool and others to develop new undergraduate curriculum—I am petitioning the provost for an exemption from the current hiring freeze so that the department can search for the linguistics specialist it so desperately needs. I argue that the department in question has several funded vacant faculty lines and, in any case, the savings in instructional monies combined with the increased undergraduate enrollments to be realized from the curricular overhaul will more than pay for the new assistant professor position. And I want to reward the department, by some concrete gesture, for its good work. But this provost never offers incentives or rewards. A firm believer in the threat of dire consequences when faculty won't toe the line, he replies only that "they shoulda done it years ago." No matter how hard I try, I can't seem to make him understand the *human* toll that change exacts and the need for positive institutional response.

What makes these bad dreams unique is that there was no relief upon waking. For almost five years, I made these and similar arguments to one provost after another, week after week, semester after semester. What I was asking for was breathing space. For a limited time, I pleaded, the College of Humanities needed to be buffered from the constant budget crises in order to take stock, set a reasonable agenda for itself, and begin the process of planning for change. Given this buffer, there would be savings and consolidations, I promised.

There would also be pedagogical and curricular innovations that would attract national notice. And most important of all, our students would benefit.

To some degree, I got the buffer in the form of modest additional monies, new faculty lines, the Board of Regents' commitment to a new building for the humanities, and approval of two new interdisciplinary graduate programs. I also managed to reduce graduate teaching assistants from two-thirds to half-time appointments while substantially increasing their salaries; and I worked to equalize teaching assignments across the college, so that no department bore a substantially heavier workload than any other. But the means by which I accomplished all this ran counter to everything I believed in.

In accepting the deanship, I had tried to model a management style based on cooperation, consultation, and team-building. It was a mode of shared community that I was also asking of support staff, faculty, department heads, and program directors. But in my dealings with central administration, it was a mode I practiced at my peril. When I went to the tower—where central administration is housed—in order to represent the College of Humanities, I became territorial, entrepreneurial, even selfish. The fact that the other academic deans were doing the same thing—some even boasted of their strategies to me— proved no consolation. I knew this was no way to run a university. Still, in the face of central administration mechanisms that militated against teamwork, I felt I had no choice.

After all, where precious dollars were at stake, my chronically underfunded units could not afford to absorb even the smallest cuts. However difficult the situation might be elsewhere on campus, I protested, our student credit hour costs were the lowest; we were more cost effective than any of our counterparts at peer institutions; our majors enrollments alone had grown by 35 percent in a four-year period, and yet our faculty numbers remained constant. Humanities faculty were teaching more students, but faculty salaries had not kept pace with national averages. Quickly, the dean's office became expert at amassing these data and organizing them into charts and tables that graphically demonstrated our desperate poverty.

I had always been tenacious, but now it became an art. I never accepted "no" for an answer but, instead, converted any provostial re-sistance into a challenge to find a better argument. Soon enough, I learned not to permit the conversation even to get to "no." When I sur-mised that things weren't going my way, I withdrew the agenda item and suggested to the provost that we both sleep on it and "give it some more thought." Then I would raise the subject again, in some other context, when no decision was at stake. And I'd take careful note of how the provost analyzed the matter, in hopes of reframing my future arguments to suit his.

If logic and hard data failed me and I thought it would help, I teased, I cajoled, I flirted, I pouted. I bought small gifts for one provost and always remembered the birthday of another. With a third provost, I learned the advantage of scheduling myself right after his meetings with a dean who had gone public with his objections to the provost's management style. After these heated encounters, I played a sooth-ing, supportive role. And the provost, hurt and wanting to be appre-ciated, usually gave me what I needed in return for my understand-ing of his difficult position. Still another provost noticeably softened when I slipped into the Yiddishisms of a long-forgotten Brooklyn in-flection that we both had once shared. Always, however, I scheduled my meetings with provosts and other senior administrators in the late afternoons, when my energy levels tend to peak while most others' are declining rapidly.

For the most part, of course, I relied on the numbers—the charts and tables—to secure budget increases and new faculty lines. The provosts I was dealing with were all scientists, after all, and neither Yiddish phrases nor soothing platitudes would substitute for hard data. Still, as I sometimes confided to my husband, the numbers and data weren't *all* I relied on. In the tower, meetings were not just a chess game of strategic moves, as one dean liked to describe his encounters with central administration. The success of my interactions with the vari-ous provosts under whom I served didn't result solely from my grasp of budget intricacies or from the tenacity on which I'd always prided myself. I had now added cunning and manipulation to my repertoire. And in this I took no pleasure.

vii.

Reflecting on my tenure as dean with the twenty-twenty vision of hindsight, I now realize that three factors made the years 1988 through 1993 more difficult than they should have been. To begin with, I was brought in to strengthen and modernize the College of Humanities after twenty years of intensive growth and improvement at the university, most of it concentrated in the sciences and in the professional schools. At the point at which the humanities were to have their turn, the university was enduring unprecedented budget cuts and ballooning enrollments. Resources were scarce, and they only got scarcer, while old habits of maintaining the science areas at all costs remained firmly entrenched. Central administration had few mechanisms for reallocating resources internally across the university, and there was no tradition of wealthier units contributing to the support of others. Thus, the inequalities in funding distribution patterns only became more glaring as state support diminished. Even with humanities undergraduate enrollments skyrocketing, those patterns remained intact. I was never able to undo them.

A second set of difficulties derived from the repeated changes of personnel in central administration. During my five years in the dean's office, I reported to five different interim, acting, or permanent provosts and to two presidents, none of whom shared any consistent vision of where the institution ought to be going, and few of whom communicated with their predecessors or successors. With the exception of the provost under whom I was first hired, a scholar trained in linguistics, each subsequent provost came from one or another of the sciences. As a result, with each new appointment, I was forced to begin again the slow, incremental process of educating a scientist about the humanities disciplines.

In terms of my administrative agenda, the third difficulty was the least significant, yet it turned out to be the most troubling on a personal level. A small group of faculty, at any time ranging in number from nine to fifteen, had opposed my appointment even before my arrival on campus. As one of them declared to my associate dean, "Whatever she's for, we're against. If she says the sky is blue, we'll say it isn't." None of the solid accomplishments of my deanship seemed to matter to this group—not the additional faculty lines in every department, not the increased wage scales and reduced work hours for graduate student teaching assistants, not the increased travel and research funding, and not even the Board of Regents' approval of a new building for the humanities. Despite the fact that all policies were developed by faculty committees, with plenty of input from everyone before being sent out for a full faculty vote, this group represented themselves as defenders of democratic rights in the face of an autocratic dean. They routinely called reporters at the *Chronicle of Higher Education* and planted stories in the right-wing press, accusing me of everything from social engineering in my emphasis on diversifying the faculty to "destroying Western civilization" in my support for interdisciplinary curricula.

Sensing I might be vulnerable with his departure, this group made its first overt move just three months after the provost who hired me left to become president of another university. A petition was circulated anonymously, asking faculty to call for an "Extraordinary Review" of the dean. Like the two petitions that followed in subsequent years, it was rejected by a vote of the faculty. Even so, the petition proved damaging: it fueled a great deal of local publicity as well as rumors that the acting provost might have to appoint a special committee to review my performance. As a result, I had to scale back my plans to develop a national advisory board for the College of Humanities, and I delayed launching a major fundraising drive that first year. This was no atmosphere in which to approach potential donors.

During my years as dean, I puzzled over this unremitting opposition but couldn't explain it. It wasn't simply political or ideological. Some in this group openly identified themselves as liberals, and others claimed to support affirmative action. My women friends saw misogyny in what was going on. Aside from the dean of the College of Nursing, they pointed out, I was the first and only female academic dean at the University of Arizona. Still, I always suspected something more. A different kind of woman, I was certain, might not have generated such vicious antagonisms. But I was a change agent—a *woman* change agent—and for some, that combination was intolerable.

The major change that I made was to democratize the decision-making process. Year by year, decision-making became increasingly inclusive and horizontal. I asked that all committees be gender-balanced, with significant participation from minority faculty and all three professorial ranks. But this group, I now suspect, had had its fill of change and found stasis more comfortable. Despite their dissatisfaction with salary compression and antiquated facilities, they were content with things as they were. Before I arrived, they ran committees, they controlled who got hired, and they determined what got taught. They were validated by what they had established. And now I had appeared, preceded by my reputation as a feminist scholar and activist. In their eyes, my attempts to introduce more inclusive decision-making meant the dismantling of old power alliances and threatened established ways of doing business.

Perhaps that explains the viciousness. In addition to putting up with the three unsuccessful petitions for extraordinary review, I received hate mail at home; and my ailing mother, at her retirement home in Florida, was anonymously mailed clippings of newspaper articles that criticized me. All the while, in national media, I confronted versions of myself that were almost unrecognizable, and I heard incredible rumors about myself circulated in the local community. Not even my dentist escaped the Tucson grapevine. One afternoon as he gingerly probed a cavity, he asked as casually as he could manage whether it was true that I was a radical feminist out to fire all the white male faculty in the College of Humanities. He said his golf partner had heard it from a friend who worked with someone at the university.

viii.

Finally, if I am to be wholly honest in this preface, I must explain why I stepped down after a single five-year term as dean. Recognizing that I would have to take on the role of a change agent and knowing that change agents have a limited time span in which they can operate effectively (after which a consolidator is required), I had accepted the position for only a single term at the outset. And I really did not want too long a break from my teaching and research. Even so, at the request of many faculty and department heads, as well as the urging of the chair of our National Advisory Board, I did seriously consider staying on a year or two longer, in order to provide continuity during yet another transition in central administration. But I finally decided against that course of action. I did so not because I was sick of battling the endless budget cuts, sick of the sheer thanklessness of the job, and sick of being pilloried in the right-wing press. The fact is, I had become *physically* sick, and I could no longer mask my growing disabilities.

When I was twenty and just out of college, I was diagnosed with rheumatoid arthritis, an autoimmune disease marked by inflammation and deterioration of the joints and soft tissues, usually accompanied by chronic pain, anemia, and severe fatigue. The disease afflicts about 3 percent of Americans, most of us women, and even with aggressive drug therapy, 7 percent of patients are disabled to some extent within five years of disease onset, while 50 percent are too disabled to work within ten years. Given the destructiveness of the disease, I understand why, in 1963, my doctors at Columbia Presbyterian Hospital in New York sternly warned me against pursuing a graduate degree at the University of California, Berkeley. The cold and damp of the Bay Area would further inflame my swollen joints, they said. The disease would leave me too tired for sustained research, and the stress of typing long papers would surely destroy my tender finger joints. But, as always, I was stubborn. I wanted to study American literature, and I wanted to teach in college. In short, I wanted to have a life, not merely a disease. Mercifully, through graduate school and most of my career, the rheumatoid arthritis remained intermittently active and occasionally disabling, but I suffered no loss of energy, little loss of movement, and pain that was generally tolerable. The progress of my disease was slow, punctuated by periodic remissions.

By the time I accepted the position of dean, however, the remissions had long stopped. In previous years, I had had to give up both tennis and cross-country skiing because my knee and hand joints became too weak. Even so, I thought of myself as healthy. My body showed no obvious signs of deformity, my energy levels remained exceptionally high, and the pain was still tolerable. I had long ago learned to block it out. I also meditated twice daily as a technique for both stress and pain management.

No one but my husband and a few close friends knew I had the disease, because over the years I perfected subterfuges for disguising it. Thus, when the provost who hired me announced that he scheduled his one-on-one meetings with the deans over 6:30 A.M. breakfasts, I was ready with a myriad of plausible excuses to beg off. What I never told him was that I required a 45-minute soak in a hot bathtub in order to massage stiff joints and get them moving. I had to swallow a variety of painkillers and anti-inflammatory drugs with breakfast, some of which brought on brief bouts of nausea. And even after the pills, it often took up to an hour for the pain to sufficiently abate, allowing me to concentrate and think clearly. But knowing none of this, like all the rest of my colleagues and coworkers throughout my career, the provost, too, good humoredly accepted my joking explanation that I simply wasn't a "morning person."

The long hours and stress of administration took its toll, however. In my third year, when I was no longer able to shake hands because even the slightest pressure on my fingers or wrist joint was intolerable, I began to tell people what was happening and to make public adjustments. In our yearly Honors Convocation, for example, I arranged for our guest speaker to shake the hands of undergraduate award recipients in my place. In my fourth year, my knees became noticeably weaker, and I began to experience swelling in my ankles for the first time. By my fifth and final year as dean, following a bout of Valley Fever (a fungal infection local to the desert southwest), the situation worsened considerably. I was tired too often and could no longer lift myself from a chair without lurching forward. The pain in my joints became more persistent. But the increasingly toxic drug regimens that I was now being offered by my doctors had such debilitating side effects—nausea, fever, dizziness—that I put off trying them until after I stepped down. I didn't want anything else to compromise my functioning.

With a kind of macabre irony, the worsening of my disease was being played out against the backdrop of multiple searches. The University of Arizona was looking for a new president and then a provost. At the same time, I was being wooed for a variety of provost and vice-president positions around the country. A recurrent theme in all these searches was "stamina." "If you only like to work fifty or sixty hours a week, don't go into administration," a fellow dean liked to joke whenever any kind of administrative search was in progress. "It takes eighty hours a week just to be a dean" was his punch line.

Reluctantly, I was coming to share those views. Simply maintaining the dean's office as I had inherited it would have been a full-time job by itself. But with my pro-active agenda, the job quickly expanded to long hours, seven days a week. In the code that my executive assistant and I developed together, a "reduced schedule" meant a week in which I didn't have job-related social events, like formal dinners or evening dinner meetings, scheduled every night. A "relaxing evening" was when the two of us remained after the office was closed at 5:30, grabbed a bite to eat at the student union, and then returned to the office for several more hours to polish off paperwork, free of the interruptions of phone calls and appointments.

After five years, with my disease markedly worsening during the last two, I had had enough. I needed time to regain my health. I wanted space to think and to contemplate—rare luxuries amid the constant crises of administration. And I wanted more time with my husband. At the farewell dinner "roast" held for me in the spring of 1993, I jokingly warned the wife of my successor that she was about to give up sex. In my experience, it wasn't entirely untrue.

I left the dean's office satisfied that I had accomplished most of what I set out to do and proud to be handing on to my successor a College of Humanities with significantly more resources than it possessed just five years earlier. But I also knew that I was handing on to him—a good friend—a fundamentally lousy job. A job whose enormous complexity was only really appreciated by your immediate staff, who see the office working on a daily basis. A job in which, no matter what good things you do for people, you will rarely hear a "thank you." A job in which you are constantly translating the budgetary and managerial concerns of central administration to a faculty concerned almost exclusively with its own teaching and research priorities—and vice versa. A job in which everyone and every constituency wants you to serve *their* interests, as though there were no others.

When Neil Rudenstine, the president of Harvard University, took an unexpected three-month leave of absence, beginning in November 1994, I followed the press coverage with sympathy. At first, newspaper accounts generally focused on the medical details. As reported in the *Chronicle of Higher Education*, "a spokesman for Mr. Rudenstine said the president was suffering from 'severe fatigue and exhaustion of unknown origin.'" To its credit, the *Chronicle* used the story as an occasion to question the very nature of the modern university presidency. The subtitle asked, "An Overwhelming Job?", and the piece concluded with the prediction by one Harvard dean that "the leave could prompt Harvard to re-evaluate the way the president's job is structured" (Heller A18). The *New York Times* coverage was even more revelatory. After acknowledging that "Mr. Rudenstine's illness has highlighted the enormous pressures on a university president generally," Karen Arenson's article went on to discuss "how complex a place like Harvard is" and how complicated would be the changes needed to "enter the 21st century." The reporter noted, however, that "the administrative structure to run Harvard, as at many other universities, seems a throwback to earlier days" (Arenson, "Harvard President's Medical Leave," 22).

Arenson did not explore the problems inherent in most universities' "administrative structure"; instead, she emphasized the inadequate staff support for senior administrators. It was a telling example. Contrary to the view of faculty—who do not fully comprehend the demands on administrators and so rail against what looks like administrative "bloat"—most academic administrators, from the department chair to the president, lack the support staff and monetary resources requisite for even a minimally satisfactory performance. As Arenson's article made clear, people from the corporate world recognize this immediately. "All of these universities are very lean," she quotes one business consultant saying. "A corporate executive would be stunned by the lack of support," he continues. "University presidents have fewer people, fewer resources, more pressure and a lot of work to do" (Arenson, "Harvard President's Medical Leave," 22).

I agreed, and I continued to follow the unfolding story eagerly. I sympathized; I empathized; I identified. Although our jobs were hardly comparable, nonetheless it occurred to me that Rudenstine and I had both been trapped, in our very different ways, within structures that, as the *New York Times* reporter noted, seem "a throwback to earlier days." Not only were we trying to take on complicated responsibilities without the resources and staff support that executives in the corporate sector take for granted, but, perhaps even more important, we were both being worn out by an organizational design in which critical decisions were made in all the wrong places by all the wrong people.

On most campuses, decisions about class size, curriculum design, and faculty advising and teaching loads—decisions with enormous long-term financial consequences—are made independently at the department or program level by largely autonomous units with great variance among them. At the same time, central administration makes decisions about how to distribute the resources that will enable or constrain those activities. During periods of economic "downsizing," a vice president for academic affairs or a vice president for finance calculates what percentage must be cut from any year's operating budget. Removed from everyday life in the departmental trenches, these administrators may even make preliminary decisions about how to allocate the cuts across campus, without fully understanding the consequences of cuts on educational practice. When severe economic downsizing leads to crisis management—as it always does—the disarticulation between these groups can paralyze a campus. The faculty act to ensure their institution's reputation as a center of teaching and/or research excellence in their particular field or discipline. Those in central administration act to ensure the institution's fiscal solvency. As far as all of these groups and individuals are concerned, they are each expressing an *institutional perspective,* even if those perspectives are fundamentally different—and sometimes at odds. As a result, even a president who is generally perceived as caring and consultative—as is Rudenstine—becomes the object of harsh attack from faculty when, in an effort to trim Harvard's annual operating deficit, he cuts "medical benefits and contributions" to the pension plan (Heller A18). Caught in the middle, of course, are the deans and department chairs who daily negotiate these frictions, trying to mediate between conflicting sets of imperatives.

When Rudenstine returned to the presidency of Harvard, I cheered. But his experience confirmed my own determination to stay away from any further forays into higher education administration. As presently constituted, these jobs are not designed for people who want some semblance of a family life or weekends free for leisure. And they certainly are not jobs for people with impaired mobility or reduced energy (which is currently my situation). In my dreams, however, I know what I would do if I could enter administration again: I would focus on dismantling the organizational structures that make these jobs so difficult, replacing an outdated segmentation of information flow and decision-making with an information-rich decentralization into inclusive decision-making. By this, I do not mean just another version of what currently passes for staff or faculty input. In other words, I am not advocating yet another faculty-staff committee hastily thrown together and overwhelmed with unfamiliar data, vested with the responsibility for "representing" the campus in making crisis-driven budget recommendations to a central administration faced with budget cuts and operating deficits. Instead, as I will elaborate in chapter 7, I mean a radical overhaul of the entire decision-making apparatus. I want to involve a fully informed faculty and staff in day-to-day management responsibilities shared with administration.

The final design would no doubt vary from campus to campus and might change over time. But the underlying principles would be clear: faculty, staff, and administration—with input from students—would work together as true partners, sharing information and negotiating priorities. And in that process, leadership, as well as decision-making, would become an inclusive collaborative activity because everyone would fully understand—and shoulder—the consequences of any decision and its alternatives.

On this kind of transformed campus, search committees for administrators would seek individuals with the wisdom to articulate shared and perhaps even multiple visions for the future, as well as those with the ability to communicate and interpret data to a wide variety of audiences. Instead of looking for the clichéd leader who can make tough decisions, search committees for administrators might instead emphasize the individual who can build community without silencing debate or disagreement, the individual who is comfortable with diversity and inclusivity, and the individual with the tact to ensure that a few prima donnas or enlarged egos (including her own) do not dominate decision-making for selfish or parochial purposes. For their part, faculty and staff would have to become knowledgeable in areas—like budget planning and enrollment management—that they had previously avoided. And faculty would need to refocus their primary professional commitment from the discipline or department to the institution and its collective student body. In turn, staff, senior administrators, and middle management administrators—those responsible for physical facilities, room scheduling, and planning—would have to learn how faculty and students spend their days.

In order to accomplish this sea change, from time to time all faculty and all support and administrative staff would find themselves in training seminars that prepare them to take on these additional tasks and responsibilities as part of their normal duties. The added workload ought not prove unduly burdensome, however, because it should eliminate the heated wranglings between faculty, staff, and administrators that already consume precious time and energy. Indeed, the "us" and "them" mentality that currently divides faculty, staff, and students from administrators should disappear altogether.

Equally important, in a structure that de-emphasizes hierarchy and truly shares information and decision-making, administrative positions should no longer require superhuman stamina and endless energy. Talented individuals with a disability or chronic disease, yet capable of handling a reasonable workload, might serve. And, whatever the state of their health, deans might even find time for research, for teaching, or for sex on the weekends.

ix.

Another dean catches up to me as I walk slowly toward the central administration office building. We are both headed for the monthly deans' council meeting. "How are you?" he asks, even as he makes clear that he is impatient with my laboring gait.

I want to answer: *I'm ready for the meeting and concentrating on it hard because laced into my every step is a pain so unremitting that I am surprised when it is not there. In fact, behind even my most casual physical movement is a willed concentration on keeping the pain at bay.* I want to add: *I'd love to join you in your brisk stride toward the tower, but all I can manage is this slow, limping walk, hips and knees burning.*

Instead, I reply with a smile: "I'm fine. Why don't you go on ahead? I'm mulling over some budget figures, and I need a few extra minutes before the meeting. Catch you there."

My old habit of denial has kicked in. If I refuse to acknowledge how badly this disease is crippling me, then it will not be so. In these final weeks of my deanship, I am also acutely aware of my lame-duck status. Central administration is stalling on several important recommendations that I've put before them, waiting for me to finish out my term and hoping for a more compliant dean to follow me. This is no time to reveal any kind of weakness.

Hours later, when I leave the deans' council meeting, to my surprise, I am smiling. I am grinning from ear to ear. It's the last meeting of its kind that I will have to attend. I won't again have to witness the hypocrisy of senior administrators who complain about meddlesome state legislators but shy away from confronting lawmakers with the fact that increased legislative micromanagement has coincided with severe cuts in the state's financial support, thus leaving the university more and more dependent on nonstate funding sources like research grants and private gifts. Why not tell legislators that they can have a say in university management in proportion to their willingness to pay the bills, I always want to ask. I won't again have to listen to the dean who admonishes us to become "lean and mean." Mean to whom, I want to ask. To the staff, the faculty, the students? I am also smiling as I leave the meeting because I know I've left a legacy behind me. Firmly in place within the College of Humanities are new, forward-looking promotion and tenure procedures that other schools are already examining as models for themselves; and child care needs are now a repeated agenda item for the academic deans. And I've decided to write a book about what I've learned these past five years, in hopes of helping some future dean struggling to keep her ideals intact.

1 Facing the Future: An Introduction

"The care of the public must oversway all private respects."
—John Winthrop, "A Modell of Christian Charity," 1630.

i.

This is a book about higher education, written for those who want to be part of its future. Most of my observations and recommendations will apply to public and private research universities, as well as to comprehensive (or nonresearch intensive) universities, because these are the institutions I have come to know best both as a student and as a professional educator. To a lesser degree, this book also reflects the current realities of four-year liberal arts colleges, public and private. But of the approximately 125 research universities in the United States—of which about forty are private and eighty-five are public—my major focus is on the public research university. These institutions are the focus of my concern because they are responsible for training most of the nation's Ph.D.s and other professionals, at the same time remaining accessible to large segments of the undergraduate population, providing superior education at relatively affordable tuition rates. Even so, despite their importance in undergraduate and professional education and their central place in the nation's research agenda, public research universities are now imperiled by budget cuts, by assaults on tenure, and by a general misunderstanding of what they do and how they do it.

That said, whether I am discussing colleges or universities—or even both at once—my remarks are informed by two carefully considered beliefs. To begin with, if we want our educational system to serve us as well in the future as it has in the past—or perhaps serve us even better—then it will require greater, and not reduced, investments of human and financial resources. An additional three million students are expected to enroll in the nation's colleges and universities between 1997 and 2015, a 20 percent increase over current enrollment levels. These students will need more professors, more classrooms, more computers, more foreign language instruction, and better equipped science laboratories if they are to receive a quality education and fulfill the employment needs of the coming century. After all, in the next decade alone, in addition to the existing jobs that already require a college degree, approximately one-third of all new jobs created will require at least that.

Who these students are is also changing. At the moment, more than one-third of students in primary and secondary schools are minorities; and in Hawaii, California, New Mexico, Texas, Mississippi, and the District of Columbia more than half of the students are members of a racial minority. Those numbers continue to grow as the twentieth century's minorities become the twenty-first century's majority. As college and university enrollments increasingly draw upon this changing population, institutions of higher education will have to accommodate the fact that, disproportionately, these students will come from poor families and even poorer school districts. This means added costs in scholarship money and loans, counseling and academic tutoring facilities, and remedial programs for basic subjects like math and English.

But it is not only the investment in improved educational quality and updated facilities for growing numbers of students or even the costs of enrolling talented students with inadequate preparation that will account for the need for increased resources. It is also the fact that institutions of higher education will be called upon to play a variety of unprecedented roles in a transnational information age. The ease with which individuals will be able to access vast quantities of information whenever they want will be matched by a commensurate demand to learn how to analyze that information, recognize recurrent patterns or connections, and extract what is truly important. In effect, the new information technologies will make higher education both more necessary *and* ongoing, if only because learning to make connections and to reason rigorously across and between the disciplines is a lifelong process requiring sensitive tutelage. The twenty-first century, in other words, will be a century in which people are constantly "going back to school" in one form or another.

The second belief behind these chapters is that accelerating technological innovation will transform all aspects of teaching and learning in ways that cannot yet be predicted. What is certain, however, even from the current successes with self-paced computer learning programs and video transmission to off-campus learning sites, is that there is no substitute for the inspiration, rigor, and focus of direct human contact between a teacher and her students. Emily Weiner, a 1995 graduate of New York's Empire State College—a college that exists in cyberspace, providing instruction online and through e-mail —made that clear when she assessed her own experience in a *New York Times* editorial. Despite her "excitement about new electronic educational opportunities" and the convenience of "on-line degrees," Weiner nonetheless came to depend on the professor at the other end for emotional and intellectual nurture (Weiner 42). In her view, the success of distance learning arrangements depends on "a person at the other end of the line who is watching to see that students are stretching themselves, choosing appropriate courses, struggling with new ideas, overcoming personal obstacles, getting smarter" (Weiner 42). But even when those ideal circumstances obtain, Weiner complained, "the fuller relationships that develop between students and teachers on a college campus will be missing" (Weiner 42). Clearly, then, the teacher as coach, as guide, and as immediately responsive presence— even beyond the teacher's disciplinary expertise—contributes to the learning process in a way that no computer program and no video, however well designed, can ever replicate.

Of course, the understandable fear of many in the professoriate today is that universities will continue trimming their costs by replacing live teachers with computer programs or with videotapes of lectures that can be replayed semester after semester—what I call "the professor in a can." We learned, however, from the innovations introduced to basic language instruction in the College of Humanities' language learning laboratory at the University of Arizona that even the most sophisticated and creative computer programs proved successful only when combined with the give-and-take of the traditional classroom.

Nothing substituted for spontaneous conversation between teachers and students in the targeted language.

The videotaped lecture series by "great professors" currently being marketed to schools and to the general public suffer from another significant liability. Because the knowledge base in any field of study is never static but, rather, dynamic and changing, these videos become obsolete almost as soon as they are canned. Although the lectures may be wonderful as performances, they will never replace professors who impart the very latest discoveries in their fields and make their students partners in the discovery process. Unlike the professor in the classroom or the laboratory, a video won't engage a student in dialogue about cutting-edge research or controversial new concepts.

The challenge facing the professoriate of the next century, therefore, is to become knowledgeable about the new technologies and their possibilities in order to adapt them both for enhanced on-campus instruction and for increased outreach to students not currently on campus. The challenge to our educational institutions is to provide incentives and continuous support to faculty willing to push the technology envelope. The challenge for policy-makers and the general public is to resist the impulse to force colleges and universities into substituting the kind of rote training that technology can cheaply supply for the more expensive education that teaches thinking and analytic skills, values and an understanding of complex relationships, which the learned professor in the classroom can facilitate. An exclusively cost-driven dependence on computers and telecourses may instruct students in a subject; but only the professor with passion and disciplinary expertise can help students understand why a subject is important to think about and *how* to think about it.

Having identified this as a book about higher education, I must add that it is consequently also a book about social responsibility. Despite all the trendy importations of corporate models into academe (like many others, my own campus embraced "total quality management"), the chapters that follow reject the notion that colleges and universities are merely training vendors, that students are end products or interim consumers, that the professoriate is a quantifiable human resource, or that prospective employers represent higher education's ultimate customers and most important constituency. In an open society, creative production and the making of new knowledge can never be reducible merely to commodities for market exchange. Markets may be excellent devices for increasing profits and personal wealth, but they are notoriously unreliable as protectors of the common good. Yet striving to define and enact the common good, since Plato, has been one of the major goals of advanced education. During my years as dean, when local business and community leaders asked whether universities should be training students to work effectively in an increasingly competitive international economy; or whether we needed to train more socially responsible participants for national and global citizenship; or whether we should concentrate on graduating individuals equipped for success in our own nation's complexly multicultural workplace, my answer was always the same: we need to be doing all three at once; we dare not separate or compartmentalize those missions; and we need to pursue each of them through high-quality curricular innovations.

What I now want to add to that answer is my profound belief that the quality of education reflects the quality of community that supports it. But at the end of the current millennium, any sense of community in this country is in short supply. Vicious corporate downsizing for the sake of short-term profits, a fraying social safety net, and widening inequalities in income distribution have turned the nation sour and cynical. Crime, violence, domestic terrorism, and smoldering racial tensions are regular features of the evening news. And, in a desperate act of scapegoating, too many citizens and politicians seem content to punish the poor as though, amid a myriad of better opportunities, the poor had stubbornly chosen their plight. It is a sad note on which to end the century.

If we have any hope of social harmony, it is a note we dare not carry over into the next century. My narrow focus on education in these pages, therefore, must be understood as grounded in the argument that the best educational system in the world is no substitute for—nor can it survive without—reinvestment in troubled communities, job creation, income redistribution, the reinstitution of a truly progressive tax system for individuals and corporations alike, and far more inclusive political and civic participation than is currently the norm. Unless we develop social programs to mitigate the economic displacements that impoverish entire neighborhoods, disrupt families, produce violence, and stunt young people's growth, educational reform will not stand proof against civil disorder.

Americans will have to get out of the habituated ruts of late-twentieth-century thinking. Social justice is not the enemy of economic growth, but rather its engine. Tax structures that continue to concentrate wealth among the few actually slow an economy's expansion by widening the income gap, depressing consumption, and depriving the dwindling middle and working classes of the opportunity to save and thereby spur investment. In fact, a truly progressive tax system is simultaneously a social good. Moreover, as the post–World War II pattern in East Asia demonstrates, "the most successful . . . economies are also the most egalitarian," and there is a direct correlation between equitable "income distribution and a strong economy" (Passell 5).

What this teaches us for the next century is that full employment at decent wages must be valued as a far greater social benefit than the lowest prices for consumers or the highest dividends for stockholders. And because the dignity and stability that well-paid employment brings to an individual translate into civic participation and political enfranchisement (not to mention social order), there need to be significant *dis*incentives in place for employers who, as *New York Times* columnist Thomas L. Friedman phrases it, *massacre their workers* (Friedman 15). By any measure, after all, American workers "work longer and harder than workers in other industrialized nations, . . . with less job security" (Meier 82), and they rank among the most productive in the world. The fact that stunning technological advances have allowed machines to replace hands and minds should mean shorter workweeks rather than fewer employees who put in overtime (as do most American workers today); and it should mean that those same hands and minds are now available to be educated to perform the tasks that technology, as yet, cannot.

A twenty-first century education can certainly make such transitions possible. But only if politicians and the general public first squarely face the consequences of current policies that protect profits before people.

ii.

I contemplate the profession that I am passing on to my graduate students with trepidation. Beyond the immediate question of whether there will be employment for these talented newcomers in a cost-cutting and downsizing academy is the larger question of how they will make a place for themselves within institutions that are already, in their view, obsolete. Often far more sophisticated than their teachers about the possibilities of technology for teaching and learning, they share with undergraduates the sense that the new technologies have the capacity to transform learning into play. Even more important, the students to whom I currently teach American literature and American studies see the university as a barrier rather than a bridge to the barrio, the reservation, and the 'hood. And they are determined to utilize the new technologies and to use their knowledge as a means of breaking down the barriers.

Perhaps as a consequence, today's Ph.D. candidates ask disturbing questions about how our society has organized itself, and they seem deeply committed to applying their studies to help solve problems like global poverty and environmental degradation. Because their intellectual ambitions have so wide a reach, these students chafe at disciplinary boundaries, pursuing dissertation topics that require professorial oversight committees made up of humanists, social scientists, and scientists in combinations that were unimaginable when I was going through my own Ph.D. training just thirty years ago. In terms of the way we have segmented disciplines and compartmentalized knowledge fields, these students are telling us, the organization of the American university in the late twentieth century cannot survive into the twenty-first century.

This is just one of many cues that major changes are upon us. As Donald Kennedy, the former president of Stanford University, wryly phrased it, "Another century's end, another revolution for higher education" (Kennedy 8). Kennedy's wearied humor notwithstanding, most colleges and universities are now expending considerable resources on *strategic planning*, the latest talisman for ensuring institutional survival into the next century. The trouble is that on most campuses strategic planning has been skewed into a search for strategies to deal with current fiscal problems while its potential to embolden creative thinking about the long-term future has been severely curtailed. As a result, the most important conversations about higher education in the twenty-first century have yet to begin in earnest. We have not generated paradigms for true interdisciplinarity; we have not planned for education's role in a society where the forty-hour week and a single career path have ceased to be the defining activities of adulthood; and we have not prepared for the internationalization of higher education.

Temperamentally suspicious of those who claim to offer blueprints, I take nonetheless seriously the fact that nearly everyone—whatever their motives or political views—seems to agree that the future demands significant changes in the ways educational institutions fulfill their multiple missions. Mindful as I am that the future is always unpredictable and that even the best-laid plans will be beset by unintended consequences, I offer the following key topics as potential entry points into the next phase of the conversation:

1. *Interdisciplinarity.* The world that today's college and university graduates will enter is a world in which the once recognizable political alignments of the Cold War have been replaced by ethnic rivalries and unstable realignments around religion and nationalism; a world in which the economic competition between a communist east and a capitalist west has been superseded by transnational conglomerates that threaten once cherished notions of sovereignty and national autonomy; a world in which resource development can also mean cascading species extinction and global environmental disaster; and a world in which the shrinking availability of potable water, clean air, and uncontaminated soil daily widens the gap between "haves" and "have nots." Trained in specific majors or programs—history, economics, environmental studies—with few formal connections across the disciplines, today's graduates can barely describe that world. Nor do they fully grasp the fact that a world interconnected by commerce and its byproducts (pollution, resource depletion, political alliances, and information) will require international perspectives for identifying problems and sensitive local understandings for solving those problems.

In order to face the complexly interwoven challenges that confront us—from racial and ethnic hatreds to quickening destruction of bio-logical habitats—the students we educate in the twenty-first century must be taught to comprehend systems, patterns, and interconnec-tions. For example, they must be readily able to grasp that the fact of male sperm counts worldwide having fallen by 50 percent since 1938 and the fact that in some areas human breast milk contains more toxic substances than is permissible in commercial cow's milk are not random or unrelated phenomena. But this kind of comprehen-sive pattern-seeking analysis is precisely what our current fragmen-tation of knowledge into disciplines and departments works against. David W. Orr, professor of environmental studies at Oberlin College, describes the situation perfectly: ". . . we have organized both curricu-lum and research by fragments called disciplines, sub-disciplines, and departments, each of which deals only with small pieces of the total picture. This is fine until we need to understand patterns and whole systems, which is the business of no single discipline, department, or specialized field. As a result, larger trends and patterns tend to be ignored within a discipline-centric context." One of Orr's proposed solutions, predictably, is "to create a genuinely interdisciplinary cur-riculum" (Orr 44, 46).

Traditionally, higher education in the United States has claimed to value creativity, initiative, and independence of thought in students, even if curricula and classroom practices have more often stressed mastery of core subjects and the performance of specific skills. But if we take seriously our professed traditional values, then—instead of alienating students from the adventure of large and searching ques-tions—the curricula of the next century can evolve into permutations that are flexible, supportive of collaborative learning and research, genuinely interdisciplinary, and inventive of new disciplines when needed. Organizational structures on campus—the old departments and programs—will similarly evolve into collaborative and flexible units. Having thus moved away from departmentally controlled em-phases on segmented bodies of knowledge, higher education in the twenty-first century can instead concentrate on teaching students how to continue learning long after graduation and how to assess what they need to know in order to tackle any problem, however complex.

2. *Education in and for a leisured society.* The crude fact of the matter is that our increasingly sophisticated technological advances displace more blue, pink, and white collar jobs than they create, and the jobs that remain are mostly low-skilled, low-pay, and part time. Such a prospect is ominous, of course, with the growing numbers of the underemployed and the unemployed experiencing themselves as both economically and politically disenfranchised. As I suggested earlier, these newly marginalized citizens withdraw from political and social engagements—ceasing to vote or to volunteer for the local little league—and some inevitably turn to crime, violence, and various forms of sabotage.

But if we develop the kinds of policies that I recommended in the first section of this chapter, we can get past the brutal economic dislocations of the current moment. With policies that encourage a more equitable distribution of wealth, full employment with substantial reductions in paid working hours, flexible work schedules, job-sharing, guaranteed income safety nets, and universal health care, the United States can transform itself into a stable, post-labor-intensive society. In other words, the nation will enjoy full employment because full-time work at livable wages will no longer be predicated on a forty-hour work week but, over time, on fewer and fewer work-week hours. And, because of continued technological advances, an individual worker's productivity will still remain high. In that case, there exists the breathtaking possibility that continuing self-education will become one of the major pleasures of those who manage their own time and who have ample discretionary time to manage. Those individuals in the next century will be able to turn to higher education not only as a means toward some vocational or professional end but, also, as an avocation, as a means toward lifelong personal growth.

How the university will reconfigure itself as a resource for this new constituency of learners and what kinds of educational services will be required are questions we have yet to pose. But we might begin by considering higher education's growing responsiveness to today's able, healthy, and energetic retirees. The challenge is not just to keep them occupied. The challenge, instead, is to provide rigorous and stimulating programs that contribute to both the betterment of society and the continuing development of the individual.

3. The internationalization of higher education. Progress toward a politically and economically unified Europe, together with rapid advances in the technologies for interactive distance learning, point inevitably toward an eventual internationalization of the entire educational enterprise and most especially toward the internationalization of higher education. As Europe moves toward a common currency, it is also exploring ways to standardize university training so that students can transfer course credits and program hours across national borders, from one school to another. In terms of higher education and professional preparation, European nations seek the kind of exchange and reciprocity that now obtains between most accredited U.S. and Canadian colleges and universities. Increasingly, that North American reciprocity has been extended to include institutions in Mexico and South America. African and Asian countries may be slower to take up these initiatives, but finally they too will want to participate in an integrated and reciprocal system of internationalized higher education.

The benefits are obvious. Despite national boundaries, students will move freely from one institution to another, depending on their research needs and interests. With easy international cross-institutional collaborations, individual schools will rely on far-flung partners to provide courses, degree programs, and faculty expertise in subject areas complementary to their own. And they can engage in multidisciplinary research ventures beyond the capacity of one campus or one country by itself. Faculty and students in the next century will thus enjoy a far richer, because more diverse, intellectual community.

Driving the process is the growing affordability of interactive learning, teaching, and research technologies. By utilizing satellite transmission, it is already feasible for a master healer in Beijing to observe and receive instruction in western surgical techniques while simultaneously advising the surgical team on postoperative herbal preparations for a patient at the University of Arizona Medical Center in Tucson. In the not too distant future, faculty and students excavating an archeological site in Greece will go online with specialists from all over the world, collaboratively analyzing their discoveries even as they make them; and, at the same time, they can connect to classrooms across the world as instructors. As today's professoriate trains its successors, therefore, we will need to encourage enhanced foreign lan-

guage skills, formalized instruction in responsiveness to and respect
for diverse cultural cues and customs, and a playful exploration of
technological possibilities. Above all, however, while retaining those
cultural and intellectual traditions that make them unique, individual
institutions will also have to reconceive themselves as vital participants in an integrated global enterprise.

Ideally, the kinds of changes that I am envisioning here would lead
to the following: outdated notions of lone researchers and isolated
communities of scholars will be transformed into the reality of international communities of socially engaged learners, locating themselves not only as members of a global human family but, equally important, as responsible partners in a healthy and sustainable habitat.

This book offers no blueprint for achieving these ends but, instead,
chapters on a variety of subjects related to these ends. The chapters
contain personal observations from my years in an academic dean's
office, anecdotes supplied by colleagues and students, hard data, and
practical strategies for dealing with at least some aspects of the immediate transition from one century to another—*but all in terms of
the future directions that I have here projected.* My purpose is to suggest ways of surviving the presently bumpy road in such a manner as
to prepare ourselves for what lies ahead.

Chapters 2 and 3 focus on the complicated issues of tenure and academic freedom in the modern university. Chapter 2 identifies the call
to abolish tenure as one facet of the organized right wing's resistance
to the changing racial and gender make-up of the faculty. Chapter 3
reviews how we went about rethinking standards and procedures for
promotion and tenure in the College of Humanities at the University of Arizona, and it offers a practical approach to maintaining high
standards for tenure while simultaneously ensuring a level playing
field for the increasing numbers of women and minorities now entering the professoriate. In its examination of the harassment to which
women and feminist scholars are still subjected, Chapter 4 reinforces
the argument for a level playing field and, as well, advances practical
measures for curtailing threats to the academic freedom of feminist
teachers and scholars. This chapter also acknowledges the unique vulnerability of women and minority faculty, because until quite recently

they were unable to participate in constituting and conceptualizing what academic freedom might entail. Chapter 5 examines the changing nature of the American family and offers a variety of campus-based family-friendly policy initiatives, including revised benefits packages, innovative approaches for funding both child care and elder care, and the use of distance learning technologies for those whose family responsibilities keep them from campus. Chapter 6 asks how we can most effectively teach the many different communities of learners now entering higher education; by recognizing *cognitive* diversity—in addition to cultural, ethnic, and racial diversity—we can teach to a student's individual intellectual strengths while helping him develop additional learning capacities. Chapter 7 surveys how during my years as dean we succeeded in beginning to set a twenty-first-century agenda for ourselves in the College of Humanities. Although much still remained to be done, the college nonetheless managed to tackle everything from curricular renewal and affirmative action hiring to expanding our international focus and changing the culture of decision-making, all within the relatively brief span of five years. The bulk of chapter 7, however, looks beyond my own experiences as dean and concentrates on future issues as wide-ranging as new forms of academic leadership and the positive potential of unionization. In the closing chapter, chapter 8, I turn to the intimate partnership between higher education and the public primary and secondary schools. The picture I draw there is a bleak one because the nation appears to be abandoning its children, allowing too many K–12 public schools to deteriorate and ignoring the need for accessible child care and preschool. It is a suicidal course, I insist. And, as in previous chapters, I put forward a program of urgent responses to urgent problems.

I would have liked the final chapter of this book to end on a more optimistic note, but present circumstances do not allow it. Instead of facing up to the challenges and possibilities of the coming millennium, we are already failing to meet the needs of future generations. The nation appears paralyzed by the very real economic anxieties of the moment and wholly forgetful of why we once so enthusiastically invested in our educational institutions. Not only did public education in primary and secondary school and beyond contribute significantly to the gross national product, enhance the income as well as

the quality of life for the vast majority of citizens, and help social-
ize—or "Americanize"—one wave of immigrants after another, but it
also came to be associated with the more abstract ideals of personal
growth and societal transformation. In *Popular Education and Its Discontents*, Lawrence A. Cremin expands on John Dewey and reminds
us that "the aim of education is not merely to make parents, or citizens, or workers, or indeed to surpass the Russians or the Japanese,
but ultimately to make human beings . . . who will participate actively
with their fellow human beings in the building of a good society" (Cremin 125). What chapter 8 demonstrates, sadly, is that we seem to have
lost any shared sense of what a "good society" might look like.

iii.

Public discussions of higher education at the end of the 1990s
have come to be dominated by two propositions. The first proposition asserts that the rising costs of college and university tuition must
point to inflated faculty salaries and to wastefulness and poor management on the part of higher education administrators. The second
proposition asserts that traditional core subjects, especially in the humanities, have been displaced by radical new curricula that undermine students' regard for the accomplishments of Western civilization
and that call into question all standards and values. Although both
propositions are gross distortions, it is not difficult to understand why
the press and the general public have accepted them so easily. The
financial argument has been fueled by the fact that "tuition at private
colleges has increased by 90 percent since 1980, and at public institutions by 100 percent. Over the same period," by contrast, "the median
family income has grown by only 5 percent" (Burd et. al. A11). The result has been what the General Accounting Office in 1996 called an
"affordability gap" in most parents' ability to pay for their children's
college education (Guernsey A59).

The curricular argument gained credence from the fact that, as in
the sciences, the last thirty years have seen an explosion of research
and new knowledge in the humanities disciplines. This new knowledge and some of the advanced methodologies of research and interpretation—again, as in the sciences—challenge long-established ways
of thinking. And while most Americans have come to accept—even

expect—periodic revolutions in scientific paradigms, few people have paid enough attention to history textbooks or American literature anthologies to notice that they, too, have changed over time. Certainly very few people were prepared for the acceleration of these changes in the last three decades. As a result, whether the demonized catchword was feminism, multiculturalism, postmodernism, deconstruction, or political correctness, those writing with the support of wealthy right-wing think tanks were able to persuade their readers that all standards of valuation were being displaced by a shoddy relativism, disabling students from distinguishing between bad literature, good literature, and truly great literature. And they told parents that, by introducing texts attentive to the seamier side of the nation's past—slavery, the genocide of native peoples, discrimination against women—humanities professors were unduly politicizing the classroom.

In a variety of different ways, the chapters that follow attempt to unravel these distortions and get at the truth beneath. As I suggest in chapter 2, the rising costs of higher education derive not from waste or poor management, and certainly not from inflated faculty salaries, but from the many demands we have placed on higher education and the consequences of recent diminished public funding. Let us remember that ever since the end of World War II—when federal investments in higher education began to increase substantially—ultraconservative and right-wing fringe elements in the Republican party tried to stem every aspect of the expanding federal government, including its role in education. But programs like the GI Bill and, after the Russians successfully launched Sputnik in 1957, the National Defense Education Act (which provided scholarship and loan money to those qualified for college entrance) were enormously popular. Because education was generally understood to be a social good and federal support a prudent investment in the nation's future, attacks on federal education spending went nowhere.

But by the end of the 1970s, emboldened by economic recession, those who had once been fringe elements in the Republican party took center stage by attacking high taxes and the allegedly wasteful spending habits of everyone who supposedly fed at the public dole, including politicians, government bureaucrats, and school administrators. The upshot was the property tax revolts of the late 1970s (California's

Proposition 13 among the earliest) and the election victory of Ronald Reagan in 1980. Supported by this increasingly vocal element in the Republican party, President Reagan enacted large cuts in income tax rates in 1981, favoring the wealthy by lowering the top brackets from 70 percent to 28 percent in seven years. At the same time, he lowered corporate taxes and later poured enormous sums into military spending, particularly the ill-conceived Star Wars missile defense system. The deficit soared, and most federal programs—including those pertaining to education—were soon starved of funds.

From the vantage point of parents trying to send their kids to college, however, little of this mattered—if it was even understood. The fact that colleges and universities were forced to raise tuition in order to compensate for the loss of federal and state support simply meant higher bills and larger debt for families whose incomes were barely keeping pace with inflation. And when radical right-wing elements began to attack what was supposedly being taught to undergraduates, the public's anxieties about college costs attached themselves to new anxieties about the value and quality of higher education. In a manner carefully manipulated toward that end, the public's confidence in higher education was compromised.

In point of fact, humanities courses have become more rigorous, and the curricular changes are hardly as radical as critics imply. As an example, like most such activities across the country, curricular renewal in the College of Humanities at the University of Arizona, to which I draw attention in chapter 7, has been relatively slow and deliberate. To begin with, traditional authors and texts remain. Chaucer, Shakespeare, Milton, and their heirs are still staples of the English department curriculum, and the writers of Spain's Golden Age still figure prominently in courses offered by the Spanish and Portuguese department. Indeed, as several surveys conducted by the Modern Language Association have demonstrated, the frequency with which established "major authors" are taught in required undergraduate literature courses has remained remarkably stable over the past twenty years.

What *has* changed is that some professors are teaching these authors within far denser historical and literary contexts. Thus, surveys of seventeenth-century English literature now examine the influence of Lady Mary Wroth's prose proto-novel *Urania* (1621) and

expand the canon that had previously been characterized as exclusively male.[1] Henry James is taught in dynamic relationship to the
popular female novelists of his era, whom he publicly scorned, but
from whom—we now know—he derived many of his plots and char-
acters.[2] Thanks to the wealth of recent scholarship, American literature courses today incorporate significant narrative traditions from
Native American peoples and three hundred years of texts by African
Americans. And American literature and English renaissance specialists alike can point to the ways in which Europe's anxious encounters
with the so-called New World and its peoples found expression in
Shakespeare's *The Tempest* as well as John Milton's *Paradise Lost.*

What students learn from all this is that literature is not some unap-
proachable storehouse of universal beauty and timeless verity. Instead,
students encounter literature as human expression deeply embedded
in and responsive to the contingencies of its particular circumstances
and historical moment. Milton's retelling of the Adam and Eve story
was given new urgency by the claim that yet another unspoiled paradise had been discovered in the Americas. Henry James was not *above*
but, rather, *part of* the popular literary culture of his day. Similarly,
students' encounter with the oldest preserved songs and stories, as
well as contemporary writings, by Native Americans teaches them
that the narrative traditions of native peoples derive from a host of different cultures, in each of which narrative serves different and unique
cultural functions (admonitory tales for children or scenarios for religious celebrations, to give only two examples). And in grappling with
story structures and symbolic patterns that are unfamiliar to them,
students from non-Indian backgrounds come to understand that these
cultural forms were constructed according to aesthetic norms quite
different from those of the European novel or the nineteenth-century
short story.

By introducing this kind of material into the literature classroom,
we are neither trashing Western civilization nor robbing our students
of the capacity to make value judgments. To the contrary, we are expanding our students' repertoire of reading and interpretive strategies,
teaching them to comprehend and appreciate the aesthetic rules and
cultural practices governing the Zuni story of emergence as well as
those governing the composition of a Shakespeare play. As a result,

they become readers of a greater variety of texts. And, as our students are quick to declare to anyone who will listen, they now possess far more complicated tools for arriving at the value judgments that they inevitably make and remake.

Finally, the right wing's portrait of some former apolitical golden age in which humanities instruction was untouched by the burdens of history and detached from the concerns of the present moment is delusory. Such a creature never existed. The ever-changing contents of course syllabi and textbooks make clear how complicated are the decisions, at any given moment, about what to teach and how. Given the ethnic diversity of the students who take my courses here at the University of Arizona, for example, were I to teach American frontier literature *without* the riveting stories and powerful writing to be found in Native American, Chicano/a, African American, and Asian American texts—limiting the readings to James Fenimore Cooper, Bret Harte, Owen Wister, Willa Cather, etc.—*that* would be a decidedly political gesture. The old, unproblematic story of a frontier that began at Plymouth Rock and progressed steadily westward to the Pacific is not only historically inaccurate; it is also a highly politically invested set of choices about where we recognize aesthetic value, who is to be valorized, and what shall be remembered. What makes the right wing nervous about today's newly revised curriculum is precisely its expansion of the frame of memory.

Having thus briefly responded to some of the right wing's distorted assertions about higher education, I should warn readers that this book is not constructed as a dialogue with the right. A variety of thoughtful scholars have already engaged that dialogue, Stanley Fish and Lawrence W. Levine prominent among them.[3] I do not need to repeat their arguments here. That said, because it deals with the radical right's assault on tenure, chapter 2 does counter right-wing views; and, because it attends to conservative attacks on feminist scholarship, so too does chapter 4, at least in part. My aim, however, has been to avoid tailoring my pages to the constraints of a right-wing discourse that is already antiquated and, instead, to focus readers' attention on the demands of the coming century.

iv.

When all is said and done, I hope this book encourages women and others from previously underrepresented groups in academia to take on administrative challenges, at least for some period in their careers. I say that even though—despite many accomplishments during my years as dean—my own experience has taught me the agonizing difficulty of acting ethically in ambiguous situations and amid profoundly divided claims on one's time, attention, and budgetary resources. The problem is compounded by the fact that, at most institutions of higher education, academic administration remains structurally male, constructed around a public role and a public sphere that subordinate or even elide the personal and the private. But the personal and the private intrude themselves nonetheless. For someone with progressive and feminist ideals, it is extremely difficult to take on a leadership role in such a context.

Still, I do not want readers to come away discouraged. If we adopt the family-friendly policies that I recommend in chapter 5, then private responsibilities need no longer conflict repeatedly with public commitments. The shape and design of campus life can acknowledge that—for students as for staff, faculty, and administrators—public and private intimately intertwine, each giving strength and support to the other. And if we change the culture of decision-making, as I recommend both in my personal preface and in chapter 7, then deans and vice presidents need no longer be confronted, at every turn, with ambiguous policy decisions and conflicting demands.

But all of this assumes that we need new models of leadership for the coming century and new models of shared governance. We need to reinvent consensus decision-making so that its inherent limitations— the tendency to suppress dissent and to level all contradictions—can be minimized. And we need to understand that the kind of leadership that can effect truly collaborative decision-making—involving faculty, staff, administrators, and governing boards—requires skills in which few academics have yet been trained. Certainly, I was not.

If we pursue this last goal, then I predict that successful administrative leaders in the next century will finally mobilize legislators and governing boards, as well as those on campus, to face, rather than avoid, deeply ingrained philosophical conflicts and long-standing institutional contradictions. This does not mean that we will thereby do away with conflicts and contradictions. It means, rather, that we will better understand their origins and motivations, thus helping us to resolve them where we can; and, in place of destroying our colleges and universities with factionalisms left over from the present century, we will learn to live with those conflicts and contradictions when resolution seems impossible at the moment. In that happy event, the campus of the twenty-first century might come to model one small facet of a "good society."

1 "60 Minutes" at the University of Arizona: The Polemic against Tenure

"It is the function of a liberal university not to
give right answers, but to ask right questions."
—Cynthia Ozick, "Women and Creativity,"
in *Motive* (1969).

i.

On a sunny November day in 1994, advance staff for CBS television's "60 Minutes" began contacting faculty in different departments at the University of Arizona. The CBS staffers were uniformly polite, asking faculty what they thought about teaching, research, and tenure. Although a few faculty were skeptical, most found the "60 Minutes" "team . . . very patient and willing to listen" (Ratliff 6). Some professors even hoped that the resulting program might highlight the unique achievements of a public research university.

A week later, the full "60 Minutes" crew arrived in Tucson. Producers and cameras followed reporter Lesley Stahl as she strolled the campus, chatted with students, examined scholarly journals in the library, and questioned the faculty who had been selected for on-camera interviews. Once the cameras began rolling, however, the questions no longer sounded neutral. As Keith Lehrer, a Regents Professor in the Department of Philosophy, described his experience to me, Stahl arrived "with a preconceived script in her head. She already knew what she wanted to hear."[1]

Judging from the twelve-minute segment, "Get Real," that finally aired on "60 Minutes" on Sunday night, 26 February 1995, what Stahl wanted to hear was the current litany of popularized misconceptions about large research institutions: Professors don't teach because they prefer to pursue research. Undergraduate courses are relegated to graduate student teaching assistants who have no training as teachers. Much of the research is frivolous, pursued only for the sake of receiving tenure. And parents subsidize this research with their precious tuition dollars. The program's opening trailer perfectly predicted what was to follow. After admiring "all these famous names" in the university course catalog, Stahl then declared, incredulous, "And the kid gets there and these professors don't teach at all?" Taking on the role of an outraged parent, she continued, "What I'm doing is subsidizing some guy's research. I thought I was forking out this money to educate my kid." As the trailer closes, an unnamed professor tacitly agrees, offering his own solution: "I'm waiting for some powerful parent to sue a university for consumer fraud" ("Get Real" 1).

University of Arizona officials were quick to respond. In a 3 March 1995 letter to the entire campus community, university president Manuel Pacheco refuted Stahl's claim that, as a parent, she might be "forking out $15,000 to $20,000" a year to send a "kid to a school where what—what I'm doing is subsidizing some guy's research" ("Get Real" 15). "Tuition at the University of Arizona is one of America's best bargains," insisted Pacheco, "$1,800 for in-state students, and $8,000 for out-of-state students" (Pacheco 1). And, as he emphasized in italics, *"tuition dollars are not spent to subsidize research.* To the contrary," Pacheco continued, *"research dollars support undergraduate education.* Eighty percent of the equipment used by our undergraduates in science was paid for by research. Research dollars have constructed buildings, outfitted laboratories and supported thousands of students with on-campus jobs" (Pacheco 2).

The president's office also circulated a fact sheet titled "Quick Response to 60 Minutes," aimed mostly at answering Stahl's claim that "teaching assistants, or TAs, have little or no training as teachers. And what's worse, in the sciences, some can barely speak English" ("Get Real" 9). The fact sheet identified the graduate students filmed for "Get Real" as lab assistants—rather than course instructors—and made clear that all international students "must pass a spoken English test before being allowed to teach" ("Quick Response" 2). Repeating an emphasis in the president's letter, the fact sheet noted that "the majority of our [freshman] lectures are taught by professors" ("Quick Response" 1).

Unfortunately, the president's letter and the three-page "Quick Response to 60 Minutes" saw only local distribution as compared with

"60 Minutes'" national audience, so that damage control was limited, at best. Equally unfortunate was the muted tone of the two documents: tempered and reasonable, when much more could have been said. For example, why not address the subtle racism—or was it only xenophobia?—suggested by the camera's exclusive focus on individuals of color, some with accents, whenever "Get Real" complained of the ineptitude of graduate teaching assistants?[2] The vast majority of graduate teaching assistants at the University of Arizona, after all, are white, native-born Americans. And, together, the Graduate College and individual departments train, supervise, and evaluate those graduate students who step into the classroom as teaching assistants.

Or why not remind Stahl of where she was when she sneered at the publication of academic research in specialized journals? For, when Stahl cited the "45 different journals on entomology, the study of bugs" ("Get Real" 13) as her example of excessive research undertaken only to achieve tenure, she made a serious misstep. Obviously, she had forgotten that she was in the library of a major land grant institution in a state whose economy depends on ranching, mining, farming, and tourism. The university's College of Agriculture is vested by the state with the responsibility for maintaining agricultural experiment stations and cooperative extension services and for conducting the kinds of research that the state's economic infrastructure requires. In Arizona, where terrain varies from arid desert to upland alpine, and where weevils threaten the pima cotton crop while the mosquito that carries dengue fever is quickly migrating in from South America, "the study of bugs" is no trivial matter.

The president's office, however, chose to ignore the claim that tenure was the cause of proliferating journals and mindless research and responded to "Get Real" solely as an attack on the quality of undergraduate education. Accordingly, Pacheco's 3 March 1995 letter noted that the "60 Minutes" "crew spent hours with renowned researchers who teach undergraduates; they talked to the faculty members who helped to launch significant improvements in undergraduate education; they heard parents on campus express positive reactions to their children's educational experience." But "none of it showed," the president protested (Pacheco 1), referring to all the footage left on the cutting-room floor.

Having thus tried to correct selected factual errors, university administrators held their breath. To their relief, in the weeks following the "60 Minutes" broadcast, the president's office was not deluged by calls from angry parents or alumni. Nor, as had been feared, did any state legislator publicly cite the "Get Real" segment as a pretext for further trimming the university's already inadequate budget. And, to date, no University of Arizona parent has filed suit. Still, this initial sigh of relief proved premature.

Although tenure had not emerged as the program's exclusive focus, "60 Minutes" nonetheless offered its audience a series of sensationalized soundbites that questioned the necessity of tenure as a safeguard for academic freedom and suggested, instead, that tenure served merely to protect job security and spur useless research. While the president's office had not responded to this aspect of "Get Real," the Arizona Board of Regents finally did. At their July 1995 retreat, key board members expressed doubt that "tenure was necessary to attract and keep top faculty," and they commissioned a study to help them determine "whether to continue to grant tenure at the three state universities" (Lamplot 1). Ironically, the regents were reacting to what had all along been the intended script of "60 Minutes." For, as a ninety-minute tape cassette made by one of the professors interviewed by Stahl reveals, "60 Minutes" had come to the University of Arizona expecting to film a polemic against tenure.

ii.

Although many faculty—from the University of Arizona and from other universities—were interviewed by "60 Minutes," only three professors were actually given any significant air time. Two were from the University of Arizona. One of these, professor of philosophy Keith Lehrer, made a tape cassette of the entire interview session, which he generously shared with me.

Lehrer surmised that he was chosen for an on-camera interview because the "60 Minutes" producers assumed that a philosopher's research could easily be portrayed as esoteric, inaccessible, and especially impractical. But when Stahl challenged Lehrer to describe his research, his answer surprised her. With at least one international nongovernmental agency eager to put his research to use, Lehrer explained, he is now trying to construct a practical mathematical model for building consensus around complicated global problems—like forging an international response to the depletion of the ozone layer. "It's fabulous," exclaims Stahl on the tape cassette. "I want to do a second story."[3] Stahl's enthusiasm notwithstanding, the only image of Lehrer's research that made it to airtime was a distance pan of a bearded professor, sitting alone in his office, eyes fixed on his computer screen. The voice-over gave no indication of what he might be working on. The emphasis, instead, is on professors who leave their students for the solitude of their research. "Research that may, of course, be very important," concedes Stahl ("Get Real" 12).

By contrast, the tape cassette records Lehrer—who regularly teaches large-enrollment lower division courses in general humanities—speaking repeatedly and passionately about the "hours and hours" of preparation for such courses. But when "Get Real" was aired, it did not include any part of this discussion, or of his questions to himself: "How can I best capture their imagination?" and "How can I best teach them?" Lehrer's statement that "working with students is the most thrilling and exciting pleasure" was cut.

The real value of Lehrer's tape cassette, however, goes beyond its confirmation of President Pacheco's claim that "60 Minutes" deleted evidence of professorial devotion to undergraduate teaching. Even more important is what it exposes of the interviewer's original preoccupation. As Stahl revealed to Lehrer at one point, "Our main focus is tenure, the issue of tenure—whether we need to keep it, change it, get rid of it."

Beginning with Stahl's first questions to Lehrer—"What is the idea behind tenure? Why did they start it in the first place?"—his tape cassette lays bare the program that had originally been in the works. No matter how cogently Lehrer responded to these questions and despite whatever new subjects he tried to introduce, Stahl repeatedly brought the discussion back to tenure. "What is the basic idea behind tenure?" she asks again, and "Why did they give professors this extraordinary protection?" Lehrer's patient explanations of the need to secure an open and free "marketplace of ideas" and his survey of the many historical threats to open inquiry—from Nazi Germany to home-grown McCarthyism—do not satisfy Stahl. "Is guaranteeing someone a job for life the best way to protect academic freedom?" she presses. In her view, the issue is not academic freedom: "The issue is job protection. The professors have the best union contract ever written."

In fact, this is the main theme of Stahl's interview with Lehrer. Because the tenure "contract says you have a job for life," no matter how you perform, Stahl keeps insisting, all other problems follow. "Tenure protects a professor who doesn't teach well," Stahl reiterates. She tells Lehrer that "administrators around the country, at large research universities, complain that because of tenure they can't reshape the curriculum." And she tries repeatedly to get Lehrer to agree with her that "if tenure were abolished," all these problems would be solved.

iii.

Despite the singlemindedness of Stahl's questions, "60 Minutes" was never able to produce a full-fledged polemic against tenure. Instead, in the segment as it was finally aired, tenure is simply implicated in the problem that receives greatest emphasis: professors who don't—or can't—teach undergraduates. On the one hand, Stahl told her audience, tenure protects "deadwood": "We keep hearing that universities can no longer get rid of faculty members who are—let's—let's not be coy about this—too old. They're burned out" ("Get Real" 14). On the other hand, the program suggests that tenure is granted for the wrong reason: it rewards research productivity over teaching performance. For "a tenured professor at any university, teaching means very little," one of the professors interviewed by Stahl tells the camera ("Get Real" 12). And although "Get Real" certainly expressed a deep suspicion of tenure for its "extraordinary [job] protection," the segment concluded by recommending only that tenured professors teach "more and better" ("Get Real" 14).

Granted that academe has serious problems that need to be addressed, tenure is not—as Stahl would have it—the source of those problems. Her intended polemic against tenure proved unworkable because Stahl's original assumptions were unworkable. As she articulated them in the "Get Real" segment and as she revealed them in her interview with Lehrer, Stahl's three central assertions do not stand up to scrutiny and, in fact, deserve the kind of discussion that will not be contained by soundbites.

Assertion no. 1. "Get Real" scored its easiest points by insisting that tenure protects "deadwood" because it forces universities to retain faculty who are "burned out" ("Get Real" 14). But as Lehrer repeatedly tried to explain to Stahl, tenure was never designed to assure lifelong employment *no matter what.* The guidelines of the American Association of University Professors, widely followed in academe, make clear that "universities can break tenure contracts . . . under certain conditions: if they find 'cause,' such as misconduct or incompetence; if they can show that they face a financial emergency; or if they close a program and cannot find jobs for displaced professors" (Mooney A19). Accordingly, as is true of the policy statements at most universities, the University of Arizona *Handbook for Appointed Personnel* (section 3.11.04) states that faculty are subject to "dismissal for just cause, or termination for budgetary reasons or for educational policy change" (Fredette 6). The termination of any faculty member's employment thus requires the university to demonstrate that it is not punishing someone for her political views, her area of study or research, or the ideas, declarations, or creative work emanating from that research.

During my years as dean, I worked with a department head and with university lawyers to initiate "cause" proceedings to dismiss a tenured professor. We were responding to a series of student complaints about poor teaching and to a record of unsatisfactory annual peer performance evaluations. Legal guidance was crucial at every step, and the department head and I were frustrated by the lengthy and cumbersome procedures, procedures that could profitably be streamlined.[4] Still, I remain grateful that the dismissal of a tenured professor is *not* an easy matter. As a feminist literary critic whose area of study has not always been welcomed by my departmental colleagues, I am all too aware of the vulnerability of those who introduce new research methodologies or put forward controversial analyses.

The best approach is to minimize the need for cause proceedings in the first place. One way to do this is for schools to devise a plan for regularly reviewing the teaching and research of tenured faculty. Such reviews might be scheduled every three to five years, thus replacing the wasteful paperwork of the often pro forma annual evaluation, and they should go beyond merely identifying weaknesses and strengths. The goals, instead, would be to identify senior faculty who could benefit from ongoing professional development activities, to address problems where they exist, and to build on areas of strength. But for tenured faculty members who show themselves to be incapable of satisfactory performance, we need to refine and update the mechanisms for cause proceedings while still maintaining their academic freedom protections. At the same time, we need to design dismissal procedures that are less accessible to legal challenges in the courts. Only then will administrators lose their current reluctance to initiate such proceedings. In other words, I am arguing not for doing away with tenure, but for making tenure work as it was originally intended—that is, as a protection for free inquiry and free expression rather than as a guarantee of employment, no matter how a faculty member performs.

After all, when tenure works properly, a junior faculty member is subjected to fair and rigorous review over a five-to-seven-year period. At a research university (and at most colleges and universities), the faculty member must demonstrate excellence in both teaching and research—or creative work—in order to be granted tenure. Tenure then functions as a set of reciprocal obligations. In exchange for faculty rights to free inquiry and free communication in the classroom, the tenured faculty member takes on the responsibility to maintain the highest ethical practice as a teacher and researcher. She accepts the obligation to share in the collective governance of her university. And she assumes the responsibility to exercise her disciplinary expertise as well as her professional judgment in the hiring, firing, and promotion of colleagues. In a nutshell, the tenured faculty member is expected to contribute to the common good of her university's teaching, research, and service missions.

Unfortunately, because no opposing views were offered on camera, the "60 Minutes" audience was left to believe the allegation made by Stahl that tenure is merely a form of job protection, shielding deadwood on the nation's campuses. But on the tape cassette Lehrer challenged Stahl's "whole issue of deadwood" ("Get Real" 14). Reminding her of his earlier service as a department head and his considerable experience on university-wide committees, he estimated that no more than 1 percent of his colleagues across campus qualified for the label of "deadwood." Admittedly, Lehrer may have been somewhat generous in his judgment, but not by much. During my years as dean, in all my discussions with students, administrators, and faculty around the country, I never heard estimates beyond 3–5 percent—not even in the most candid and heated conversations. Without question, tenured professors who are no longer active in their field, who no longer keep up with the latest research, or who no longer have enthusiasm for teaching *are* a problem, no matter how small the actual numbers. But, as Lehrer tried to explain to Stahl, even some of these professors can be encouraged to retool in new subject areas, or they can be usefully reassigned to advising or other nonteaching duties, thereby allowing the university to continue to make use of their considerable experience and expertise. The more interesting point to be made, though, is how well tenure has worked. If it is accurate that the rigorous reviews required for tenure have produced a faculty where, over all, 95 percent or more of the nation's professors remain active and engaged through their entire career, then that's a pretty impressive success rate.

Assertion no. 2. While scoring points with the unsubstantiated allegation of "deadwood" faculty was relatively easy, the producers of the "Get Real" segment must have ascertained that they would score no points with the argument that tenure undermines a school's ability to respond to changing curricular needs. This argument never saw airtime, although on the tape cassette Stahl makes the charge explicit when she tells Lehrer that "administrators around the country, at large research institutions, complain that because of tenure, they can't reshape the curriculum." It is surprising that this did not see airtime because schools routinely justify hiring faculty into adjunct rather than tenure-track positions by claiming to require flexibility in meeting changing student enrollment patterns. As reported in the 2 June 1995 *Chronicle of Higher Education,* for example, Florida Gulf Coast University, "scheduled to open in 1997," will experiment with "two- to five-year employment contracts" in order "to fulfill specific short-term needs." "For instance," one administrator told the *Chronicle,* the school "might offer such a contract to a candidate whose assignment would be to help start a new academic program" (Cage A15).

Putting aside the exploitative nature of appointments that turn serious teachers into academic nomads, periodically moving from one multiyear position to another, and putting aside the fact that part-time and term-contract faculty rarely become part of the community of the institution to which they are so temporarily attached, it simply is not the case that tenure stands in the way of rapid curricular change. Instead, we must look to the organizational structure on most campuses. Ossified disciplinary distinctions, whose roots date back to the nineteenth century, have evolved into semi-autonomous budgetary and administrative units called departments or programs. Even during periods of adequate funding, a Department of English or a Chemistry Program claims to "own" the time of its faculty and resists reassigning either human or other resources across departmental or college lines. During periods of diminished funding, these units protect themselves at all costs, withdrawing from cooperative ventures with, say, a Women's Studies Program or a Department of Biochemistry and thereby thwart the development of innovative cross- and interdisciplinary courses. Historically, programs, departments, and colleges were genuinely useful entities, both for administrative convenience and as reasonable means for organizing knowledge. At the end of the 1990s, however, this inflexible structure is no longer either practical or intellectually defensible.

The challenges about to confront the students of the twenty-first century cannot be addressed solely within established disciplines. Nowadays, cultural, social, environmental, and scientific problems necessarily cross discipline boundaries or integrate established disciplines in unprecedented ways or even require the development of wholly new disciplines. In my experience, most faculty chafe at the insularity of their exclusively disciplinary culture. They don't want to grow stale by teaching the same subject in the same manner year after year, and they are eager for the intellectual stimulus of teaching and research collaborations with colleagues from different departments.

Thanks to a fast-developing data technology that favors flexibility over rigidity, even the most complex large research university possesses the potential to respond in a timely fashion to changing student enrollment patterns and to emerging cross-disciplinary research areas. Because it is now much easier to track information about human and financial resources, physical space, capital equipment, and student credit hours, it is also easier to redesign faculty teaching responsibilities, alter prior patterns of room and equipment assignments, and generally reconfigure a curriculum in a manner that both responds to student needs and simultaneously frees faculty from the sometimes stultifying confines of a "home" department. While required courses will still be covered (or supplanted by new courses) and established majors remain available (even if in modified form), innovative faculty can now enjoy the option of moving beyond department boundaries to form cross-disciplinary "clusters" of new courses around emerging fields or in response to some pressing academic or public need. Students registering electronically receive immediate information about new curricular options, and they can also be informed, well in advance, when or if changing requirements affect their own course of study.

If Stahl really wanted to point a finger of blame for the slowness of curricular change, therefore, she should have aimed not at tenured professors but at unimaginative administrators who have been slow to take advantage of new technologies in reorganizing a campus and even slower to work with faculty in modifying entrenched departmental and college bureaucracies. As a result, following administrative cues, many faculty—especially those who are untenured—hesitate to defy departmental authority. The professors who do push the envelope, more often than not, are protected by tenure. Indeed, without the activism of influential tenured faculty, it's doubtful that most schools today would be offering any of their successful cross- and interdisciplinary programs.

Assertion no. 3. Finally, Stahl contradicted herself when she identified tenure as the cause of the alleged imbalance between teaching and research in today's large universities. Based on what she had learned from her interviewees, Stahl herself clearly identified diminished funding as the real source of the problem. As Stahl explained to her "60 Minutes" audience in the first few minutes of the piece, "The University of Arizona gets $250 million a year in government and private research grants, nearly half its total budget. It and all other big universities couldn't operate without that money. Lately government and private grants have been shrinking, so that the pressure on professors to bring in money is even greater" ("Get Real" 10–11). The only problem with the comment is that Stahl didn't go far enough.

Federal aid to education in this country has declined by 30 percent since 1980. And when, during a period of economic slowdown, President Ronald Reagan curtailed revenue-sharing with the states, he effectively shrank most states' ability to fund any nonmandatory public programs—including higher education—to prior levels. The combination of shrinking federal supports and the states' inability to make up the shortfall was nothing less than catastrophic for public universities. Especially hard hit were schools like the University of Arizona, where enrollments continued to rise sharply. By the late 1980s, when I first became dean, enrollments in our various humanities majors had been growing by 35 percent over a five-year period, but our share of state support was actually shrinking. Many of our students were from less affluent, nontraditional backgrounds. But, during that same period, federal support for student aid had been drastically reduced. And, because we were never able to secure construction dollars, the main building in which the humanities are housed remained both antiquated and too small. We didn't have enough classrooms during peak-demand weekday hours; our new state-of-the-art language laboratory had space for only half the computer workstations required to accommodate students enrolled in foreign language courses; and in some departments two or three faculty shared offices designed for one. By 1992–93, when I decided to step down as dean, state appropriations for higher education all across the country were not only failing to keep up with inflation—an old story—but now, for the first time, there was an actual decrease in funding.[5]

Large public universities found themselves in an impossible situation. Not only was it politically risky to raise tuition, but it was also educationally irresponsible: the majority of the students we serve could not afford significantly increased expenses. In such a strapped financial climate, a renewed emphasis on competing for externally funded research dollars was inevitable, and professors who could bring in large grants were highly prized. Again, however, tenure did not cause this imbalance in rewarding research over teaching. At the University of Arizona, for example, where in past decades almost three-quarters of the school's annual budget had come from state appropriations, by the time "60 Minutes" hit campus, only half of the school's budget was state-funded. The other $250 million, as Stahl made plain, came from "government and private research grants." The overhead or indirect cost recovery (ICR) accompanying these grants was distributed across campus, keeping the lights on, supplementing the instructional budget, and equipping classrooms and laboratories alike. That is why, in his 3 March 1995 letter, President Pacheco tried to stress that *"research dollars support undergraduate education"* (Pacheco 2).[6]

While eminently popular, the view that tenure—and tenure alone—accounts for the current imbalance between teaching and research falsifies a great deal of recent history. The fact is that it was the post–World War II "conversion of military research into university science" —and not research performed merely in the competition for tenure— that "added tremendous impetus to the domination of the research university by research" (Kennedy 10). As Donald Kennedy, president emeritus and Bing Professor of Environmental Science at Stanford University, points out, "largely as a result of the public investment in scientific research and the faith that such work could support national economic goals, the [research] institution became a significant instrument of U.S. policy quite apart from its educational mission. The birth of microelectronics, biotechnology, Silicon Valley, national competitiveness, regional economic renewal"—all these, says Kennedy—"spell[ed] out a new iconography for describing the role of higher education in American society" (Kennedy 10).

Kennedy narrates the end of a story that properly begins in the nineteenth century when American higher education successfully melded the English college system with the research-oriented German graduate school. The result was a unique new institution for the education of the young *and* for the production of new types of knowledge. In the twentieth century, unlike most of its counterparts abroad, the U.S. government invested heavily in these institutions for its research needs, seeing this as far more cost-effective than developing and staffing independent research centers of its own. With additional investment from the private sector, the modern research university became a national hub for research and creative work in all fields and disciplines, from the sciences to the fine arts. Despite the many successes of this academic-governmental research complex, and despite the fact that the government still depends on universities as its research machine—"university research developed the smart bombs used during the Gulf War," Lehrer reminded Stahl—a conservative Congress now says it doesn't want to pay the bills. In 1995 and 1996 budgets for the National Endowment for the Arts, the National Endowment for the Humanities, and the National Science Foundation—each of which supported a great deal of university-based research—were slashed severely; and future funding for the first two remains in jeopardy even after President Clinton asked Congress for budgetary increases for both in his February 1997 State of the Union address.

Research universities continue to compete for whatever research dollars remain available—they cannot afford to do otherwise—but, at the same time, many schools are beginning to rethink their participation in the academic-governmental research complex. They wonder if they can any longer afford what Donald Kennedy called "a new iconography." Prominent research institutions like the University of California at Berkeley and Syracuse University, for example, have increased faculty teaching responsibilities and publicly announced that teaching will receive greater weight in promotion and tenure decisions. And, as Stahl conceded in "Get Real," "at Arizona, the administration is trying hard to get its professors back in the classroom" ("Get Real" 11).

The major point to be made here, however, is that the current animus against tenure is not simply the outcome of random economic forces that make contracted lecturers seem more cost-effective than tenured professors who pursue research. The economic situation itself is being manipulated so as to make the public research university *appear* unaffordable. Consider, for example, that the entire budget of the National Endowment for the Humanities was only $172 million in 1994. But that small outlay, in addition to the NEH's public programs and many library projects, funded "fully two-thirds of the research in the humanities in this country," providing money for things like "curriculum development and seminars to improve teaching" (Kerber A80). Slashing the NEH budget by 40 percent, as recommended by a House-Senate conference committee in 1995, makes no significant impact on the multitrillion-dollar national debt, but it guts most universities' ability to support faculty research in all the humanities disciplines.[7] Or consider the fact that as the Arizona economy recovered in the mid-1990s, with state revenues exceeding expenditures, Republican governor Fife Symington and a conservative Republican-controlled state legislature decided to use the surpluses to provide state income tax reductions for the affluent and to establish a "rainy day fund" for future needs. There was no discussion of restoring lost funding to the state's three public universities. And consider the fact that this pattern repeated itself in New York State in January 1997 when, confronted by a $1.3 billion budget surplus, Republican governor George E. Pataki "proposed cuts in the operating budgets for New York's two public university systems," which had already endured several years of reduced funding (Healy, "N.Y. Governor Proposes," A22).

Still, Stahl may be correct: as funding for public higher education continues to be purposefully squeezed, doing away with tenure might well seem to save a few dollars and put more term lecturers or part-time adjuncts into the classroom as teachers. But such a move also begins to dismantle the very fabric of the modern research university at precisely the moment when most other industrialized nations are massively increasing their expenditures for research and development.[8] Doing away with tenure would surely slow the pace of research in general and chill all but the safest research by eliminating the single most effective protection we now have for risk-taking and innovation. And, given the fact that the nation's research universities train over three quarters of the Ph.D.s who staff the other 3,900 institutions of higher education (Kennedy 13), would Stahl really want to banish the risk-takers and innovators from their ranks?

Stahl seems never to have recognized the abiding contradictions in her arguments. Without tenure, there would be a noticeable decline in the numbers of "all these famous names teaching in the sciences, in the humanities" ("Get Real" 10), the names Stahl was so quick to admire in the university catalog. What makes those names "famous" or at least recognizable to Stahl and to the parents of prospective students is their prominence as researchers, creative artists, originals. And it is that sometimes unpredictable, sometimes unwelcome capacity for originality, for going beyond the borders of current thinking, that tenure, for all its flaws, is designed to protect. Even Stahl acknowledged on camera that "academic freedom . . . really is the bedrock that tenure is built on" ("Get Real" 14).

iv.

If burgeoning student enrollments, the escalating costs of maintaining a school's physical facilities, and declining state and federal supports explain most of academia's current ills, why are report-ers like Stahl turning the spotlight, instead, on tenure? Wouldn't it make more sense to question who suffers when classroom buildings decay, when lab equipment for basic chemistry classes becomes out-dated, and when NEH-sponsored seminars to improve teaching in the humanities are canceled? By not asking such questions, even a dis-tinguished program like "60 Minutes" echoed, however inadvertently, right-wing columnist George Will's view that all manner of "academic malpractice" derives from "the smugly self-absorbed professoriate that . . . is often tenured and always comfortable" (Will A13). And the most troubling question of all remains unanswered: why has tenure sud-denly become a contested issue?

Moderate, liberal, and progressive left faculty and administrators have interpreted the assault on tenure as just one more facet of an organized right-wing attempt to reshape research and teaching on the nation's campuses.[9] No doubt the best publicized example of that at-tempt was alumnus Lee Bass's ill-fated $20 million gift to Yale. Ac-cording to a 23 March 1995 letter to all Yale graduates from Yale's president, Richard C. Levin, at first "the gift was intended to endow faculty positions and a new interdisciplinary survey course in Western Civilization." Even though Yale already boasted a vast array of courses in Western civilization, the gift was eagerly courted. But then *Light and Truth*—characterized by *Newsweek* as "an obscure periodical run by a handful of conservative Yale students"—ran an exposé of Yale's allegedly "clumsy handling" of the gift (Hancock 58). And, as President Levin explained in his letter, now "Mr. Bass sought a new and addi-tional condition—the authority to approve the appointment of faculty to teach in the program." At this point, Levin continued, the gift had to be returned. "We simply could not delegate authority over faculty appointments to a donor" (Levin).

Levin's decision was widely applauded by students, faculty, and alumni because it acknowledged that, due to specialization and com-plexity in the academic disciplines, even great wealth does not qualify donors and alumni to judge the abilities of potential new teachers and scholars. A wealthy private institution like Yale could afford thus to honor the intellectual integrity of retaining the responsibility for hiring and tenure in faculty hands, supervised by university-wide faculty committees and by academic administrators. In the future, however, institutions with less solid endowments—which includes most public universities—may not be able to afford that luxury. For, "as government aid shrinks," noted the *New York Times* in its coverage of the Bass story, "universities have become more dependent on private giving, which constitutes a significant source of revenue"; in a period of scarcity, even gifts that come "with more strings attached" will be hard to turn down (Arenson, "Alumni Generosity," 5). And attaching strings is precisely the goal of the National Alumni Forum, led by Lynne Cheney, former chair of the National Endowment for the Humanities under Presidents Reagan and Bush and now an advocate for cutting the very endowment that she once headed. Capitalizing on the financial desperation of colleges and universities, Cheney's National Alumni Forum is organizing conservative alumni to target their donations to influence everything from academic program development to faculty hiring. As Andrew Gold, writing in the conservative journal *Campus*, stated flatly, "One of the primary aims of the Princeton [alumni] organization is to secure more conservative faculty" (Gold 2). *Newsweek* reported yet another approach to purchasing campus influence, an approach promoted by "the Intercollegiate Studies Institute, Inc., a $3.5 million conservative organization," which was also the publisher of Yale's conservative gazette, *Light and Truth* (Hancock 58). "Dedicated to purging 'the pervasive forces of multiculturalism' from the nation's campuses," according to *Newsweek*, ISI contacts conservative alumni at targeted institutions, "among them Princeton, Stanford and Duke" (Hancock 58), asking them to "withhold their annual donations—and funnel the cash to ISI instead. The result," concludes *Newsweek*, "is that controversial decisions on campus can be disproportionately influenced by wealthy, and most often conservative, alumni" (Hancock 59).

At the same time, wealthy conservative foundations—like the John M. Olin Foundation—have mastered how to choreograph a school's educational direction. James Piereson, executive director of the Olin Foundation, "currently provides funds for more than 50 university programs" and explained his strategy to the *New York Times.* "'We don't tell them who to hire,'" Piereson told the reporter, Karen Arenson. Instead, "'we start with a professor who is already in place and wants to do what we want to do. If all goes well, we renew the grant. Then maybe the program will grow internally and bring on more faculty'" (Arenson, "Alumni Generosity," 5).

What the right has come to understand is that—like the rest of the nation—academia sits poised at the edge of a major demographic fault line. Affluent and predominantly white students will continue to cluster in the elite private colleges and universities, while the public institutions will enroll a more diverse population. The faculty available to teach is also undergoing shifts in its own makeup. In order to control how that changing faculty distributes itself, as well as to control what that faculty can actually accomplish, right-wing foundations and alumni groups are targeting private institutions, pouring millions of dollars into narrowly tailored conservative professorships, endowed chairs, research centers, and instructional programs. Public institutions will be targeted by many of the same tactics, but, for now, they are being subjected to severe budget cuts, at both state and federal levels, with conservative legislators pushing them to restrict or abandon tenure as a means for maintaining solvency. The timing of all this is not accidental, nor, as I have tried to suggest, is it primarily motivated by financial exigency. Instead, the polemic against tenure represents one more anxiety-laden strategy for containing the impact of the nation's changing demographics, at least on campus.

The first wave of demographic change in academe over which the right sounded alarms was the so-called feminization of the professoriate. In the two decades between 1971 and 1991, the percentage of doctorates awarded to women climbed from 14 to 37 percent, and in some fields—like psychology and foreign languages—significantly more than half the doctorates awarded in 1991 were awarded to women (Brown 190). Moreover, in the brief span "between 1989 and 1993, the number of women awarded PhDs increased by 20 percent, while men PhDs increased by only 2 percent" ("Growth in Number" 5). Again, in 1994 and 1995 "women continued to make up a growing proportion of the doctoral pool" while "the number of men receiving doctorates rose only slightly" (see Magner, "More Black Ph.D.'s," A25). Even so, the spectacular growth in the percentages of women earning Ph.D.s did not translate into proportionately more women within professorial ranks.

What those who rail against the "feminization" of the professoriate fail to note is that many of these women Ph.D.s never seek careers in academe and that, in the case of those who do, promotion and tenure reviews still reject them more often than they do men.[10] In 1995, women outnumbered men at only one rank: lecturer.

No less equivocal are the even smaller, but sometimes much publicized, gains of people of color. Black women earning Ph.D.s between 1983 and 1993 increased by 31 percent; after a slight decline in 1991–92, in 1992–93 the number of doctorates awarded to all African Americans, male and female, rebounded by 15 percent ("Growth in Number" 5). According to an American Council on Education analysis of data collected by the National Research Council, "from 1982 to 1992, the number of doctorates awarded to Asian Americans jumped by 83 per cent, to 828 from 452." The same analysis also showed that doctorates "earned by Hispanic Americans rose 41 per cent during that decade, to 755 from 535" (Robin Wilson, "Hiring of Black Scholars," A16). And while "most of the growth in the number of doctorates granted between 1987 and 1992 was fueled by the increase in foreign nationals studying in the United States on temporary visas," between 1992 and 1993 "the increase was primarily in U.S. women and U.S. minority students" ("Growth in Number" 5). By 1995, the last year for which statistics are available as this book goes to press, "American universities awarded a record number of doctorates to black Americans," so that "they received about 5 per cent of the Ph.D.'s granted to U.S. citizens" that year (Magner, "More Black Ph.D.'s," A25). In fact, "minority students earned 13.7 per cent more doctoral degrees in 1995 than in 1994" (Gose A38).

But citing percentage increases alone obscures the real picture. For example, in 1992–93, in all fields and disciplines, a total of 3,867 doctorates were awarded to Native Americans, Asian Americans, African Americans, and Hispanic Americans *combined*, as compared to the 26,700 doctorates awarded that same year to whites ("Earned Degrees" A37). And in 1994, of all the doctorates granted to U.S. citizens by American universities, 79.6 percent went to whites ("Who Got Doctorates" A18).

A 1995 Department of Education survey of over 800 selected colleges and universities, *Faculty and Instructional Staff: What Are They and What Do They Do?*, reveals even more starkly that despite modest gains in Ph.D. distribution, not much has changed in the makeup of the faculty. Broken down by ethnicity, race, and gender, the percentages of full-time faculty members remain overwhelmingly white and male:

	Men	Women
White	58.9%	27.9%
Black	2.6%	2.3%
Asian	4.0%	1.3%
Hispanic	1.7%	0.8%
Native American	0.3%	0.2%

("Surprise!" 3)

A more recent nationwide survey found that in 1995–96, minority professors accounted for only "about 10 per cent of the professoriate, inching up from 9 per cent in 1989"; and, unlike their white peers, "minority scholars in the survey were more likely to be squeezed into the lowest echelons of academe," with many "working at two-year colleges instead of more prominent four-year [colleges and] universities" (Schneider, "Proportion," A12, A13). Unfortunately, the real numbers are not what most people (including staff, faculty, students, and alumni) ever see. Instead, what get into the public media are the successes of schools' efforts at diversification, thus giving women and minority faculty a visibility disproportionate to their actual numbers. And when the best of these new scholars bring original and sometimes troubling questions to their chosen disciplines—especially in the already contested arts, humanities, and social sciences—the organized right is quick to exploit this, stirring deep-seated white anxieties about both the direction and the pace of intellectual change on the nation's campuses.

From those who are politically motivated to distort what is happening as well as from those who find new intellectual directions unsettling, we now hear scenarios of fragmenting disciplines and exaggerated tales of wholesale disregard for established traditions. Shakespeare displaced by Madonna, Beethoven by rap and salsa. Or, as Cheney claimed in 1988, "the concept of Western civilization, . . . this central and sustaining idea of our educational system and our intellectual heritage is being declared unworthy of study" (Cheney 6). The portrait that emerges is of a once-coherent academic culture now incapable of assimilating, without permanent damage, the radically new and different. Instead of providing welcome ferment, unfamiliar scholars with their sometimes unfamiliar ideas are seen as intrusive, shattering, dangerous to continuity.

However irrational, the conservative response to these anxieties parallels the impetus behind California's Proposition 187. Without overtly naming the anxieties that motivated it, Proposition 187 was an attempt to contain the reality of the nation's changing ethnic and racial makeup by targeting immigration: notably, in a period when the actual rates of immigration are not particularly high but when the sources of immigration have changed substantially—from Europe to Asia and Latin America. Those who now attack tenure are similarly silent about their own motivating racial and cultural anxieties. But their goal is to contain the first signs of a shift in the makeup of the professoriate, just as the percentages of doctorates awarded to white males are beginning to slip slightly. What I am trying to stress here is that it is not accidental that the assault on tenure gained momentum after two decades of growth in the number of doctorates awarded to women and at a moment in which the pool of Ph.D.s that will provide the next generation of professors contains quantifiably more people from previously underrepresented groups.

A chilling pattern emerges. For women and so-called minorities, the front end of the academic pipeline can be tightened by eliminating race, sex, color, ethnicity, or national origin as criteria for preferences in both undergraduate and graduate admissions and scholarships.[11] At the same time—as in California's Proposition 209, disingenuously named the California Civil Rights Initiative by its supporters—there is no prohibition against granting preferential treatment on the basis of such other criteria as being an athlete or a wealthy alumnus's grandchild.[12] At the far end of the pipeline, in the professorial ranks, women and minorities will be squeezed out by the elimination of affirmative action hiring goals, and tenure will be in short supply.

The success of these strategies is already apparent. Based on "a fall 1992 faculty survey sponsored by the Education Department's National Center for Education Statistics," researchers have found that a

new generation of full-time faculty look very different from their seniors. In 1992, those who were still "in the first seven years of their
academic careers" included increased percentages of women and minorities. But while "compared to their senior colleagues, these faculty
members are much more likely to be women and somewhat more
likely to be members of minority groups . . . *they are less likely . . .
to hold tenure-track jobs*" (emphasis mine). Indeed, "a third of [these]
junior academics are not even in positions where they are eligible for
tenure" (Magner, "The New Generation," A17, A18).

It is often assumed that the growing polemic against tenure in the
1990s is intended to dislodge the so-called tenured radicals of the 1960s
generation. But the right's fantasies notwithstanding, radicals are relatively rare in academe, and, anyway, that particular 1960s cohort will
begin retiring in large numbers within a decade. Instead, the dismantling of tenure is aimed at those who have yet to attain a firm foothold
within academe but who now seem poised to enter. By seeking to
make tenure less available at public universities and by influencing the
choice of tenure candidates at private institutions through gifts and
endowments, conservative forces have launched a campaign to substantially affect, if not wholly control, who gets to do the teaching and
what gets taught in the next century. Many who advocate restricting
or abolishing tenure are betting that without the job security afforded
by tenure, those from still-marginalized groups will find academic employment too uncertain to attract them. And without the academic
freedom protections of tenure, even those few who do enter the professoriate will be less likely to challenge the established norms and
procedures of their fields. What eliminating affirmative action hiring
goals might not achieve, and what budget cuts and hiring freezes have
only imperfectly accomplished,[13] the abolition of tenure surely will.
By doing away with tenure, some people truly believe that the borders
of academe can be secured.

v.

Tenure makes it possible for a professor of biochemistry to
experiment with the genetic manipulation of viruses when conventional wisdom in her department advocates the pursuit of vaccines to
combat AIDS. Tenure allows a professor of clinical psychology to con-

tinue to publish her research on the prevention of child sexual abuse despite the views of a prominent trustee of her university, who proclaims his distaste for the entire project. When teaching his courses on the philosophy of religion, Williams College's Mark Taylor—named by the Carnegie Foundation for the Advancement of Teaching as its undergraduate professor of the year for 1995—agrees with those who "interpret religion as providing structures and patterns that give meaning. . . . but another interpretation" he offers students is "that religion calls into question all meaning" (Judson 43). It may not be a popular view, but tenure empowers Taylor to confront his students with ideas that are both provocative and controversial. And he knows he can't be fired for doing that. Tenure is thus the most effective device that higher education has yet devised for maintaining academic freedom, keeping our campuses havens of free inquiry and open expression.

Without tenure, academic freedom is imperiled. The First Amendment rights of assembly and free speech and the due process protections of the Fourteenth Amendment have never been viewed by legal experts as sufficient, by themselves, for defending academic freedom as institutional practice. And while the courts do tend to treat tenure as a legal concept, they generally regard tenure as contractual, conferring certain rights and privileges of employment but *not* conferring protection for speech and due process or protection in the search for truth. Even "the U.S. Supreme Court has never granted academic freedom full constitutional status," notes Robert Poch in his comprehensive overview of the subject, *Academic Freedom in American Higher Education: Rights, Responsibilities, and Limitations* (iii). The best protection that the professoriate has, therefore, is the 1940 Statement of Academic Freedom and Tenure, composed jointly by the American Association of University Professors and the Association of American Colleges. That statement firmly establishes tenure as the functional guarantor of academic freedom. It seemed the only mechanism that would suffice.

Those who have joined the polemic against tenure often give eloquent lip-service to the concept of academic freedom but then fail to explain how it will be sustained once tenure disappears. "Do you think that if tenure were abolished that [*sic*] the university would survive and be just as wonderful as it is?" Stahl can be heard asking Lehrer on the tape cassette. What she never suggests—as does no one else—is what might replace it.

Unfortunately, we know what is already beginning to replace tenure —and it has little to do with academic freedom or concern for quality education. Desperate for solvency as state and federal support diminishes, America's colleges and universities are bracing themselves for the estimated additional three million students who are expected to enroll between 1997 and 2015. Elite private colleges and universities —like Harvard, Yale, and Stanford—have embarked on multibillion-dollar fundraising campaigns directed at wealthy alumni. But most public institutions, by contrast, have given up arguing their case to state legislators or in the media and, instead, they have taken what savings they can from restructuring administrative processes, closing entire academic programs, and consolidating student support services. And bowing to political pressures, they are going after their biggest fixed cost by paring staff positions and by replacing retiring faculty with *non*-tenure-eligible appointments that carry increased teaching loads. As a result, more and more faculty openings are being filled with relatively low-wage adjuncts, part-timers, and term contract instructors or lecturers.

The trend is most pronounced at two-year community colleges, like the Community College of Vermont "where all 400 faculty teach part-time and earn $1,000 per course" (Lesko B5). But four-year colleges and universities are also increasingly relying on non-tenure-track faculty, especially for introductory courses in the liberal arts and in some technical and professional fields. "At public universities in Florida, for example," says Philip G. Altbach, a senior associate of the Carnegie Foundation for the Advancement of Teaching, "60 percent of lower-division undergraduate courses are taught by non-tenure-track faculty members, many of whom are part-timers. . . . The proportion of part-time faculty members in the United States has been increasing steadily," he concludes, estimating that in 1995 it stood "at about 35 percent nationally" (Altbach B3). More recent estimates go as high as 45 percent (see Tomasky 46).

At most colleges and universities, part-timers and adjuncts are ineligible for health and retirement benefits, and they receive no secretarial support for the preparation of course material. On some campuses, they aren't even assigned an office and have no quiet place to meet with students. Full-time adjuncts or lecturers on year-to-year contracts usually have an office and are eligible for some benefits, but they are also routinely assigned large classes and mind-numbing teaching loads. Rarely do they have time to keep up with the latest developments in their field or enjoy any kind of research support. In some instances, they have no say in the design of the courses they are hired to teach and may even be wholly unfamiliar with the assigned textbook. Whether part time or full time, contracted for a semester or for three years, such faculty are viewed as temporary by colleagues and administrators alike and, as such, they rarely serve on committees, attend faculty meetings, or participate in "the myriad other activities that make a university function" (Altbach B3).[14] Exploited and individually isolated, this growing population of teachers cannot conceivably develop meaningful educational relationships with their students, find the time to pursue any research agenda, let alone harbor a warm departmental attachment or institutional loyalty. Whatever their initial enthusiasm for teaching, they soon burn out. If abuses in the tenure system sometimes protect deadwood in the senior ranks, the characteristics of *non*tenured employment guarantee deadwood at a far earlier age.

Except where union contracts or other unusual circumstances intervene, these faculty members can be hired and fired at will, whatever the quality of their job performance. A university administration may claim that it has cut costs and gained greater flexibility in meeting student enrollment patterns, but what the school has really achieved is a pliable faculty. Those who can be hired and fired at will generally teach what they are assigned, shy away from experiment and innovation, and avoid risk-taking in their teaching and their scholarship (if they have the luxury of research time). Had circumstances like these prevailed for the past fifty years, many of the nation's great research advances would have been derailed and students would still encounter what Linda Kerber, recent president of the Organization of American Historians, has called "the two-tier institutional setting of the 1950s." In that setting, distinguished faculty as well as "research and scholarship were the province of a relatively few elite universities," which mainly served the children of privilege and influence. Public support for higher education in the post–World War II era, however, substantially narrowed the gap between "our elite institutions . . . and others" so that, as Kerber put it, differences between institutions became "less marked and educational opportunity for [all] students [was] greatly enhanced" (Kerber A80). But if the conservative right succeeds in eroding tenure and circumstances like these become the norm, then we will surely witness the precipitous disappearance of the conditions that enabled public colleges and universities to strive for excellence in the first place.

The decline of the public university at the beginning of the twenty-first century is frightening in its implications because it presages a future in which quality higher education will be available only to those who can pay for it. Knowledge, power, prestige—and all decisions concerning the direction of the nation's research—will become ever more concentrated at the top of the social pyramid. "The way to do that," mused Lehrer some time after his "60 Minutes" interview, "is to make the public think that less should be spent on public higher education." Reviewing the segment several months after it first aired, Lehrer concluded that this was precisely "what 'Get Real' attempted to do. The moral of the show was: public universities are a waste of money, why spend money on them? Only the poor really need them."[15]

vi.

To be sure, tenure is not a perfect system. Beginning in 1975, I was repeatedly denied both promotion and tenure by the Department of English at the University of New Hampshire, despite the department's own evaluation of my teaching, scholarship, and service as outstanding. The department claimed that I lacked "collegiality," a term that was never defined and did not appear in any university document. As a result, at what should have been a well-earned midcareer transition, I was forced to file a Title VII discrimination suit against the university, draining my time, energy, and bank account from 1975 until the university offered an out-of-court settlement in the fall of 1980.[16] What I came to understand in the process is that the initial promotion and tenure review can as easily be a gate-keeping device for excluding unfamiliar people and unpopular ideas—in my case, a Jewish feminist literary critic—as it can be a safeguard for bold creativity and intellectual innovation. In some cases, moreover, tenure has certainly allowed the continued employment of incompetent teachers and burned-out scholars. And during periods of crisis, tenure has not always protected academic freedom. Amid the Joseph McCarthy red-baiting of the 1950s, tenured professors suspected of communist sympathies and some who, on principle, refused to sign loyalty oaths were routinely dismissed from U.S. colleges and universities. In 1971, following the U.S. invasion of Laos, Stanford University fired tenured American literature scholar H. Bruce Franklin because of what the school's hearing board characterized as Franklin's "convictions" concerning Stanford's role in the Vietnam war effort (Franklin 39).

But all of these represent *abuses* of the tenure system, not its goals. As abuses, they are subject to correction and *must* be corrected. Like the College of Humanities at the University of Arizona, other institutions have also revised their tenure and promotion procedures so as to introduce both greater openness and greater fairness into the review process.[17] The widespread interest in comprehensive posttenure reviews should soon produce mechanisms by which incompetent faculty can be helped either to retool or to retire. Or, where necessary, posttenure reviews can help speed up procedures for dismissal "for cause." And, by learning from past abuses, the professoriate can insist on a stricter regard for the academic freedom protections of tenure in all university documents, thereby preventing politically motivated dismissals in the future. With these correctives in place, and until something demonstrably better comes along, tenure is surely preferable to the conditions of employment now being introduced to replace it. Indeed, what "60 Minutes" may have demonstrated—albeit unintentionally—is that only tenure provides the conditions necessary for the academy to address its many problems.

The reason that "60 Minutes" could not produce its intended exposé of tenure is that tenure made their segment possible. Near the end of "Get Real," following one professor's harsh criticism of academia, Stahl questioned why he didn't fear retaliation for his comments. "Why aren't you afraid of the slings and arrows of your col-leagues?" she asked. "Because I have tenure," he replied ("Get Real" 14). It was perhaps the segment's finest moment, pointing to tenure as the sanctuary for the very kind of free expression that, however unwel-come, forces the academy to look at itself critically and make changes.

3 Raising Standards While Lowering Anxieties:
Rethinking the Promotion and Tenure Process

Alice: "Would you tell me, please, which
way to go from here?"
Cheshire Cat: "That depends a good deal
on where you want to get to."
—Lewis Carroll, *Alice's Adventures in
Wonderland* (1865).

i.

"Maybe I should just pack it in right now," the young woman
suggested hesitatingly. "When I started graduate school, I left a pretty
good job in publishing—and I'm sure I could still get that job back,
if I tried." She was standing, third in line, in a hotel corridor outside
the entryway to a large suite in which job interviews were being conducted. Indeed, all along the corridor of this midtown Manhattan conference hotel, men and women stood (or sometimes sat on the floor)
next to doors or entry foyers, waiting their turn. No one was smiling.
The word was out that the 1992 Modern Language Association (MLA)
Job List had fewer entries than any year's list since 1976. What troubled
this young woman, as she explained to me, was not just the paucity of
jobs but the prospect that, even if she found a position, she still might
not enjoy a full career. In her eyes, women in academe seemed to be
faring no better in 1992 than when her mother had attempted to climb
the tenure ladder twenty years earlier. "If all the statistics are right,"
she insisted, "then very few of us have any chance of making it to full
professor. So why bother even trying?"

Just starting out her professional career, this newly minted Ph.D.
had every reason to be concerned. A 1991 article by Debra Blum in the
Chronicle of Higher Education had revealed that although the total
number of women in tenure-eligible ranks in all fields and disciplines
steadily increased since the early 1970s, their proportion of the total

faculty nationwide nonetheless remained relatively steady (since the total itself increased). As a result, the greatest gains were registered at the rank of assistant professor, where the proportion of women went from 24 percent in 1972 to just over 30 percent in 1989. At the full professor rank, however, as Blum pointed out, only 13.6 percent were women in 1989 (see Blum, "Old Issues Unresolved," A20). Figures compiled in 1992, just as this young woman first entered the job market, were even less encouraging. In an article in the 24 January 1993 *New York Times* that appeared three weeks after the MLA meeting, Anthony DePalma reported that "women make up only 11.6% of full professors nationwide. . . . And even that figure is misleading," he continued: "The more prestigious the institution, the fewer women there are" (DePalma 11). The example offered was the Ivy League where, as this reporter noted dryly, "women make up 7% to 13% of full professors, excluding those in the medical schools" (DePalma 1). To his credit, DePalma emphasized the discrepancy between these figures and both the numbers of women college students and the numbers of women earning doctorates: "While women make up more than half of all college students, they make up just 27.6% of faculty members"; but "the pipeline argument" could not explain these figures, "since women receive 36% of the 38,000 doctorates conferred each year" (De-Palma 11).

Even before DePalma's article appeared, statistical studies from the MLA's Commission on the Status of Women had confirmed that women were making "dramatic gains at the PhD level" between 1970 and 1986, a period in which "they almost doubled their share of the doctorates granted in English and increased their representation among foreign language degree recipients by just over half" (Huber 59). But as Bettina J. Huber cautioned in a summary essay, those same studies also indicated that while "women made significant gains at all ranks between 1977 and 1987," their gains "were less dramatic at the full-professor rank" (Huber 59–60). In reviewing these data, Huber cited a number of factors, including the "rapid shift in undergraduate interests" to vocational studies in the mid-1970s, the shrinking college age population, and the consequent "severe contraction of the academic job market, which hit the humanities particularly hard because of the simultaneous decline in majors. . . . It would appear, therefore,"

Huber observed, "that just as women were starting to join the faculty in significant numbers, the doors of the academy were swinging shut" (Huber 58).

Notwithstanding the stagnant job market that began in the 1970s and has continued through the 1990s, the dramatic increases in the percentages of women earning doctorates should have resulted by now in some statistically significant realignments at the senior ranks. But the explanation offered by Huber in 1990 holds true at the end of the decade, and not just in the humanities disciplines: "women have been hired in relatively large numbers at the assistant-professor level since 1980, but once in tenure-track positions, they have advanced more slowly than men to tenured ranks and full professorships" (Huber 66). As the century draws to a close, therefore, women are still predominantly clustered in the generally untenured ranks of assistant professor and lecturer. Unless hiring and promotion patterns change dramatically, data from the U.S. Department of Education lead one to predict a growing bulge of under- or unemployed women Ph.D.s. According to that department's projections, the percentage of doctoral "degrees awarded to women is expected to grow from 37.9 percent in 1996 to 49.5 percent by 2006." And even though this gain is "not quite large enough to reach parity with men" ("The Future" 7), it nonetheless signals the markedly increased number of women available for academic employment. While optimists can always tease modest signs of progress from these and other recent statistics, overall the picture remains bleak. Whatever their field or discipline, women continue to hit the proverbial glass ceiling at two crucial points: in the initial promotion and tenure review and then, again, in advancement to full professor.

Given this picture, the young woman who stopped me in the hotel corridor in 1992 was right to have second thoughts about her chosen career path. She and every female graduate student with whom I have had similar conversations in subsequent years faced not only a depressing job market but, in addition, twenty years of stalled progress in admitting women into full partnership within academia.

To be sure, under pressure from affirmative action laws and organized women's groups—and often with genuine good will—colleges and universities around the country have attempted to increase the numbers of women and minority faculty hired and promoted. The problem with these efforts is that they have been largely aimed at simply adding women and others from underrepresented groups to institutional structures designed by and for a white male professoriate. Thus, even when a disproportionate number of women and minority faculty fail to succeed in the promotion and tenure process, few schools have felt compelled to examine the process itself. Instead, the common response is to abandon aggressive affirmative action recruitment altogether or to hire another cohort of junior women and minority faculty in hopes that these *new* people will better adjust to or "fit into" the system as it currently exists.

Only rarely is such institutional inertia an expression of viciousness or intentional insensitivity. There is another, more obvious explanation: those now in power in academe are those for whom the promotion and tenure system *worked*. Indeed, it is the very system that conferred their present status. The urgent need for change, therefore, is felt only by those for whom the current system is not working, or at least not working as well. But these individuals are usually without a voice in policy-making. And when these individuals do raise their voices, more often than not, they are dismissed as "uncollegial," while their legitimate charges of systemic bias are greeted by accusations that they are merely trying to lower academic standards. As a result, women and minorities continue to be disproportionately underrepresented in the senior ranks across all fields and disciplines, and existing promotion and tenure documents remain unexamined at most institutions.

ii.

To the best of my knowledge, there exists no comprehensive national survey of the obstacles to advancement encountered by women faculty. Nonetheless, anecdotal wisdom abounds, and most academics have a ready list of problems facing women in the promotion and tenure process. What follows is hardly exhaustive, but it does summarize my own observations and those that colleagues have shared with me over the years.

Unfamiliar research areas. Many women and minority scholars have been drawn to the academy by their interest in subject areas that are innovative and still developing, including, for example, women's studies, ethnic studies, African-American studies, or disability studies. While these fields can prove personally rewarding to junior scholars and their students, and while these scholars' work adds substantially to the creation of new knowledge, both their research materials and their experimental methodologies can be unfamiliar to senior departmental colleagues who abide comfortably entrenched in more orthodox approaches. In too many cases, *unfamiliarity* breeds contempt (or, even worse, suspicion and devaluation). When the promotion and tenure review begins, senior professors may be unable to recognize a junior colleague's contribution to an emerging field, instead dismissing her work as eccentric or merely faddish.

Hidden workload. Whatever their rank, women and minority faculty repeatedly find themselves burdened with responsibilities that have never been demanded of their white male peers. The consequences for junior faculty can be career-threatening. An assistant professor in her fifth year who ought to be concentrating on preparing her promotion and tenure file for review may feel compelled, instead, to devote long hours to mentoring a first-year colleague—especially if there are no women available in the tenured ranks. Minority and women junior faculty alike find themselves mentoring women and minority graduate students as well as undergraduates—even when these students are not in their classes or are not their own dissertation advisees. Although these kinds of activities drain substantial stores of time and energy, I have rarely encountered a woman or a minority faculty member who felt she could turn away from such responsibilities. As an African-American colleague at another institution explained to me years ago, "If we're going to open up the pipeline and get these young folks through it, then I've got to make sure they have a friend and a helping hand along the way. In my department, I'm the only black person—so who else would they turn to?"

National surveys demonstrate that women and minority faculty tend to spend more time on student advising and in office hours.[1] My own observations over the years have led me to conclude that the majority of male faculty are comfortable scheduling ten, fifteen, and twenty-minute slots for students during office hours but that women, by contrast, rarely give a student *less* than twenty minutes. Indeed, during my own years as a faculty member, before I became a dean, I regularly spent more than six hours each week in office hours. Like many of my women colleagues, if I deemed it potentially helpful, I afforded students time to talk about personal matters that were impinging on their academic performance. Most male colleagues shied away from such conversations.

Because women and minority faculty are often numerically underrepresented in their home department and across the campus generally, they tend to be overburdened with committee assignments. In the laudatory attempt to seek diversity, most universities try to include at least one woman and one minority member on almost every committee. That this may amount to no more than tokenism does not diminish the fact that the few women and minority faculty available are consistently overutilized in committee assignments. And when the appointment to a committee is couched in terms like "If you don't serve, there won't be any voice for women's issues," it is very difficult for even the most junior assistant professor to decline. In fact, the stronger the faculty member feels regarding issues of gender, ethnic, or racial equity, the more susceptible she is to burdensome invitations. At the same time, that faculty member must be on guard against the trap of being asked to speak "on behalf of" her race or gender, constantly reminding her committee colleagues that she speaks—as they do—as an individual. In trying to maintain her individuality while simultaneously bringing unique or alternative group perspectives to any committee, the lone woman or token minority often exhibits heroic capacities for overcoming her marginal status and inserts a vital new voice into the discussion. But she always walks a psychological tightrope, and the emotional cost is enormous.

Perhaps less well understood is the fact that women and minority faculty spend more time than their white male peers in preparing for committee meetings. The only woman in the room may be asked to take the minutes. (And, unless she refuses or suggests a rotation system, she will be asked to take on this task repeatedly.) More important, because the woman or minority faculty member has often been invited to serve on the committee specifically to represent women's or minority perspectives, this individual feels compelled to do the extra work that will make those perspectives comprehensible. As a result, unlike their white male peers, these committee members spend hours researching statistics, gathering reports, or surveying colleagues in order to bring a firm database to an upcoming meeting. The majority on the committee may rest content to put forward their personal observations and opinions; the woman or minority member does so at her peril. She knows that in order to be persuasive she will have to present irrefutable evidence. And because she knows that her lone voice is too often lost within the larger group, she also knows that, in order to be heard, she will have to spend additional hours in one-on-one conversation, personally lobbying key committee members on "her" issues. Inescapably this makes her role both more stressful and more time-consuming.[2]

Less subtle indicators of the "hidden workload" are the differential course assignments given to junior faculty. Again, anecdotal evidence will have to serve in the absence of survey data. Many junior women tell me that they are assigned fewer graduate seminars than male peers and are repeatedly asked to teach large undergraduate courses or endless sections of basic French or English composition. By comparison, male peers enjoy course assignments closer to their areas of research interest, and department chairs are often more responsive to the men's need for lighter teaching loads as they complete a book or an article. When I have pointed out this phenomenon to department chairs, men and women alike, they acknowledge that such disparities exist, even in their own departments. Their most common explanation is that male junior faculty approach them directly and request lighter teaching loads when they are heavily involved in completing a research project before the tenure review. By contrast, junior women faculty rarely make such requests explicit. Moreover, women appear to be more cooperative and flexible in accepting course assignments, while men declare themselves limited to their specialty. And department chairs—both men and women—readily admit that they do not carefully enough monitor such disparities or consciously seek to offer women the same opportunities as men. In most cases, it may be an innocent oversight—but for the woman who is its victim the oversight can be devastating.[3] Not only does she enjoy less research time than her male peers but, when she is reviewed for tenure, she may be judged a less valuable colleague because she has not demonstrated proficiency in teaching graduate seminars or advanced undergraduate courses in her particular field of expertise.

Unquestionably the most obvious aspect of the "hidden workload" is the fact that, even in two-wage-earner heterosexual families, women continue to shoulder the major responsibilities for home-keeping and child-rearing. The young male assistant professor, full of enlightened views and feminist sympathies, "helps" his wife at home with the cooking and childcare. But the young woman who is an untenured assistant professor typically spends up to twice as many hours as her husband in organizing these same chores, and, more likely than not, it is *her* book—not his—that gets left unwritten on the dining room table.[4]

Lack of access to informal male networks. Senior male faculty express no hesitation at inviting a new junior male colleague to join them for a beer at the end of the day or to try out for the noon basketball league at the gym. And many powerful male bonds have been forged at the Friday-night poker game. Women are rarely invited to partake of such activities. Married women are generally invited only to social gatherings to which spouses (or other guests) are also invited. And single women are sometimes altogether shunned (or, even worse, "hit upon" sexually). As a result, the informal networks of friendship and collegial exchange that silently influence the promotion and tenure review remain largely unavailable to women. As long as informal networks provide opportunities for senior males to advise their younger colleagues on publication venues, recommend fellowship opportunities, facilitate introductions to other major researchers, and assess the collegiality and the intellectual worth of their juniors, the prevalence of these male-only gatherings continues to be a serious problem for women.

Differential standards. A frequent complaint from women who have experienced difficulty in the promotion and tenure review is that they were held to higher or different standards than were male peers going through the review at the same time. A woman's ten articles in prominent refereed feminist journals may be deemed less consequential than a male colleague's three articles in more familiar (even if non-refereed) journals. In the humanities disciplines, males are usually tenured on the basis of an original, single-authored book published by a reputable university press. The woman whose book has also been published by a university press is often asked, in addition, to demonstrate that she is now embarked on a further scholarly project. The variety of differential standards becomes even more problematic where the evaluation of "quality" is wholly subjective. How, for example, do we compare the archival recovery of a forgotten woman author and the most recent exegesis of a William Faulkner short story? The familiar may be judged of superior worth simply because it *is* familiar.

The most common complaint from women who have had difficulty in the promotion and tenure process, however, is that they were being held to standards to which the senior members of their promotion and tenure committee were never held. In other words, the males on the committee were requiring levels of scholarly productivity from junior women that they had never demanded of themselves. When trying to vent their outraged sense of injustice, women in such situations repeatedly offer the analogy of Alice in Wonderland, wandering through a landscape in which the rules are always arbitrary.

Let me offer just one example. At a small midwestern university, Professor X, a promising young Americanist, was denied promotion and tenure despite consistently high praise from students and despite the fact that she had won a dissertation prize at the Ivy League institution from which she had received her Ph.D. and had published an original book with a major university press, as well as five articles in well-respected refereed journals. Not a single member of her all-male promotion and tenure committee had published a book and the chair of the committee had only one article to his credit, a brief review essay in a small journal. The committee had expressed itself as unimpressed with the quality of her book, in part because it introduced what they perceived as nonliterary concerns into a discussion of canonical American texts. As Professor X later said to me, "They just don't understand feminist or American Studies interdisciplinary approaches."[5]

When I was invited to the same institution as a commencement speaker, the chair of this young woman's promotion and tenure committee happened to be seated to my left at the awards dinner. At some point in the conversation, I expressed my surprise that Professor X had not received promotion and tenure. "Oh," replied the tenure committee chair, "I haven't published any books myself, you know, but I have my standards." He then proceeded to explain that Professor X's book had not received universally laudatory reviews. I responded, in vain, that no scholarly book ever does. But only someone who had himself produced a book for peer judgment would know that.

Inappropriate statements by external referees. Without malice or intent, even the most supportive referees sometimes write letters that hurt the woman candidate for promotion and tenure. A statement like "She is one of the top women in Shakespeare studies today," rather than "She is one of the top scholars in Shakespeare studies today," is a typical example. By measuring the woman scholar *only* against other women in her field, the external referee subtly suggests that her work cannot support larger comparisons. Too often, referees may discuss a woman candidate's nonacademic assets, such as her charming personality, her ability to throw a great party, or the excellence of her fudge brownies. These may be well-intentioned expressions of personal warmth, but they undermine the profile of the candidate as a serious professional. And review committees are quick to interpret such sentences as covert signals that the candidate's professional talents are weaker than her personal ones.

Other letters by external referees can be intentionally damaging. Many referees try to hide their biases, while others openly identify themselves as hostile to or ignorant of feminist approaches, cross-disciplinary analyses, or women's studies. Yet, in both cases, such referees proceed to evaluate a candidate's publication record as though their comments were wholly objective. If, in their haste to read dozens of candidates' files, members of a promotion and tenure review committee overlook a referee's admission of prejudice—or if the committee members are not aware of that bias—they will give the referee's negative comments a weight they should not have.

iii.

Because change in academe is gradual and incremental, any overhaul of the promotion and tenure process that seeks to address the obstacles I've listed here must itself also be gradual and incremental. Understanding this, the College of Humanities at the University of Arizona decided to re-examine promotion and tenure in two separate steps, beginning first with a clear set of *criteria* and then moving on to the invention of new promotion and tenure *procedures*. The first step, in fact, strategically prepared the way for the second. The faculty, department heads, and I all felt reasonably confident that we could build consensus around appropriate criteria for evaluating teaching, research/scholarship, and service because we had ready referents in national norms and discipline expectations at peer institutions. Had we begun with a wholesale invention of new procedures, by contrast, the effort would have been sabotaged by some individuals' suspicions that we were simply attempting to find ways to promote women and minorities without regard to quality. By beginning with a criteria document, therefore, we constrained anxieties that standards would be lowered in what was already an aggressive campaign to recruit and retain women and minority faculty.

After an eighteen-month collaboration between faculty and department heads, a document was hammered out that both clarified and upgraded criteria for promotion and tenure within the College of Humanities. Among other things, the criteria document explicitly acknowledged the new kinds of scholarly productivity that we were striving to accommodate. For example, our new "Promotion and Tenure Criteria" recognized traditional forms of publication, including books, articles, and monographs; in addition, it accepted the fact that, in certain humanities disciplines, "an innovative textbook, software programs, video presentations, translations, or the like" might well be "of such high quality as to constitute a significant contribution to the field in the opinion of nationally recognized experts" ("Promotion and Tenure Criteria" 9). We thus made room in our promotion and tenure criteria document for people whose research resulted in the curatorship of museum shows or in innovative software for foreign language instruction.

The criteria document also emphasized the need to have a candidate's record assessed by those with expertise in her field. Although the document largely shied away from procedural issues, the faculty saw the need to guarantee—even in this document—the fairness of the review process. As a result, the criteria document stipulated that "in every case, the candidate must be guaranteed fair representation by scholars sharing his or her area of academic specialization" on departmental promotion and tenure committees ("Promotion and Tenure Criteria" 3). Because of the signal importance of this guarantee, departments with limited areas of specialization began to appoint to their promotion and tenure review committees those from other appropriate departments or programs who were knowledgeable about a candidate's field or methodological approach. This informal practice was later codified as part of the procedures document.

Finally, the criteria document raised one more quasi-procedural issue: the need to protect women and minority faculty from a debilitating "hidden workload." In one of the boldest statements in that document, all department heads and the dean were put on notice that "care must be taken . . . on the part of both candidates and administration, not to overcommit assistant professors by demanding a level of service that interferes with their development of a coherent research program and of teaching skills." The document explicitly cautioned that, "while women and minorities are under-represented on the faculty, it will be particularly important to resist the temptation to overutilize their contributions to service" ("Promotion and Tenure Criteria" 7).

Soon after the new "Promotion and Tenure Criteria" were adopted by faculty ballot in the spring semester of 1990, each department within the College of Humanities began to revise its own department-level promotion and tenure materials accordingly. Equally important, junior as well as senior faculty quickly recognized that guidelines were now required to help us implement the review of our enhanced and upgraded criteria. In other words, having agreed—as a community— to clarify and raise our standards as well as to embrace new forms of scholarly productivity, we needed a set of procedures that would truly "level the playing field." As dean, I was concerned that, after refining and raising the threshold of expectation, we also lower the anxiety level by assuring all promotion and tenure candidates that the review process, as much as possible, was scrupulously fair *and* designed to ensure their success so long as they met our clearly articulated written criteria.

iv.

In May 1992, after marathon committee meetings and nine drafts, the College of Humanities voted to adopt its first promotion and tenure procedures document. This second document was the result of a collaboration between all department heads and program directors, the faculty as a whole, and the newly formed Faculty Planning and Policies Advisory Committee. Appointed by me specifically to provide me with advice and counsel on a whole range of policy issues, the committee was gender-balanced, with minority participation, and included faculty from all three tenure-eligible ranks (assistant, associate, and full professor) in equal numbers. Every program and department was represented, along with a full spectrum of faculty views and political dispositions. (In subsequent years, at the committee's recommendation, half of its members were elected by the faculty.) A large and potentially unwieldy group, the committee broke into subcommittees, divided up its many tasks, and began work on its first charge: drafting procedures for fair and open promotion and tenure reviews. Over a two-year period, the committee circulated successive drafts for faculty-wide comment, and committee members presided over open forums to allow for further faculty input. The committee also met regularly with the department heads and program directors.

The committee's charge was not an easy one because few units on our own campus or nationwide had documents that could serve as models. Still, the goal of the group was clear: they wanted to build on the spirit of the criteria document and address the obstacles that had traditionally thwarted the successful advancement of women and minorities. They also wanted to protect the career advancement of those in nontraditional or marginalized areas of study—like the lone linguist in an English department or the single Portuguese specialist in a Spanish department. To accomplish this, they did a great deal of reading, gathering relevant materials from other universities and from professional organizations. Probably of more importance, they did much sharing. Once the group felt sufficiently comfortable with one another and a certain level of mutual trust and respect had been established, individuals on the committee began to talk about their own career histories. Several women revealed details of experiences that had been both personally and professionally wrenching and talked frankly about the difficulties they had encountered because of their gender. One woman's candor emboldened another to speak out in turn. And by the end of their first year together, three men on the committee told me privately that they had come to understand the plight of women and minorities in the profession. As one senior male observed to me, "I think this is what you feminists call consciousness-raising."

Perhaps because the committee had developed this quality of candid exchange and had watched one another go through a sea-change in attitudes, many members were unprepared for the outright hostility directed against them by some on the faculty when an initial draft was circulated. One open forum degenerated into a three-hour "encounter session," the subcommittee chair reported, with ten very vocal faculty members assaulting the committee with "sputtering" invective and personal attack. "It was an ugly outburst of self-protection," one committee member later told me. "They just don't want anything to change, they're scared," added another. The major objections, according to the committee members, centered on recommendations to involve promotion and tenure candidates in the choice of external referees and to set minimum qualifications for those faculty within the college who would serve on promotion and tenure review committees. As some faculty apparently viewed the matter, junior faculty could not be trusted to supply names of appropriate off-campus experts in their field, while service on review committees was seen as an automatic right conferred by tenured status rather than as a professional responsibility earned by merit.

Recognizing that there would be resistance to any redesign in promotion and tenure procedures, the Faculty Planning and Policies Advisory Committee repeatedly redrafted their recommendations with a view toward mollifying anxieties and incorporating responsible suggestions. But they gave up the illusion that their hard work would be universally applauded. Their perseverance in circulating all drafts for additional input (thus ensuring widespread faculty ownership), their willingness to meet with each department, and their continued openness to debate and discussion finally proved persuasive to a large majority of faculty ready for meaningful change. In the end, reason and good will prevailed.

With each redrafting, I consulted with the university attorneys' office in order to ensure that we remained in compliance with university and Board of Regents policies. In only one instance was there a problem. Together, the Faculty Planning and Policies Advisory Committee with the department heads and program directors had recommended enhanced procedures for stopping the tenure clock that included paid "family responsibility" leaves. The draft of that recommendation spelled out provisions for stopping the tenure clock on the basis of "family care responsibilities . . . or other appropriate reasons" and made it possible for a faculty member to remain on full salary during any leave period (up to two semesters) connected with "family care responsibilities." Those who proposed these paragraphs were convinced that until and unless women faculty were permitted paid family care leaves while their tenure clock was stopped—and men faculty were given an incentive to do the same—the playing field would never be level. Despite the persuasiveness of these arguments, university attorneys restricted us to the terms for stopping the tenure clock that had appeared in a recent memorandum from the provost. And they told us that because the state of Arizona had no policy for granting paid family care leaves, we could not—as state employees—institute them on our own.

As a result, the first version of the "Promotion and Tenure Procedures" carried a copy of the provost's memorandum at the end, along with a statement that urged the development of campus-wide paid family care leave policies in the future. Amended by faculty vote in later years, the "Promotion and Tenure Procedures" document dropped the provost's memorandum (because improved provisions for stopping the tenure clock had now become university-level policy); and our recommendation for paid family care leaves became a topic of discussion across campus, as other deans began to take notice of our arguments. In the meantime, as I discuss in chapter 5, the College of Humanities pursued other methods for achieving equity in family care issues.

The amended version of the "College of Humanities Promotion and Tenure Procedures" appears as an appendix in this book, so that readers may go through the document in detail. Let me point out some of its salient features. First, the procedures offer a plausible level of fairness by enjoining the dean to appoint to the college-level promotion and tenure review committee "only faculty members who have met the current criteria by which the candidates under consideration are being judged." Most—but not all—faculty have welcomed this condition because it secures the most professionally active and engaged faculty in the crucial task of evaluating their junior colleagues. Second, candidates no longer suffer the anxieties of protracted uncertainty because, "At each stage in the review process, every candidate is to be informed, promptly, of the recommendations (including any minority reports) made regarding her or his tenure and/or promotion." The principle of openness enunciated in that sentence is further guaranteed by the stipulation that candidates receive verbatim copies of all committee recommendations as well as the department head's recommendation to the dean and the dean's recommendation to the provost. At both stages, moreover, the candidate can compose a written response to be included in the promotion and tenure file; among other things, this gives the candidate an opportunity to correct any factual errors that may have crept into a head's, a dean's, or a review committee's letter. According to one senior faculty member, this lifting of what he called the "veil of silence" not only introduced real accountability into the process for the first time, but in addition the new openness contributed substantially to improved morale among his junior colleagues. All along, this had been one of our major goals.

Other significant features of the document include the following:

• Candidates for promotion and tenure are integrally involved in helping to identify appropriate internal *and* external reviewers. The purpose here is to ensure that a reviewer known to be irretrievably hostile to a candidate's field of study or hostile to the candidate personally is not invited to sit on a departmental committee or submit an external letter of reference.

• Moreover, in addition to being consulted in the choice of external reviewers, candidates are also assured that their external referees are appropriate persons to review their work.

• Any unprofessional or inappropriate information about a candidate that appears in an external referee's letter must be clearly noted as such in the department head's letter. The referee's letter can then be weighed accordingly.

• Informal or "overload" participation in an interdisciplinary program such as Women's Studies, African-American Studies, or American Indian Studies, etc., is evaluated as part of the promotion and tenure file. The candidate thus receives full credit for *all* of his or her contributions.

   • And, like the earlier criteria document, the cover page of the "College of Humanities Promotion and Tenure Procedures" mandates that, "immediately upon assuming their duties, all newly-hired tenured or tenure-eligible faculty members" will receive copies of these and other pertinent promotion and tenure materials. From their first day, faculty thereby know what is expected of them and how they will be evaluated.

   Admittedly, the promotion and tenure procedures document of the College of Humanities at the University of Arizona represents no panacea. Written policies are only as fair and unbiased as those who implement them. Even so, because the document was developed within a larger matrix of strategies designed to enhance the performance of women and minorities—including the cluster hiring of women and minorities, a buddy system, blind-submission research grant competitions for faculty, awards for innovative curriculum development, and a gender-balanced Faculty Planning and Policies Advisory Committee— it played a significant role in contributing to an environment in which *all* faculty could *know* that they were invited to succeed. Together with these other strategies, the new procedures effectively changed the culture of decision-making during the years that I was dean and helped us as well to build a sense of community. What we wanted, after all, was to encourage the best from every faculty member and to transform what had once been a gate-*closing* function into a gate-*opening* function for everyone who was qualified.

4 Paying the Price of Antifeminist Intellectual Harassment

"Ginger Rogers did everything that Fred Astaire did,
but she had to do it backward in high heels."
—Ann Richards, former governor of Texas (qtd.
in Kaufman 162).

"Many of us have modulated our voices out of fear.
I have. I am ashamed of it."
—Beth Kalikoff, Ph.D. in English (Kalikoff 41).

i.

On 11 June 1993 Jane Schaberg, a professor of religious studies
at the University of Detroit Mercy, was awakened after midnight by
the sound of fire engines. She hardly expected them to stop at her
house. When she looked out her bedroom window and saw flames,
however, she realized that her 1987 Toyota Tercel, parked out front,
was on fire. A rag had been stuffed in the gas tank and then ignited.
The police report listed the motive as "revenge." But to Schaberg it
was simply what the *Chronicle of Higher Education* characterized as
"the latest salvo in a nasty battle raging over her scholarship" (Robin
Wilson, "A Scholar's Conclusion," A7).

In 1987, the scholar and former nun published *The Illegitimacy of
Jesus*, a historical and literary critique examining internal evidence
that the writers of the Gospels were handing on a tradition in which
Jesus was not miraculously conceived but, rather, illegitimately conceived, perhaps as the result of the rape of Mary. By crediting divine
love as intervening in the fate of Mary and her child, with God reliev-
ing Mary's humiliation through His special relationship with her son,
Schaberg offered a theology of God's caring for the socially outcast—
and thus endangered—mother and child. Understandably, Schaberg's
thesis was controversial, and not just in Catholic circles. Schaberg received hate mail, threatening phone calls, and she became a target
of public attack by Detroit's Archbishop. Most troubling to Schaberg

in all this was her university's lack of a forceful stand and its refusal to unequivocally support the value of serious scholarship, whatever its findings. In response to rumors of alumni threatening to cancel their contributions, according to Schaberg, the school's administration began distancing itself from her and her work, both through public statements and internal silence (Schaberg 1993). "I didn't know the university was going to cave in like this," she told the *Chronicle of Higher Education.* And although, because protected by tenure, she still had a job at the Jesuit school, she acknowledged that her "will [was] a bit broken" (Robin Wilson, "A Scholar's Conclusion," A7). In fact, Schaberg stepped down as head of religious studies because of what she experienced as Detroit Mercy's continuing lack of support.

While the torching of her automobile is surely an extreme response to a scholar's findings, unfortunately it represents only one event in the escalating campaign of intimidation directed at feminist teachers and researchers in a variety of fields all across the country. Stories are legion about right-wing organizations moving onto campuses in order to finance publications whose sole purpose is to attack (and, they hope, shut down) a women's studies program.[1] In such a volatile atmosphere, some faculty take the path of least resistance by looking the other way when colleagues openly discourage students from taking courses in women's studies. Many schools harbor senior faculty who refuse to sit on qualifying examinations or to serve on dissertation committees if the candidate employs feminist approaches. Deans and department chairs still quietly reassure recruitment committees that once they've hired one woman, they need seek no others, thus encouraging a revolving door of tokenism. And in a typically incongruous situation, at Scripps College, "a women's college dedicated to the education of women," professor of English and the well-published feminist critic, Gayle Greene, has seen her "course in feminist theory [repeatedly] . . . refused credit as 'the senior seminar,'" while a supposedly "real theory" course "taught by a white male" *was* given senior seminar status (Greene 17).

Should anyone suppose that the resistance to feminist scholars and their work is grounded in reasonable concerns for academic excellence, the public statements of those who oppose such work prove otherwise. The "self-proclaimed conservative watchdog," Peter Shaw, for example, served on the National Council on the Humanities, the 27-member advisory board of the National Endowment for the Humanities, during Lynne Cheney's tenure as chair of the Endowment. Reflecting on his own predilections in the awarding of NEH grants, Shaw told the *Chronicle of Higher Education* in 1994 that "what I truly believe is that second-rate traditionalist scholarship is ultimately more valuable to the country than first-rate feminist works" (Burd A25).

Not surprisingly, this cumulative resistance has surfaced at the very moment that a graying professoriate of mostly white males looks toward retirement. Between 1995 and 2010, according to Department of Education projections, over 300,000 faculty are expected to retire, leaving vacancies in all fields across higher education. At the same time, in almost every discipline, women have been making "dramatic gains at the Ph.D. level," almost doubling "their share of the doctorates granted in English and increas[ing] their representation among foreign language degree recipients by just over half" (Huber 59–60). As a result, especially in the humanities disciplines, the 1990s are certain to be the last decade in which tenured white males over fifty control what gets published and who gets tenured.

The transition, however, is proving extremely difficult because, as a rule, academics are not comfortable with rapid change. But these changes have taken hold within a single generation and are massive in both their intellectual *and* their social implications. For, beyond challenging the orthodoxies of their chosen disciplines, the increasing numbers of women faculty also demanded that the academy scrutinize its daily behaviors and customary procedures. Once commonplace in hallway conversations and over faculty club luncheons, exchanges of sexual banter, sexist humor, ethnic jokes, and racial slurs were no longer without consequences. Sexual overtures to students or demands for sexual favors from untenured colleagues could now result in a sexual harassment charge. And whole departments splintered over outdated promotion and tenure procedures that gave them no way to evaluate the junior colleague who had designed a traveling museum exhibition or studied the works of a long-forgotten woman author.

If resistance to the magnitude of change was predictable, the fierceness and tenacity with which some groups and individuals have chosen to express that reflex was not. Dr. Bernice Resnick Sandler,

Senior Scholar in Residence with the National Association for Women in Education, has reported that, at some colleges, posters announcing any lecture or course with a feminist theme are routinely destroyed or vandalized (Sandler 7). In one instance in the spring of 1988, the chair of the Women's Law Association at Harvard put up a poster publicizing a weekly luncheon series in which the topic was "The 'F' Word: To Be or Not to Be a Feminist." Within hours, according to Sandler, the words "a feminist" were crossed out, and the new title was "The 'F' Word: To Be or Not to Be Fucked" (Sandler 7).

On other campuses, any negative reviews or published critical comments pertaining to the work of feminist faculty are duplicated and mailed out anonymously. At a small New England college recently, a feminist professor in the French department took great pleasure from the fact that her critical theory book had received laudatory reviews in the major professional journals. Thus it was with some surprise that she and her students arrived on campus one day to discover a poster-sized blowup of the only negative review to have appeared, prominent in the department's hallway display case, safely locked behind glass. The nastiest sentences in the review were underlined in red. It was three weeks before the key to the display case could be located and the poster removed. In the meantime, she heard from students that some of her colleagues were reciting portions of the negative review to their classes and making fun of her work based on the distorted readings of this particular reviewer. When she shared her anger with feminist faculty in other departments, the French professor discovered that the feminist critics in the English Department (both male and female) had long been the subjects of obscene verses circulated almost monthly by unknown persons. And her colleagues in the School of Nursing told of needing to take extra security precautions for their labs whenever their grants supported research on women's health issues.

Given this kind of anecdotal evidence, it is hardly surprising that national reports from every source regularly document "that the experiences of women on campus are substantially different from those of men" (Sandler 1). Nor do we wonder that "a study of graduate students at the University of Michigan revealed that women are more likely to consider the university as alienating and less likely to describe it as accepting than are men" ("Chilly Climate" 2). National studies notwithstanding, few administrators in higher education have measured the full scope of the problem or examined their own responses as a possible contributory factor. It is difficult to command a provost's undivided attention or to invoke institutional responsibility, after all, in the face of seemingly unrelated and random events, however disturbing. Those who do not want the larger problem accurately named and understood, moreover, actively encourage the misunderstanding that each event is isolated, sui generis, and without aim or method connected to anything else. But the real problem may be just here, in the institutional habit of uncritically accepting "problems" as *only* discrete events rather than probing for larger patterns.

The appeal from a feminist assistant professor denied promotion and tenure because her research area was unfamiliar to her department colleagues, for instance, rarely is viewed by the provost as having any connection to the vandalizing of posters announcing a women's studies speakers' series. To be sure, a dean or provost may acknowledge that there is a "climate problem" on campus. But this may only compound the situation by further masking the fact that women's— and especially feminist—intellectual activities are being repeatedly attacked and hobbled. Accordingly, unaware that others on campus are enduring different forms of the same malice, the targets of such harassment too often perceive themselves as alone and isolated. Without an adequate support network, they tend to internalize the harassment as a legitimate value judgment on their capabilities. At the best, these individuals reach out to family, friends, and sympathetic colleagues for help and guidance; and though their self-confidence remains deeply shaken, they develop coping mechanisms to see them through. At the worst, the vulnerable untenured assistant professor shies away from the activity that brings with it so much pain and struggle, even putting aside her most cherished research project.

For their part, faculty and students outraged at the attacks on feminist faculty and feminist activities are forced to respond on an ad hoc basis to each specific event. In May students organize a letter campaign on behalf of the outstanding feminist scholar who has been denied tenure, and then in September a women's faculty group files a complaint with the campus police to protest the repeated destruction of posters advertising the women's studies speakers' series. Unquestionably necessary and helpful, such ad hoc activities lead only to piecemeal solutions (if at all), and they never identify the larger problem.

ii.

At the 1991 meeting of the Modern Language Association, that organization's Commission on the Status of Women sponsored a forum and associated workshops on the topic "Antifeminist Harassment in the Academy." Within this complex topic, the commission encouraged participants to recognize "anti-feminist *intellectual* harassment" as a specific and independent category. While the commission members fully recognized that different modes of harassment often overlap and reinforce one another, their stress on the word "intellectual" was intended to distinguish certain kinds of events from more commonly understood forms of harassment, including sexual harassment, emotional battering, and physical threats.

As the speaker asked to address antifeminist *intellectual* harassment, I suggested that whatever form this kind of harassment takes— vandalizing posters or the threat of physical violence—its object is always to foreclose further feminist inquiry and, more generally, to shut down women's access to unfettered intellectual activity in any field or discipline. Publicly humiliating a colleague by anonymously circulating scurrilous verses about her and torching a scholar's parked car, in other words, are means—punishing means, to be sure—but means to the further end of intellectual silencing. And intellectual silencing, I insisted, was anathema to every definition of the academic freedom that our colleges and universities claim to protect.

Thus at the heart of my 1991 remarks to the Modern Language Association audience was an appeal for the preservation of the principle of academic freedom undiminished by bias, prejudice, or discomfort with difference. Over the years, however, I have come to understand that this principle is inordinately difficult to grasp because until its practice is historically situated, or until its practice takes meaning within a specific context, academic freedom remains only a vague, rather amorphous, abstraction. Retaining *Catcher in the Rye* on a freshman English reading list, for example, enacts (and thereby defines) the concept of academic freedom only when a school or teacher enunciates the reasoning behind rejecting some local call to ban the novel. But while most teachers of literature nowadays would be quick to defend J. D. Salinger's controversial 1951 work under the flag of academic freedom, far fewer professors (especially if they are untenured) would risk defending Rita Mae Brown's 1973 novel, *Rubyfruit Jungle*, with its exuberant and unapologetic lesbian narrator. This is because the teaching, research, and scholarly practices that, to date, have been traditionally protected by the concept of academic freedom—that is, the practices that make the concept recognizable and constitute its meaning—have largely been practices forged without the participation of women (especially feminists), African Americans, Asian Americans, Native Americans, Latinos, (open) lesbians and gays, or the disabled. (Indeed, this is true of almost all the practices of the academy.) Having enjoyed no role in defining the concept of academic freedom, these groups—and their interests—are understood to be protected by it only insofar as their products and activities *conform to the accepted products and activities of the past.*

By that statement, I do not mean to imply a simplistic correlation between a scholar's ethnicity or sexual orientation and his or her area of research interest. Not all Native American students care to become experts in Native American literatures (most of my Indian undergraduates are headed to medical school), and the majority of my Mexican American colleagues are not in Latin American Studies but in the sciences. Even so, any influx of students and faculty from previously invisible or underrepresented groups allows for a critical mass of individuals who do, in fact, begin to question the terms of their institutional invisibility. As a result, when scholars from previously invisible or underrepresented groups interrogate the inherited paradigms of their disciplines and try to introduce new curricular, creative, or intellectual directions that include *them*, the very unfamiliarity of their efforts renders those efforts vulnerable to charges of narrow partisanship or political contrivance. And their activities are not defined as falling within the protections of academic freedom. But, in truth, these new areas of interest—feminist inquiry, ethnic studies, queer studies, or the emerging field of disability studies—are no more or less narrow, political, or partisan than earlier categories of research and analysis whose adherents insisted upon inclusion: for example, the steady addition of United States authors to the "English" literature curriculum or, more recently, the development of programs in Holocaust studies. By forcing a rethinking of old intellectual habits, new areas of inquiry have the potential to revitalize moribund corners of established disciplines. And, no less important, they challenge us to reconstitute the meaning of academic freedom yet once more by enrolling colleagues in scenarios that declare that these new areas of research and scholarship *matter*. For feminist scholars, now threatened by various forms of intellectual harassment, this process is urgent.

In order to preserve our few hard-won spaces for women's research, scholarship, and innovative pedagogy—and in order to create more adequate spaces for the future—it is essential to develop a workable definition of the term *antifeminist intellectual harassment* so that, as it is named, it can be readily recognized and effectively contained. Building on the groundbreaking work of the MLA commission, I offered the following tentative definition in 1991 as at least a place to start:

> Anti-feminist intellectual harassment, a serious threat to academic freedom, occurs when (1) any policy, action, statement, and/or behavior has the intent or the effect of discouraging or preventing women's freedom of lawful action, freedom of thought, and freedom of expression; (2) *or* when any policy, action, statement, and/or behavior creates an environment in which the appropriate application of feminist theories or methodologies to research, scholarship, and teaching is devalued, discouraged, or altogether thwarted; (3) *or* when any policy, action, statement, and/or behavior creates an environment in which research, scholarship, and teaching pertaining to women, gender, or gender inequities is devalued, discouraged, or altogether thwarted.

Implicit in this definition is the understanding that the harmful policies or behaviors may be enacted by women as well as by men, and that men—as well as women—may also be the targets of such harassment. No less important, this definition does not require that the agent of the harassment—whether a person or a university policy—be burdened with the guilt of intentionality (*intention* being difficult to prove even in the best documented circumstances). Instead, following the early legal precedents established under Title VII of the 1964 Civil Rights Act, this definition concentrates on effects and consequences.

The lawyers with whom I have consulted on the specific wording of this definition were variously enthusiastic and cautionary. Some see it as a civil rights–based elaboration of well-accepted principles of academic freedom, while a few have questioned its implications for certain free speech protections. My purpose for generating the definition was not to establish some new point of law, however, but to raise the level of awareness by identifying a complex problem with diverse manifestations. Thus, under this definition, promotion and tenure procedures that worked well two decades ago may now be understood as potentially harassing if those procedures provide no mechanism for evaluating newer forms of scholarship and research productivity (interdisciplinary women's studies research, for example, or a computer program instead of a book) in which many feminist and minority faculty are now engaged. Obviously, the procedures were not originally designed to devalue these kinds of scholarly productions; the procedures were simply designed before such productions become possible. Even so, where a department or college evades responsibility for periodically revising and rethinking its promotion and tenure procedures, my definition reminds them that such inaction can have the *effect* of devaluing the work of many newer scholars, feminist and minority faculty prominent among them. And the *consequence* may be a campus environment hostile to excellence in a wide variety of academic areas and hostile, too, to those innovative women faculty who dare to push beyond the encrusted conventions of their disciplines.

iii.

After first offering this definition at the 1991 Modern Language Association meeting, I have been continually contacted by numbers of women who generously shared their own stories of antifeminist intellectual harassment. What these women emphasize is that, despite its apparent randomness and the seeming lack of connection between incidents, this form of harassment is nonetheless extremely costly to the women who are targeted and increasingly pervasive in its cumulative effects across the profession. From that generosity of response, I have culled three very different career episodes—episodes that might not at first appear to have anything in common. But if my definition of antifeminist intellectual harassment is applied, the episodes reveal a chilling commonality.

In reconstructing the stories for this essay, I have altered some details in order to protect the privacy of individuals. Because the graduate student is now an untenured assistant professor, her field of study as well as her graduate school affiliation are extensively disguised. The story of Dr. Jean Jew has been pieced together from public sources, including articles in *Newsweek* and the *Chronicle of Higher Education*. The longest and most detailed story, that of an administrator, is a composite: two remarkably similar experiences have been combined as one. My five years as dean unquestionably made me particularly sympathetic to these narratives, but nothing from my own years as an administrator figures into the history of "Sarah Smith." I have written about my experiences in the personal preface to this book, not here.

1. *Diana Franklin.* An advanced graduate student going through her first round of job interviews at a Modern Language Association meeting, Diana Franklin (not her real name) repeatedly found herself in the same uncomfortable situation. In several interviews, one or more of the faculty present challenged her to defend the theories of the well-known African-American feminist critic who served as her dissertation director. In more than one interview, reported Franklin, she had never been given any opportunity to discuss her own research or teaching interests. Instead, the conversation was dominated by individuals who objected to a particularly controversial article that her dissertation director had published recently in a prominent journal. During this grilling, the other members of the interview committee sat silent.

The chilly reception she encountered in these interviews, however, jarred sharply with the assumptions of some of her colleagues in the corridors. There, ominous rumors circulated about the lack of jobs and the oversupply of applicants. But Diana would be exempt from such worries, commented a number of the young white men waiting with her in the little clusters outside of hotel suites. "You've got it made," they asserted. "Everyone's looking for women and minorities—you don't even have to publish. I don't stand a chance as a white male—no matter how much I've done already."

2. *Jean Jew.* As reported in the *Chronicle of Higher Education* (Blum, "Medical Professor," A15-16), Dr. Jean Jew, an associate professor at the University of Iowa medical school, was awarded tenure in the Anatomy Department in 1979. Despite the award of tenure, Dr. Jew continued to experience harassing behaviors from some of her departmental colleagues, behaviors that had begun in 1973. She repeatedly filed formal requests with administrators to have the matter resolved, but no action was taken until 1984. That year a university committee appointed to investigate her complaints found that she *had* been harassed. The faculty committee's findings notwithstanding, the university still took no action. Finally, in 1985 Dr. Jew sued the University of Iowa for failing to respond promptly to her cries for help. Her suit charged that faculty members in her department—especially one individual—spread false rumors that she had engaged in a sexual relationship with a former department chair and received preferential treatment from him in exchange. According to her attorney's brief, these rumors created a hostile work environment for Dr. Jew that resulted in the curtailment of her research activities and the subsequent denial of her promotion to full professor.

As the trial progressed, it became clear that Dr. Jew had been harassed not only by the colleague intent on spreading false rumors about the supposed relationship with a former department chair. According to *Newsweek*, "others in the department joked about her ethnic background. Jew is an American of Chinese descent. Explicit sex-based graffiti about her appeared on the walls of the department's men's room when she was being evaluated for promotion. In 1979, another professor, apparently drunk, yelled at her as she walked down a hallway in the department, calling her a 'slut,' a 'bitch,' and a 'whore'" ("Diagnosis" 62). Despite such damaging testimony, as the *Chronicle of Higher Education* wryly observed, "her case dragged on and . . . the university fought her every step of the way" (Blum, "Medical Professor," A15), resisting court intervention in promotion and tenure as a matter of principle and claiming to defend the First Amendment rights of the colleague who had slandered her. For the university, in other words, this had become a case about protecting freedom of speech—even if that speech was sexist, racist, or slanderous—rather than protecting an accomplished faculty woman from sexual harassment. When, finally, in October 1990 the court ruled in her favor, and Jean Jew had reason to hope that her ordeal might be over, the university announced its intention to appeal. The Board of Regents had released a statement reiterating that the case raised First Amendment issues, and the board thereby contested the clear implication of the judge's ruling that the university did indeed have a "responsibility to police its professors' activities and speech" (Blum, "Medical Professor," A16). Five years after filing suit, Dr. Jew's situation still remained unresolved.

3. *Sarah Smith.* A nationally prominent feminist critic in the field of British modernism was hired away from one school, where she chaired the English Department, in order to assume the deanship of the College of Fine Arts and Letters at a small private midwestern university famous for its championship basketball teams. As such, Sarah Smith (not her real name) was the first woman ever to be appointed as an academic dean at her new institution (the dean of students being the only other high-ranking female administrator on campus), and she was the first dean of Fine Arts and Letters to enjoy national visibility based on her scholarship and her extensive publications on feminist critical theory. When she was hired, in fact, the university's president told her he'd chosen her *because* of that record. He hoped her scholarly reputation would attract high caliber faculty and thus upgrade certain departments within Fine Arts and Letters, and he hoped that her feminist commitments might energize what he viewed as only sluggish progress toward improving the school's record in tenuring and retaining women and minority faculty. Indeed, the president strongly implied that Sarah Smith was to take his comments as a mandate. Which she did.

Moving swiftly while employing a widely consultative style, Dean Smith asked the school's affirmative action office to work with a variety of faculty committees, department heads, support staff, and students in order to develop a three-year faculty recruitment plan in Fine Arts and Letters that would result in increased numbers of women faculty and faculty from other underrepresented groups. She asked an elected faculty governance council to review promotion and tenure procedures for any inadvertent biases against women or minority candidates. And she modestly increased financial support for a fledgling women's studies program, including assigning them two tenure-track faculty lines on which to recruit. Although a few faculty, and even some department heads, were vocal in their complaints that the new dean was "moving too fast" or practicing "social engineering," the majority of staff and faculty remained supportive and cooperative.

After several months in which she concentrated on getting to know faculty in the sixteen departments and five programs within Fine Arts and Letters, Dean Smith came to realize that her positions on certain issues were being distorted and erroneously represented to faculty by some of the department heads who had been most vocal in their opposition to her. After redoubling her efforts to reach out to these men, however, Dean Smith had to admit to herself that two would never be team players and one simply could not abide a woman in authority. Because all administrators at this institution serve on annual contracts at the pleasure of their supervisor; and because she'd seen her male colleague deans routinely remove department heads and appoint new ones in their place, she requested the resignation of two department heads at the end of her first year. Preferring to accept resignations rather than summarily inform them of the nonrenewal of their administrative contracts, Smith talked with each man at length, and, in exchange for his resignation, she offered a package that included a semester's paid research leave, a period of reduced teaching assignments, and a generous research budget—to ease the transition out of administration and back to full-time faculty status. Once the terms had been agreed to by both parties, the dean announced her acceptance of both men's resignations and praised their years of administrative service. Her fellow deans (still all male) commented on her generosity but boasted that when they saw the need to remove a department head they just "threw the bum out on his ass," without face-saving resignations or transitional packages. Even so, in her second year, Smith repeated the same scenario with three more department heads. With that, and with the appointment of less authoritarian administrators in their place—two white women and one African-American male, among them—the dean felt she now had a congenial working team.

But three of the former department heads went to the student newspaper and accused Smith of forcing them out in favor of "less qualified" women and minorities. No mention was made of the transition packages they had accepted or, in one instance, of the vote of no confidence in the head taken by his faculty only months before. Instead, the dean was labeled as "unskilled in administration," a "tenured radical hostile to men," "temperamental," and "too controversial." And, for the first two years of her administration, Smith saw herself caricatured in a recurring cartoon in the campus and local papers. Dressed in shorts and a tee shirt with the Fine Arts and Letters logo, she was pictured on a basketball court, dribbling the heads of two or more of her former administrators.

When the department heads' charges and the cartoons were picked up by several national education publications, as well as by the right-wing press, a woman who had always prided herself on a low-key, nonconfrontational style encountered an unfamiliar portrait of herself as "abrasive" and "controversial." Rarely did these stories mention the policy implications of her actions or compare her treatment of department heads with treatment meted out by male deans at the same institution. And, of course, no one interviewed the president to inquire about—nor did the president volunteer—the implied mandate under which the dean had been hired. Still, confident that the majority of the faculty remained comfortable with their new role in recommending affirmative action recruitment priorities and assured, further, by the elected faculty governance council that their members all saw the wisdom of reviewing tenure and promotion procedures, the dean shied away from reporters and continued to work with students, staff, and faculty to implement recommended changes. She did not defend herself to the press, nor did any senior university administrator call her to account.

Toward the end of a relatively quiet third year, therefore, it came as a shock when the president requested Smith's immediate resignation. Her tenure as dean had become too "volatile" and too "publicly controversial" to be effective, he explained. Dean Smith resigned in May, making no statement to the press, and took a long summer vacation, after which she resumed full-time duties as a professor in the English Department. In July, the vice president for Academic Affairs named a new dean. He was one of the department heads whom Sarah Smith had asked to tender his resignation, a man who had been an unsuccessful candidate for the position when Smith was appointed.

iv.

While it is easy to condemn these events as deplorable, it is likewise easy to dismiss them as isolated and unrelated. For the women who lived through them, however, these stories represent only tiny strands teased out of even larger tapestries of harassment and intimidation with which they contend daily.

Consider the graduate student—smart, attractive, articulate. But by the time Diana Franklin attended the Modern Language Association meeting, she had already spent five years stifling her rage and turning away from colleagues' hints that her two graduate school fellowships had been awarded on the basis of her color or her gender, rather than her straight-A record and her two published articles in refereed journals. As a teaching assistant in freshman English, moreover, she'd received no counseling from faculty or course supervisors on how to handle a returning older white male student who repeatedly disrupted the class, challenging her authority on both gender and racial grounds. And now, at her first Modern Language Association meeting, added to the hostility of some of the job interviewers and the disturbing assumptions of some of her fellow job-seekers, Franklin also encountered the misguided good will of one of her most supportive teachers. A bit tipsy from the evening's cocktail party, this kindly older professor put one arm around her shoulder and, in an avuncular fashion, confided that he'd helpfully de-emphasized her "feminist side" in his letters of recommendation by commenting at length on her charming personality and the "delicious fudge brownies" she baked for the department's yearly spring picnic.

Or consider Dr. Jean Jew's career history. Given the scarcity of women in most fields of medicine and science, Jean Jew called upon heroic reserves of determination just to get through the grueling semesters at the Tulane University medical school. Then, for most of her years as a faculty member at the University of Iowa medical school, she was forced to live daily with rumors and their aftermath. Not only was she the object of open sexual speculation among her colleagues. In addition, the gossip drove off potential research partners as colleagues shied away from joining her or inviting her to participate in large collaborative projects. This, in turn, diminished her capacity to attract substantial research grants and pursue her work. And without grants she could not support graduate student research assistants and advisees, thus limiting her opportunity to train the next generation in her particular area of neuroscience.

Sarah Smith was older and, she thought, toughened by experience. But her brief years as dean also took place within a larger pattern of challenge and struggle. She had completed her Ph.D. at a prestigious Ivy League university that, in those days, never awarded fellowships or teaching assistantships to women and, in fact, discouraged women from going beyond the masters degree. Her husband, like so many bewildered men of his generation, had never understood her desire for an independent career, and, on the very day that Smith successfully defended her dissertation, he announced that he was filing for divorce.

A single mother with a small child, Smith at first had difficulty locating a tenure-track position, and when she did find one, she spent years earning half the salary of her male colleagues while routinely being assigned heavier teaching loads. Working around the clock at two full-time jobs—being a parent *and* an academic—she managed to publish a series of influential books and articles and was finally elected chair of her department. In that capacity, she had worked with the faculty to update promotion and tenure documents, revise graduate and undergraduate course offerings to reflect the latest scholarship in the field, and she quickly recruited a number of outstanding women and minority faculty. With support from the dean, she also analyzed faculty salaries and made adjustments where past inequities based on gender were still in evidence. Her well-known successes in these areas contributed to making her a desirable candidate for a deanship.

But, as the first female academic dean at her new institution, Smith found it almost impossible to break into the camaraderie that marked the long-term relationships between most of the male deans. As a single woman, she was oftentimes overlooked for their "married couples-only" dinner parties. And never did any of the other deans invite her for lunch, dinner, coffee, or a drink—as they regularly did with one another. When she began inviting them to lunch, one at a time, her fellow deans each reciprocated—once. After that, it always took *her* initiative to get any of them to meet her for coffee or lunch (the only invitations they would accept, as two made explicit), in order to discuss concerns of mutual interest in an informal setting. When she sat with her fellow academic deans at the president's monthly Academic Policies Council, she heard them habitually interrupt or speak over her even while she was still talking—something they rarely did to one another. And whenever she introduced issues pertaining to women or minorities, or when she asked that some pending budget reallocation be analyzed for its impact on women or minority students, she would later be told—by one or another of the deans who had been friendlier to her—that she should be wary of developing a reputation as a "one issue administrator."

My point here is simple: the stories that women choose to tell about the difficulties encountered, owing to their sex, in their professional lives have force and resonance *because* those stories are not experienced in isolation. Each incident emerges out of a larger matrix that again and again had a corrosive effect on the integrity and self-esteem of the woman in question, challenging her capacity to perform her job (or research) effectively, undermining her ability to develop any sustained sense of professional competence, and draining her creative energies in the endless need to invent stratagems of self-protection. And, sadly, the individual anecdotes reveal yet another set of connections. When measured by my earlier definition of antifeminist intellectual harassment, each anecdote detailed above illustrates the reach and depth of that harassment, as well as the price we pay for it as an academic community. That price is perhaps most accurately totaled if we reverse the order of the anecdotes, beginning with the woman we might have expected to represent meaningful influence and authority.

The short-lived tenure of the feminist dean of Fine Arts and Letters illustrates the pitfalls of bringing a lone woman into a highly visible position, asking her to correct an entire history of problems, and then offering her no support network. And it reminds us of the cynicism with which some university presidents and provosts make grand gestures of hiring feminist and minority administrators specifically to respond to a poor affirmative action record, only to back away when these individuals encounter predictable pockets of resistance in their efforts to initiate the required changes.

Because of this, Sarah Smith's story also plays out all sections of my definition of antifeminist intellectual harassment. Though fully within the regulations by which this campus functioned, her summary dismissal by the president had the long-term effect of discouraging other feminist scholars there from even considering a move into administration; and it had the short-term effect of eroding the former dean's ability to speak with an influential voice on matters of discrimination, gender equity, and the need to support a developing women's studies curriculum. In addition to thus inhibiting women's freedom of action and expression, the president also effectively derailed a set of innovative policies that had already resulted in the increased hiring of women and minority faculty within the College of Fine Arts and Letters. And he shut down an environment newly receptive to cross-disciplinary research areas, including women's studies. To be sure, the president's only conscious motives may have been to placate conservative alumni threatening a withdrawal of financial support or to calm a Board of Trustees made nervous by unwanted publicity. But, in fact, both in his manner of removing Dean Smith and in his tacit approval of her replacement, the president reconstituted an earlier environment on campus in which research, scholarship, and teaching pertaining to women and gender inequities was understood to be a low priority, and perhaps even hazardous to one's professional health.

Even as Jean Jew's story raises questions about the adequacy of the University of Iowa's internal grievance procedures and the effectiveness of its affirmative action office, her story also challenges us to justify the personal toll exacted by the ongoing stress and financial burden of a lawsuit.[2] "Her pursuit of sexual harassment complaints against the university and individual administrators," noted the *Chronicle of Higher Education*, has left Dr. Jew "drained financially and emotionally," her reputation as a competent scientist shattered (Blum, "Medical Professor," A15). As a result, as with so many Title VII cases, the real benefits of Dr. Jew's perseverance will be enjoyed by women who may not even know her name. Her suit forced the University of Iowa's affirmative action office to organize training programs on sexual harassment issues and to develop specific sexual harassment policies. The *Chronicle of Higher Education* also reported that the institution was clarifying and streamlining its complaint procedures and intended to provide all employees with informational booklets on what constitutes sexual harassment (Blum, "Medical Professor," A16). However belated, such remediating steps are to be applauded—even though they do not address, or even recognize, the pernicious *intellectual* harassment to which Dr. Jew was also subjected.

Although Jean Jew's research does not focus on women or address questions of gender, the treatment she received at the University of Iowa's medical college—and the university's lack of response—still falls within my definition because that treatment had the effect of curtailing her research activity. The department's rumor mill made most graduate students wary of working with Dr. Jew. For that same reason, Dr. Jew was unable easily to collaborate with colleagues on research projects. Thus she was forced to pursue her work under burdens not faced by her male colleagues and under burdens that inevitably had a chilling effect on the progress of that work. While all of this, combined with the years of litigation, had personal consequences for Dr. Jew— inhibiting her intellectual potential and robbing her of years of professional productivity—it also had consequences for the women and minority students for whom, under other circumstances, she might have served as mentor and friend.

In the science fields and on medical school faculties, women— especially women from nontraditional backgrounds—are notoriously underrepresented. Amid all the curricular reforms and community outreach programs that have been devised to correct this situation, one strategy has been universally endorsed: bringing more women and minorities into visible faculty and research positions. But by turning Dr. Jew into an object of gossip within her department, and thus effectively isolating her, the University of Iowa undoubtedly deprived some eager graduate student of the very support she needed for survival there. Or, even worse, the treatment accorded Dr. Jew may have warned another talented young Chinese-American woman that science and medicine were simply minefields too dangerous to enter. As the only woman faculty member in the Anatomy Department at Iowa during most of her years there and as one of only three women in a 22-member department in 1994, Dr. Jew herself commented that "one of the reasons these sorts of problems about gender in the workplace persist is that there are so few women here to begin with" (Blum, "Medical Professor," A16).

Like Jean Jew, the graduate student at the Modern Language Association meeting had enjoyed a strong and supportive relationship with her mentor as she completed her dissertation. It was only during her first foray into the larger profession that Diana Franklin found herself intimidated and silenced. For, whether they consciously intended it or not, the job interviewers who grilled her about the work of her feminist adviser effectively issued a covert warning: "Women who display the intellectual daring of your adviser," they seemed to be saying, "are dangerous and too controversial to be admitted to *our* department. We have no place for such women or for anyone they train." This experience, coupled with the condescending admission from one of her strongest references that he had purposefully understated her "feminist side" in his job letters for her, forced Franklin to reassess the dissertation topic she had once chosen with unalloyed enthusiasm. *Should* she de-emphasize or even altogether omit from her dissertation some of its more unsettling speculations? *Should* she, she wondered, modify her research agenda until she was safely tenured? Turning over the alternatives as she dozed on the flight back to California, Diana Franklin finally realized, with a start, that academe no longer felt to her like the haven of intellectual freedom she thought she had found.

v.

When I asked a mixed group of graduate students on my home campus if they'd ever heard the phrase "antifeminist intellectual harassment," they all said no. When I asked what they thought it might mean, one young woman quickly replied, "Oh, that's easy—business as usual." No one disagreed.

When I circulated the three numbered anecdotes to friends and colleagues around the country, asking if these stories seemed like legitimate instances of antifeminist intellectual harassment, I was struck by another uniformity of response. Very few recognized my harassment category, but every correspondent was convinced that one or more of the anecdotes was based on events at her or his campus (including the story of Jean Jew, where the institution was identified).

Because such events are now both familiar and ubiquitous, each of my correspondents had ready remedies. In response to Diana Franklin's story, there were recommendations that all advanced graduate students receive formal training on handling interview situations, while faculty serving on search committees be required to attend mandatory affirmative action seminars. Jean Jew's story elicited a variety of procedural recommendations, including, for example, an ombudsperson's office with selected staff trained to deal expeditiously with charges of sexual harassment. Sarah Smith's story brought the expected outcry against the suspected interference of right-wing alumni. But it also brought practical suggestions for the development of on-campus training and mentorship programs aimed at preparing women of color, white women, and all faculty from underrepresented groups for responsible roles as academic administrators. Most passionate, perhaps, were the pleas that professional and campus women's groups take responsibility for sponsoring workshops on individual survival strategies. "Someone needs to teach junior women how to reach out to senior colleagues and make them allies," one of my correspondents noted. "It's especially important for untenured women to go to conferences, sign onto e-mail, and develop a national network for themselves," wrote another.

Clearly, the three anecdotes suggested to each of my correspondents a checklist of independent activities that might prove useful on her or his own campus. And while no refusal of antifeminist intellectual harassment is ever *un*important, it may be possible to secure an even more lasting impact through a concerted effort to embed an intolerance of such harassment into all of a school's pronouncements about itself. I would recommend, therefore, an additional, comprehensive approach. The object here is to educate the campus and local community to recognize antifeminist intellectual harassment, whatever its mode of expression, and to create a context in which interested parties can speak *as* and *for* the institution in condemning it. In short, change the sound of the institution's voice. This is neither as ephemeral nor as difficult as one might initially suppose.

As a singular and monolithic entity, "the institution" simply doesn't exist. Instead, "the institution" is merely a grammatical convenience that projects the illusion of coherence and integration. The truth is that whatever the putative institution does is really the outcome of complicated ensembles of complex relationships between and among groups and individuals. Marked by loosely bounded and overlapping areas of action and responsibility,[3] with power vacuums everywhere belying the appearance of hierarchy, the college or university campus is unique in its potential to be represented by a variety of (even competing) constituencies. As a result, many different groups and individuals—the president, the Board of Trustees, elected student government officers, the head of the Black Student Association, the chair of the Faculty Senate, the librarians' committee, the campus disability caucus, the Support Staff Council, organized alumni groups, and so on—all claim at different times to be speaking *for* the college, *on behalf* of the university, or *in its best interests.* And rightly so. This sense of ownership is what prompts groups and individuals to take conscious responsibility for the environment that their actions, attitudes, behaviors, and decisions are creating for them and others.

Once this is understood, the prospect of taking on the institution's voice in order to combat antifeminist intellectual harassment becomes less daunting. And two tasks emerge clearly: first, such harassment must be widely identified and repeatedly explained; and, second, opposition to it must be projected as the *institutional* norm. That said, the vast array of governance structures coupled with the sheer variety of higher education entities in this country make it impossible to devise any universal blueprint for taking on these tasks. Interested groups at different colleges and universities will have to examine their own unique situation and explore local possibilities. As they do so, however, I would urge them to consider including some version of the following four strategies as an interrelated package, with all four—as much as possible—going forward at the same time. My experience as a dean taught me that it is always far more profitable to be overly ambitious rather than hesitatingly cautious.

1. Multiyear conference and follow-up assessments. By first employing informal internal networks—like women's studies bag lunches and e-mail—a small group can initiate an ongoing campus-wide dialogue on antifeminist intellectual harassment. Through these and other informal communications, the original group can begin to identify larger numbers of potentially interested groups and individuals. The object is to develop the widest possible coalition—such as the women's faculty association, the women's studies faculty, an appropriate student government committee, the affirmative action office, the organized librarians, etc.—so that, together, these groups can seek both internal and external funding for a multiyear conference. The more groups involved, of course, the greater the impact, and the more numerous the opportunities for tapping diverse funding sources.

Wherever feasible, the conference should announce itself as an examination of antifeminist intellectual harassment and its damaging consequences for the campus community. Conference flyers and posters might include a brief definition of the term, thus helping to educate even those who do not attend—and preparing those who will. At a school where this focus cannot win wide support, organizers would be well advised to design the conference as an examination of both the history of and the present threats to the concept of academic freedom and to position antifeminist intellectual harassment as a significant example of those threats.

Whether the conference is offered as a national or local event, it is essential to engage participation from every campus constituency— faculty, undergraduates, graduate students, librarians, support staff, and administrators. Ideally, the academic vice president, the president, the chancellor, and members of the Board of Trustees will all see the wisdom of accepting invitations to appear as featured speakers or as members of panels. Publicity for these events must be carefully planned, and press coverage courted in advance.

However well attended and however comprehensive the press coverage, one-time events (even when scheduled over two or three days) have only limited usefulness—unless, that is, they are designed to initiate an ongoing process. For antifeminist intellectual harassment to continue to be recognized and rejected, it will have to be the focus of a second and very different kind of conference two years after the first. And in order to galvanize the campus into condemning that harassment, the first conference must set in motion a series of integrated activities that will have the effect of diminishing the opportunities for such behaviors. The second conference thereby becomes an occasion to examine the problem again and, even more important, to offer a progress report on how the campus has responded to it.

As the first conference is being planned, the program committee must ensure that the conference goes beyond merely defining the problem and pointing to its prevalence. In addition, that committee should seek out representatives from student, staff, and faculty governance groups (and unions, where appropriate) as well as members of the university's legal office to serve on specific action-oriented sessions. These sessions might examine the institution's own policy documents to determine if they include adequate safeguards against antifeminist intellectual harassment. And these same sessions should function as occasions for encouraging designated groups and individuals to take responsibility for reviewing campus codes of conduct, faculty handbooks, and other like documents in order to determine if some new or clarifying language might be helpful.

Given the expense of mounting any kind of conference nowadays —and especially a multiyear event—several schools in a given geographic area might cooperate in joint sponsorship, thus sharing the expenses and, at the same time, increasing the audience. Or, where a school already enjoys a well-established (and funded) annual women's studies conference, that conference might be adapted as the occasion for these "special events." In that case, it will be important to attract an audience beyond those who regularly attend women's studies activities.

The school in which antifeminist intellectual harassment is a recurring problem probably will not be hospitable to the multiyear conference outlined here, however, even as a participant with several other schools in the area. Interested faculty at these institutions should turn instead to the women's caucuses and women's commissions within their disciplinary professional organizations. Either separately or together, these groups also have the capacity to find conference funding or, at the very least, to command a substantial portion of their professional organization's yearly conference program. And while such an organization-sponsored conference ordinarily would not scrutinize the policy documents of a single campus, the conference could certainly examine discipline-related policy statements at a variety of schools. And, as the feminist literary biographer Emily Toth has pointed out to me, a university initially wary of hosting a conference on antifeminist intellectual harassment might become far more amenable after the subject has been aired through a series of professional meetings and rendered "topical."[4]

2. *Reviewing promotion and tenure policy documents.* In order to ensure that women continue actively to participate in the ongoing creation and re-creation of every discipline's knowledge base and in

order to ensure that the energizing variety of feminist approaches is fully represented, promotion and tenure policy documents must undergo careful and regular review. As illustrated in chapter 3, committees examining these documents will want to ascertain that criteria for promotion and tenure make room for work in nontraditional areas—where feminist scholarship has been particularly prominent—and acknowledge the value of cross- and interdisciplinary research and scholarship. Especially in the humanities fields, these committees should also see to it that promotion and tenure criteria allow for the evaluation of scholarly work that appears in formats other than the article, the monograph, or the book. Much important new research is now being presented through the production of documentary videos for educational television, museum exhibitions, and innovative instructional computer programs. No less important, the tenure and promotion procedural documents should declare, unequivocally, that the candidate's internal and external reviewers will include those knowledgeable in her field and that her participation in a women's studies program (or African-American or ethnic studies program, etc.) will be fully credited and evaluated.

Finally, any examination of promotion and tenure policies must include a careful "reading-between-the-lines" in search of covert messages suggesting that one tenured feminist is enough. This often unspoken mind-set assumes mistakenly that feminism is monolithic, adhering to some narrowly defined set of questions and methodologies. The language for containing and constraining the development of a fully polyvocal feminist dialogue in a department may be camouflaged in terminology about "programmatic needs" and "avoiding duplication." But, in fact, an English Department's legitimate concern over the wisdom of hiring a second specialist in pre-Shakespearean drama when enrollments are falling should not be confused with the tenuring of a feminist theorist in medieval studies and a feminist critic in nineteenth-century American literature, each bringing a different set of theories and methods to her classes and to the department as a whole. In this context, feminist inquiry is not by itself a field of study, as is pre-Shakespearean drama; rather, feminist inquiry is constituted by sets of interrelated (and sometimes oppositional) theories and methods for re-examining and even renewing already well-established subject areas. Additionally, by cutting across area and discipline boundaries, feminist theory—in all its current diversity—has come to represent both a critique of and a challenge to the enterprise of theory itself. The tenuring of a feminist theorist would thus secure for a department strengths very different from those of the feminist medievalist or the feminist Americanist.

3. *Bringing more women and members of underrepresented groups into higher education administration.* Anyone who is unfamiliar or perceived as "nontraditional" within an otherwise homogeneous group inevitably takes on a visibility disproportionate to that individual's actual activities within the group. He or she will be subjected to more intense scrutiny, along with quicker judgments about her performance, and her motives will be interpreted less as a function of her professional role than as an expression of her "difference" or "uniqueness." According to those who have studied the concept of *surplus visibility*, moreover, the greater the decision-making authority vested in her position, the more conspicuous that individual becomes.[5]

At the same time, every student of organizational psychology knows that institutions feel "safe" to people only insofar as they see themselves—or those like them—as empowered within those institutions. In order both to diminish the debilitating consequences of surplus visibility and to enhance *everyone's* comfort within higher education, it is essential that campuses make a concerted effort to recruit members of underrepresented groups, and especially feminist-identified men and women, for all layers of administration, management, and policy-making. But that recruitment must avoid tokenism and, instead, be focused on purposefully creating a designated critical mass of change agents.

To be sure, what constitutes a critical mass will vary from campus to campus, although one third of any specifiable group is usually a minimum target. I stress the concept because only a critical mass of mutually supportive individuals is capable of sustaining them through difficult periods while, at the same time, reaching out widely to create an ongoing atmosphere welcoming to diversity and open to all serious intellectual activity. And only a critical mass convincingly demonstrates to the larger community the role of the campus as a haven of academic freedom for many different kinds of people. The human face of these administrators, we may hope, might even help to make both feminism and diversity less threatening by building bridges of personal relationships, especially with types of individuals previously subjected to caricature and the mockery of cartoons.

This evolution beyond mere tokenism is demanded by the nation's changing demographics, of course. At the City University of New York, the nation's largest public urban university, 40 percent of the entering students nowadays "are black or Hispanic and trace their ancestry to the Caribbean" (Honan 16), while slightly over half the undergraduate population nationwide is female. But the move beyond tokenism also derives from the fact that, as an affirmative action strategy, tokenism has backfired badly. Not only were individuals destroyed and careers derailed in the spotlight of surplus visibility; but highly qualified white women, women of color, and others from underrepresented groups witnessed the costs of these struggles, internalized the experiences as their own, and reconsidered any aspirations they once might have harbored regarding an administrative career for themselves in higher education. The end result was that few women and fewer feminists believed that they had been seriously invited to any permanent place at the decision-making table. In order to avoid passing on these silent messages of inevitable failure, therefore, and in order to make it possible to move larger numbers of women and others from underrepresented groups into administrative positions, schools must develop internship programs for staff and faculty alike.

Ideally, on-campus internship and administrative mentorship programs should be open, on a competitive basis, to the entire eligible campus community. I say this because such programs face two challenges. The first is to convince potential women and minority recruits that the institution is genuinely committed to change. To accomplish this will require an outlay of significant resources, usually in mentorship hours or formal training sessions, rather than large sums of money. And it will require the speedy appointment of some of the program's women and minority graduates to appropriate administrative or managerial positions. Otherwise, women and those from underrepresented groups will remain reluctant to invest themselves.

The second challenge is to prepare *all* participants in an administrative training program to respond to the special stresses of bias, stereotyping, discrimination, and surplus visibility that will be encountered by some of them. To put it another way, until women and those from currently underrepresented groups are no longer anomalies in higher education administration, the on-the-job problems encountered by white women and women of color *because of who they are* really can be mediated successfully only through the sympathetic interventions of colleagues who appreciate the full complexity of the situation. In other words, white males and males of color must learn how to become allies of their feminist colleagues in administration, and they must be taught appropriate responses to the particular difficulties of surplus visibility that a female president or a feminist dean will inevitably encounter. At the same time, all administrative trainees can be taught to understand and contain the scope of surplus visibility that a male from any underrepresented group will also encounter. Only in this way can administrators learn to share meaningful colleagueship across the divides of difference.

Effective administrative training programs are rarely expensive, and they can be implemented relatively easily. With only a limited budget to cover such items as "a small library of reference books on women and leadership, copying, occasional lunches and snacks, and a field trip to meet with state leaders in Harrisburg," for example, Kutztown University in Pennsylvania initiated a Women in Leadership program in 1993. Enrolling twenty-eight women in its first year—and more in subsequent years—"the program's goals are to empower women on campus by: 1) providing information on sexism, the glass ceiling and the campus climate for women; 2) developing their leadership skills by studying leadership styles, communication and conflict resolution; and 3) developing understanding of the roles of campus and system leaders including chairs, deans, provost, chancellor and president" ("Kutztown Leadership" 8). Additionally, schools in the same region can pool resources by establishing exchange—or "loaned administrative trainee"—programs. And many schools already take advantage of national resources like the annual Summer Institute for Women in Higher Education Administration, held at Bryn Mawr College and sponsored by Higher Education Resource Services of Mid-America.[6]

Statewide cooperation should not be overlooked, either. Thanks to two years of modest funding from the state legislature, the Florida Department of Education was able to develop the Educational Leadership Enhancement Grant Program, targeted at attracting "more women and minorities into the upper echelons of higher education administration." In 1994, the first year of funding, six different leadership projects in nine schools reached "more than 60 women and minorities in Florida's public community colleges and universities." According to an article in *Women in Higher Education,* most of these projects involved "internships, mentoring and career counseling, and a series of seminars to build leadership and networking skills" ("Florida Invests" 2).

Whatever the design or scope of the program, however, every institution that has supported or participated in either on-campus or off-campus administrative training programs has learned that their continued success is determined, over time, by the institution's efforts to recruit program participants for visible managerial and administrative positions. Were the women and minority graduates of an administrative internship program repeatedly passed over for openings at the home campus or lured away to administrative posts at other schools, the home institution would not only be losing out on its best investment. It would also appear to be acting in bad faith.

4. *Continuing the commitment to feminist intellectual inquiry within the academy.* For all its petty turf battles and its inherently reactionary conservatism, its overheated interpersonal squabbles and public mendacities, the academy still remains the single institution in the United States that at least *claims* to protect access to unimpeded intellectual inquiry—for everyone in the society and on behalf of the society as a whole. While the growing incidence of outright hostility toward feminist scholars and their research puts that claim to the test, that same hostility also challenges feminists ever more fiercely to seize our right to participate in the creation and re-creation of knowledge. Thus, in my view, the indispensable requirement for combating antifeminist intellectual harassment is the creative, energetic, ever-expanding persistence of feminist inquiry itself. Whatever else we do— including our efforts to ward off the harassment—our scholarship, research, and teaching innovations cannot be put aside.

All by itself, academic freedom is a difficult ideal to sustain. It is an ideal, after all, that holds the potential to undermine established systems of power, to unravel the society's most cherished myths about itself, and, indeed, to challenge the structures of knowledge on which the academy once securely positioned itself. Because the best of feminist work shatters to its very foundations a full panoply of powerful cultural conventions—from class arrangements to gender hierarchy to men's imputed mastery over nature—resistance to that work will be as powerful as the privileges and cultural beliefs being protected. But the impact of our scholarship and teaching—the persuasiveness of our critical scrutiny, the compelling evidence produced by our research, and the disturbing questions that linger in the student's mind long after our classes are over—will contribute to changing people's beliefs and perceptions, altering forever their categories of analysis and understanding. Indeed, as most feminist scholars rather ruefully remark, the ubiquity of the harassment we now encounter is testimony to our effectiveness in bringing substantial change to the various disciplines and to the educational institutions that once tried to keep us out. Feminist research and theory must inform the strategies of response to intellectual harassment, of course; but feminist research, scholarship, and teaching are themselves the most important parts of that response. Or, to put it another way: the moment we abandon our research, our pursuit of better interpretations, our thoughtful reappraisal of all received truths, our insistence on asking how we know what we think we know, in that moment antifeminist intellectual harassment will have prevailed.

vi.

All stories, even anecdotes, deserve endings.

As she returned from the Modern Language Association meeting to her tiny apartment in California, Diana Franklin made up her mind. By the time the next school year was to begin, she needed to have a full-time faculty position with a decent salary. Despite her fellowships and her years as a graduate teaching assistant, she had accumulated considerable debt. And her parents required financial help as they worked to put the younger children through school. The entire month of January, therefore, was given over to revising sections of her dissertation, and especially the two sample chapters she was sending out to prospective employers. Her purpose was not to censor her conclusions but, where possible, to reframe those conclusions in language that was less daring, less provocative. In several places, she also carefully deleted any hints about the kinds of feminist projects she intended to pursue in the future.

After making five campus visits, Franklin received three firm job offers, two from departments of English and one a joint appointment with English and African-American Studies. She accepted the latter, because she felt her research might be better received within an interdisciplinary African-American Studies program than within a conventional English Department. In fact, she continues to wonder whether the English Department at her new school would have sponsored her candidacy had the search committee read her dissertation chapters in their original form. Franklin knows she is secure, for the time being, she says; but it doesn't *feel* that way. And, she adds, as she rewrites her dissertation for book publication, she has to struggle against censoring herself at every turn.

Despite the continued harassment and against all odds, Dr. Jean Jew tenaciously pursued her research agenda. Her circumstances compromised her opportunities for external funding, but still she succeeded in bringing in grants, thereby demonstrating not only her dedication but also the quality of her work as judged by the larger scientific community. These successes notwithstanding, it was with profound relief that in October 1990, five years after she filed suit in federal court and thirteen years after filing internal complaints at the University of Iowa, Jean Jew heard a judge deliver a scathing indictment of the university's failure to take "prompt, appropriate corrective action" on her behalf (Blum, "Medical Professor," A16). But her relief quickly disappeared as she heard university attorneys state their intention to appeal. At that point, groups from within the university community who were sympathetic to Dr. Jew organized in earnest, circulating copies of the judge's findings to every faculty member. The *Des Moines Register*, which had been following the case closely, "printed a full page of excerpts" from the judge's ruling, according to *Newsweek*, and ran an editorial urging the university to give up its appeal. Finally, in November, after pressure from a variety of constituencies, the university dropped its plans to appeal and, as *Newsweek* put it, "paid for its laissez-faire attitude. . . . The university issued a humbling public apology and agreed to pay Dr. Jew $50,000 in back pay, $126,000 in damages, and $895,000 in fees and expenses to her attorney" ("Diagnosis" 62). And, as the judge had ordered, she was promoted to full professor.

In response to the judge's decree that the university "take all reasonable steps to ensure a hostility-free work environment" for Dr. Jew (Blum, "Medical Professor," A16), the university's president at the time, Hunter Rawlings III, promised to do just that, adding that "Dr. Jew deserves our apologies and our respect for her stand" ("Diagnosis" 62). For her part, Jean Jew remained skeptical. "It's so much easier to hand over money than to do what's right," she commented; in her view, "the hardest part of all" was still to come: actually correcting the problem ("Diagnosis" 62).

After returning to faculty status in the Department of English, Sarah Smith remained only two more years at the school where she had once been dean of the College of Fine Arts and Letters. Her articles on facilitating change and renewal in higher education caught the attention of two executive search firms and a number of educators across the country. Smith's experience as a department chair and a dean, combined with strong recommendations from faculty and administrators who had worked closely with her, added to her attractiveness as a candidate for senior administrative posts. A small private liberal arts college in the Pacific Northwest lured her away as provost. Four years later, a similar institution in the Northeast named her as its president. Within a few years of becoming president, Smith established a solid reputation as both a fundraiser and an academic leader. And she emerged as an eloquent national spokesperson for equity issues in higher education. "But I'm very, very tired," she told me, and "I don't think I can keep this up much longer. That experience as Dean of Fine Arts and Letters," she continued, "affected my health and used up all my reserves of energy. It almost broke me."

Jane Schaberg, the image of whose torched Toyota Tercel opened this chapter, miraculously remains both unbroken and undaunted. Continuing her groundbreaking studies of the New Testament, she recently used a sabbatical leave to work on a book-length analysis of Mary Magdalene traditions.

If there are lessons to be learned from these women's stories, they surely are not lessons about the triumphs of antifeminist intellectual harassment. On the contrary: in each instance, a strong determined woman surmounted the harassment and survived, even succeeded. But there *is* a cautionary lesson to be learned, nonetheless: in each instance, the woman paid too high a price—a price that never should have been exacted in the first place. The energies of those who will be needed to lead the academy into the twenty-first century should not be so carelessly squandered.

5 Creating the Family-Friendly Campus

"The goals of the feminist movement have
not been achieved, and those who claim
we're living in a post-feminist era are either
sadly mistaken or tired of thinking about
the whole subject."
—Margaret Atwood, *Second Words*, 370.

i.

A national study released in October 1996 cited the University of Arizona as among the top twenty-nine campuses in the United States for its efforts to "help faculty members and administrators balance the pressures of work and family life." Junior faculty struggling to raise families while simultaneously preparing for tenure review, staff personnel who require family-sensitive policies different from those designed for faculty and administrators, and individuals caring for a chronically ill parent would object that the university still has a long way to go before *their* lives will experience any balance. But whatever the shortcomings of present policies, everyone seems to agree that our designation as one of "the most family-friendly . . . institutions" (Robin Wilson, "A Report," A13) represents a rapid turnaround and illustrates how much can be accomplished when a university finally makes a commitment to examine the family needs of its faculty, staff, and students. Certainly it wasn't always this way.

When I entered the dean's office in July 1988, I had an emphatic mandate from central administration to diversify the faculty by increasing the numbers of women and individuals from underrepresented groups in the tenure ranks. But I had the financial resources to hire at the assistant professor level only. I knew I needed incentives to attract the best and the brightest of these highly sought-after newly minted Ph.D.s, many of whom (I also knew) would be hearing the tenure clock tick alongside their own (or a partner's) biological clock and be thinking about children. When I made inquiries in the university's Human

Resources Office, I was assured by a staff member that family care was not an issue on campus and that a recent campus-wide survey indicated no immediate need for any additional child care services. That office's distribution of information about private providers in the area met the current demand. I was doubtful. In my own office, there was evidence of a range of child care needs.

Even after we adjusted individual schedules and offered flex-time options, on certain occasions—generally the state's grade school holidays or teacher in-service training days—our office looked like an elementary school, with a five-year-old cutting recycled paper into notepads, while a seven-year-old tried to change the color images on his mother's computer screen. Whether as single mothers or as the wives of men with full-time jobs, several secretaries could not afford the loss in pay or the deduction of precious vacation time that would result from their staying home on scheduled school closings. And because university wage scales are chronically low, private day care was beyond their means. Bringing their children with them to work was their only realistic option except when their children were sick, in which case these women had no choice but to lose a day's pay (or give up a paid vacation day) and stay home. No one else was available for caretaking.

I had also become aware of the little girl who spent her nights in the basement ladies' room of the student union. One evening, when my executive assistant and I had worked late in that building, we encountered her, sprawled on the linoleum floor of the ladies' room entry, silently drawing with crayons on a large pad of white paper. She looked up and smiled when we addressed her—first in English, then in Spanish—but she responded to none of our questions. From members of the custodial staff, we learned that the girl, seven years old, slightly retarded and slow of speech, was the daughter of one of the women on the night crew cleaning team. The entire crew, along with the child's mother, took turns checking on her regularly. The crew members had identified the bathroom as the safest place for her because, if left anywhere else, the child might wander off in search of water or toilet facilities and get lost. In about an hour, we were told, the girl would fall asleep, and her mother would cover her with a blanket. The mother was single and without any family in the area, one custodian volunteered, and the night shift job was the best she had been able to secure. Without it, she would be forced back on welfare. Finally, to quiet our obvious unease, the same custodian suggested that, if things went well, the mother might be reassigned to the day shift, and then a neighbor could be asked to take care of the child after school.

It was a chilling encounter that continued to resonate as I heard stories about junior faculty who regularly brought their infants or small children to class or as I watched young student parents—men and women alike—perched on the sills of open windows in ground-floor classrooms, trying to attend to the lecture within while also keeping an eye on a small child playing just outside. Seeking to understand how a campus-wide child care survey could generate data that so starkly contradicted my own observations, I learned that the questionnaire had been sent to a randomly selected group of faculty from the tenured and tenure-eligible ranks only. No staff or students had been included. Once I understood how the data were compiled, it was no surprise to me that over 80 percent of the respondents expressed no urgency on the subject. In 1988, the professoriate at the University of Arizona, like the professoriate nationwide, was still overwhelmingly white, male, and over fifty. Not only did the recipients of the questionnaire represent the demographics of the past, but, in addition, the vast majority of those who responded were men who had never themselves been primarily responsible for any child's daily care.

Happily, during the years of my deanship, the demographics of the future asserted themselves, and organized faculty women's groups, staff women, student government leaders, and a few well-placed women administrators became increasingly vocal on the issue of child care. With a transition in the president's and provost's offices, a new administration found itself pressured to look at the question anew. This time, "600 University of Arizona employees who currently use child care services" were surveyed. According to the front-page story in the 11 February 1994 issue of the student newspaper, the *Arizona Daily Wildcat*, "about half of the employees reported having problems with child care affecting their work responsibilities, while 57% reported having their work affected by someone else's child care problems." The report accompanying the survey recommended an on-campus child care facility "open for extended hours on weekdays and open on weekends to accommodate working parents and students"

(Hartmann 1, 4). Independent surveys by the university's Commission on the Status of Women estimated 2,203 child care users in the employee population and "between 2,500 and 3,500 parents who are . . . students," all with a variety of different needs, including summer child care, sick-child care, and drop-in care facilities (Leibold 3).[1]

To be fair, the University of Arizona was not alone in its earlier inability to ask the right questions or to target the right audience for those questions. As was true at most of the nation's higher educational institutions, until quite recently the University of Arizona's policymakers were rarely those who shouldered significant responsibility for family care—whether the care of children or the care of an aging parent—and a workplace constructed around a male wage-earner with a supportive wife at home remained for them both familiar and comfortable. Long after that model was no longer feasible, in everything from meeting schedules to timetables for intellectual achievement, the academy—including my own university—continued to operate on outdated assumptions about typical family configurations. As a result, few senior administrators nationwide viewed family care issues as a pressing priority, even though predictions of two major demographic shifts should have caught their notice.

Those shifts are now upon us, and no workplace—certainly not academe—can turn away from the projection of the National Commission of Working Women that "by the year 2000, 80 percent of women in their prime childbearing years (between 25 and 44) will be in the labor force" (Coiner 213). Nor can any employer afford to ignore the fact that, by the year 2025, a full 20 percent of the United States population will be 65 or older, and "nearly half of those will be 75 or older" (Park A40).

But while radically shifting demographics and the collective voices of women (and a few men) may finally be focusing campus administrators on a spectrum of family needs, the question of how to respond to those needs is being framed in a crisis atmosphere of sliced budgets and demoralizing scarcity. Endless task forces and countless committees puzzle over how to finance benefits packages for domestic partners, how to pay for child care centers, or, at state-supported campuses, how to subsidize on-site child care in the face of local laws that prohibit public entities from competing with the private sector. And because most central administrations have been unprepared for this increasingly insistent demand for campus-based family services, they find themselves forced to respond before assessing what precisely is required or before determining how to ensure quality in the delivery of such services. Without sufficient hard data and without an adequate conceptual framework, discussions in deans' councils and presidents' cabinets degenerate into predictable debates over money and competing campus priorities, while what is really at issue never surfaces: the evolving reshapings of family structures and the consequent redefinitions of family needs. In other words, rather than face up to a complex set of challenges relating to the changing structures of the American family, the institutional focus remains fixed, almost exclusively, on dealing piecemeal with one or another limited (and, it is hoped, affordable) component—like maternity leave, child care, or domestic partner benefits.

Having served on the statewide Commission on the Status of Women, created in the fall of 1989 by the Arizona Board of Regents to improve "the conditions of employment for women at the state's three public universities" (*Reaching the Vision* 4), I am convinced that the means exist to make the required accommodations. During the Commission's two and a half years of fact-finding, it became clear to me that colleges and universities everywhere—large and small, public and private, residential and commuter—were responding to the same demographic shifts and were experimenting with a variety of strategies. And although no school we examined had developed anything close to a comprehensive response to changing family structures, it was nonetheless evident that even the most resistant administrators on any campus had come to understand that, as we race into the twenty-first century, our old ways of running a campus will no longer serve.

Mine is an improbable voice in these matters, I admit. Although happily married for over a quarter century, my husband and I have no children. And although I sometimes conferred with my mother's doctors regarding her prescriptions and medical tests, I was never responsible, in any extended way, for her daily care. Even so, as I look back on a full, generally satisfying, and often frenzied life in academe, I find myself questioning which of these circumstances was really freely chosen and which the unacknowledged by-product of a career path that always demanded too much. Other women academics, I know, have broken under the strain of trying to do it all.

The urgency in this chapter does not derive from personal experience, therefore, but it is certainly personally felt. Over the years, I have had too many conversations with bleary-eyed junior colleagues who were trying simultaneously to raise their children and to finish a book manuscript before tenure review. Nowadays, I regularly receive letters from women colleagues my own age—in their fifties—who tell me they eagerly contemplate early retirement because they are just too exhausted to go on.

That women in academe were in crisis became brutally apparent to me in 1986 when professors Lois Banner, Eileen Boris, Mary Kelley, Cecelia Tichi, Lillian Schlissel, and I designed a questionnaire to assess "the uneasy balance" between the "personal lives and [the] professional careers" of women who were members of the American Studies Association and the Organization of American Historians. In answer to the question, "How do you find time to rest? to exercise? to maintain social contacts?", 25 percent "of the respondents indicated some degree of difficulty in finding time for one or more of these." For the summary report of the data, published by the American Studies Association in 1988, I wrote, "typical responses to the question about rest were 'rarely,' to the one about exercise 'sporadically,' and to maintaining social contacts, 'marginally.'" The difficulties were acute for women with children, "whether they were single parents or part of a two parenting household" (Banner et al. 6). Sobered by what historian Joyce Antler, in an afterword to the report, called an "often disturbing picture of how women in the academy view their lives and careers" (Banner et al. 25), I made the move into academic administration determined to work with students, staff, faculty, and other administrators in a shared effort to find institution-based solutions.

ii.

"Women simply cannot be persons within the
present system of work and family, and they can
only rise to liberated personhood by the most
radical and fundamental reshaping of the entire
human environment in a way that redefines the
very nature of work, family and the institutional
expressions of social relations."
—Rosemary Radford Ruether, *Liberation Theology*, 116.

To conceptualize what I am calling the "family-friendly campus" means *re*conceptualizing what we include in the term *family*. An
urban single mother with a part-time job in the campus cafeteria, for
example, may well find herself sharing child care and food purchases
with a nearby relative in similar circumstances. As anthropologist
Carol B. Stack observes, theirs may not be a traditional "co-residential"
single family unit, but "the two households" clearly function "as a
single domestic unit of cooperation" (Stack 552). In another nontraditional family configuration on my own campus, a professor of classics
has just taken into her home the critically ill mother of her former
husband. Although the professor and her husband are long divorced
and never had any children, she still maintains a loving relationship
with the woman who had once been her mother-in-law, and she now
wishes to care for the older woman in her last years. Consider also the
department secretary, a single mother who has designated a close, gay,
male friend and colleague as the legal father of her adopted child. As
instances like these make clear, the family of the twenty-first century
will no longer be identified solely by blood ties, by legalized affiliations, by cohabitation, or by heterosexual arrangements. As a result,
campuses need to take advantage of the facts and figures that can be
supplied by groups like the College and University Work-Family Association, founded in 1995, and the Families and Work Institute, a
nonprofit group in New York City, in order to develop more inclusive
definitions of "family." And administrators need to begin the process
of redesigning benefits packages and family care policies narrowly tailored for the heterosexual nuclear family (or even the heterosexual extended family). As they are now written, most policies in this area are

already hopelessly anachronistic, with some inviting legal challenge on the grounds of discrimination.

Ironically, discriminatory language and anachronisms surface even when schools attempt to address family needs through such laudable programs as child care, tenure-clock delays, flex-time, half-time tenure track appointments, and family care leaves. Too often, the policy statements for these programs revert to a vocabulary that assumes rigidly gender-inflected family roles. By adopting the language of the so-called "special needs of women," or by designating only a single "primary caregiver" as eligible for certain benefits, college and university administrators (even if unintentionally) reinforce outdated family patterns and all but ignore the responsibilities of men in childrearing and family care. Indeed, *every* senior administrator of my acquaintance, male or female, unhesitatingly admits that the primary caregiver envisioned as eligible for leave to look after a sick child or an incapacitated family member is always *female*. In this regard, higher education administrators differ very little from their counterparts in the corporate workplace where "many CEOs still see careers as inherently masculine and parenting as inherently feminine" (Jones 56).

To be sure, some special provisions for women—like paid medical maternity leaves for childbirth and early infant care—must remain in place and be expanded. But all other family-sensitive policies, including provisions for paid extended infant care leaves in cases of birth, adoption, or foster care placement, and leaves to attend a sick family member, should be developed within the guidelines of Title VII of the 1964 Civil Rights Act and Title IX of the 1972 Education Amendments to that act. Both sets of laws declare unequivocally that campus workplace privileges must be accorded to women and to men equally. Legality, however, is not the only issue. With women having entered the academic workforce at all levels in increasing numbers, it becomes a practical necessity to ensure those women's effective performance by tenaciously rejecting the notion that it is always and only women who bear the major responsibility for caretaking in the family.

Such notions are ubiquitous, of course. A 1987 study of corporate employees indicated that while there were no statistically significant differences in the hours that men and women devoted to the workplace, there were "major differences . . . in the amount of time spent on home chores and child care. Married female parents spent 40 hours at work, and an additional 45 hours in home chores and child care." Married male parents with full-time working partners, by contrast, spent an average 44 hours at work, but only "14 hours in child care, and 11 hours in household chores" (Jones 56–57). A decade later, nothing had changed. A national survey of 1,246 couples conducted in 1995 by Patricia Ulbrich, a sociologist at the University of Akron, revealed that "women, whether they work for pay or not, spend an average of 32.3 hours on housework a week, not including childcare," while "men spend an average of 8.7 hours per week" ("Data Bit" 4).

The 1986 survey conducted jointly by the American Studies Association and the Organization of American Historians documented a similar situation in academe. Amid uniformly "poignant" remarks about homemaking tasks and child care and in answers crowded with anecdotes about physical exhaustion and career setbacks, women respondents revealed that "nearly forty percent of [them] . . . took on between seventy and one hundred percent of the responsibility for the care of their children." Younger, beginning graduate students noted that among their older, married peers, it was always the women "in the marriage who sacrifice" (Banner 4, 6). Because few campuses have begun to address these realities as policy issues, it is not surprising that a study published in 1996 only confirmed what the 1986 survey had uncovered. In interviews with 124 female assistant professors, nearly 43 percent of them regarded "time required by children" as a "serious" impediment to obtaining tenure; another 18.1 percent saw childrearing as "somewhat" of an impediment (Finkel and Olswang 123). At least in part, the asymmetrical distribution of family care responsibilities may also explain why, as of 1993, "the average number of years women took to earn a doctorate after receiving a bachelor's degree [was] 12.2 years"; but "the average number of years men took to earn a doctorate after receiving a bachelor's degree" was only "9.9 years" ("Fast Facts" 10).

Given this kind of overwhelming statistical and anecdotal evidence, most academic administrators have finally come to agree that gender-based inequities should be countered by policies that allow—and, more important, *invite*—men to share in family care responsibilities. In defining those responsibilities, however, too many administrators still focus exclusively on infant and child care policies, thereby ignoring another major demographic shift: our society is aging. "By 2030," according to Denise Park, director of the Center for Applied Cognitive Aging Research at the University of Georgia, "the United States will actually have more older adults than children" (Park A40). While these statistics have already prompted some schools to begin developing enhanced lifelong learning programs and even specialized degree programs for the elderly adult population, the statistics also indicate that families of the twenty-first century will become increasingly responsible for the care of aging and infirm members. Schools have been slower to respond to this eventuality. But, in fact, colleges and universities would be wise to look ahead and review benefits packages and family care policies *now*, while prudent advance financial planning is still possible. University medical centers and colleges of nursing might be brought in as prospective partners in elder care educational programs and benefits, another move that requires planning. Indeed, as the numbers of children dwindle and the numbers of those over sixty-five increase, elder care services may be even more in demand than child care.

If, as I have been arguing, conceptualizing the family-friendly campus means reconceptualizing our understanding of "family" and family roles, it also entails recognizing the students we now serve. This means refining our concept of "campus" with a twenty-first century student body in mind. While a relatively small group of elite private institutions will continue to attract a predominantly upper-middle class undergraduate student body in the 18–22 age range, and while these schools will continue to graduate full time students in four years, those conditions are no longer typical. "Since the 1970's," as Barbara Jacoby editorialized in the *Chronicle of Higher Education*, "college populations have changed dramatically; 85 percent of today's undergraduates commute to campus, nearly half are 25 years old or older, and more than half attend part time. In addition, two-thirds are employed, some working full time or at more than one job to pay their college expenses" (Jacoby B2).

Significant within this changed population are the increasing numbers of students who would welcome access to off-campus or distance-learning sites that offer degree programs. Such students include those

with chronic illnesses or disabilities that make on-campus life difficult, those in rural areas whose family or job responsibilities make it
impossible for them to travel any distance to campus, and those jug-
gling work and family responsibilities who need convenient part-time
educational options. With the rapid development of satellite, CD-ROM,
and computer technology, high quality interactive distance-learning
services for these students can be designed to include rigorous formal
assessment procedures as well as frequent contacts with faculty mentors. And because, as one graduate of an online degree program con-
fessed, "It can be lonely going to school sitting at your own desk"
(Weiner 42), computer-equipped satellite campuses can be located in
public schools, on military bases, in properly equipped public libraries,
or even in private workplaces to simulate at least a semblance of
shared classroom experience. The new technology, in short, allows for
maximum flexibility. A student *can* sit at her own desk at home, com-
municating by telephone and e-mail with faculty who have tailored a
course of study specifically to her needs. Or, along with others, she can
take one or two courses in the evenings or on weekends at a nearby on-
line satellite campus and, over time, complete a degree program similar to what she would be offered on a traditional campus. Residence
requirements can be nonexistent or a matter of months—for examinations and to allow face-to-face contact with professors. While the initial start-up costs for this technology are still relatively high, the costs
are dropping daily, and student fees easily cover operating expenses.
Once the technology is in place, moreover, schools can pool resources
and create new degree programs by combining courses already taught
on various campuses, delivering these courses electronically both to
distance-learning sites and to on-campus classrooms at the same time.[2]

The overwhelming majority of students to take advantage of the
extended campus, not surprisingly, will be women, many of them
parents, all of them part-timers. Of course, part-time enrollments for
both men and women have been growing steadily since 1970—"128
percent, compared with 38 percent growth among full-time students,
according to the National University Continuing Education Association"—but what has swelled that growth is the fact that "enrollments
among women over 35 quadrupled between 1970 and 1991" (Feemster 28). As those numbers continue to rise, they exert even more

pressure for services that offer working women and women with children both greater accessibility and more flexibility in scheduling. "I needed a school that would let me incorporate work projects into my study program," explained a woman in Bellingham, Washington, who completed her degree electronically from the State University of New York's Empire State College; "I also needed to fit my schoolwork into the time constraints of caring for my two sons, 10 and 3" (Weiner 42).

The value of distance-learning services notwithstanding, older students with families can also profit from a variety of experiences on the more traditional campus. The geography of the campus, after all, provides instant access to a library, quiet study areas, and personal conferences with instructors; perhaps most important, the campus represents that rare protected space which enables the open exchange of ideas and the excitement of shared explorations. Unfortunately, the working woman of thirty-five, with a child to raise on her own, rarely feels either comfortable or welcomed in the current environment of most four-year colleges and universities. As one such woman explained to the *New York Times*, "I didn't see myself in school" because "I wanted to be in a situation where I was taking classes with my peers, not with kids my daughter's age" (Feemster 28).

To accommodate the bulge of students in their late twenties and thirties who return to college after a break of some years or who first begin a degree program, and especially to accommodate those who must work and care for children at the same time, community colleges have been singularly innovative in developing highly specialized weekend and evening programs. Students at Oklahoma City Community College, for example, can now enroll in "classes 24 hours a day," thus turning the campus into what its president calls "the college where learning never ends" (Shea A44). Even so, as the sheer numbers of older and part-time students continue to increase—as all indicators would lead one to predict—and as many of these students seek education beyond the associate degree, liberal arts colleges and research universities also will have to expand, rethink, and revise their programs and schedules. At the moment, there is little incentive to do this, because federal aid and most local and private scholarship funding favor the younger full-time student. But it is precisely this outmoded tilt that must be adjusted, with higher educational institutions lobbying actively in Washington and, where feasible, reviewing the aid distribution formulas of their own endowments and alumni organizations. Additionally, local employers might be approached for contributions to twenty-first-century scholarship funds earmarked especially for the working student; and, at the same time, schools can encourage employers to provide tuition vouchers for workers who upgrade their skills through a bachelor's degree program.

Scholarships, scheduling, and programmatic redesign for the older student can prove of enormous financial benefit to colleges and universities because they generate an entirely new cohort of grateful "instant alumni." Patricia McGuire, the president of a small, private women's college that experimented successfully with specialized degree programs, told the *New York Times*, "It takes younger graduates years to become regular contributors. Some of the part-timers will write us a check [right after graduation] and write: 'If it weren't for Trinity, I couldn't write any checks like these today'" (Feemster 29).

Having made the case for distance-learning services as well as on-site specialized programs to accommodate the older, part-time student, I also want to emphasize the wisdom of redesigning the residential campus to accommodate these same undergraduate students on a full-time basis—including single parents with children. The most obvious benefit of full-time status, of course, is the relative speed with which the degree can be completed (followed, presumably, by immediate increased earning capacity). The intangible benefit derives from total immersion in a learning environment and, with that, an enhanced *quality* in the learning experience—especially if that immersion can be shared with others in similar circumstances. The 35-year-old single mother or father who resists returning to school because s/he fears the absence of supportive peers may be far more enthusiastic if the on-campus living site could provide those peers, along with cooperative living arrangements for the children. After all, why should the student with children be deprived of the late-night discussions of books and ideas, the dormitory gabfests about teachers and courses, and the varied out-of-class exchanges that are remembered later as the intellectual exhilaration of college life?

As imminent enrollment pressures force residential campuses to renovate dormitories and build new ones, planning for future construction should begin now to include floors with communal spaces—shared kitchens and eating, play, and study areas—all serving one- and two-bedroom suites designed for single parents and their children. The introduction of families into traditional dormitories could have unexpected benefits for everyone. A woman who said "I never thought I'd turn 40 living in a residence hall," nonetheless discovered that "having a family around humanizes a campus." The newsletter *Women in Higher Education* reported her observation that dormitory students behaved better as a result of her family's presence and that "the student residents . . . adopted her children, decorating their own dorm rooms for holidays and encouraging the children to trick-or-treat down the halls at Halloween" ("Getting a Terminal Degree" 7).

In addition to the usual sources of funding for dormitory construction—state appropriations, revenue bonds, or endowment income—for this kind of low-income family accommodation, schools might consider seeking eligibility for grants and low-cost loans from the U.S. Department of Housing and Urban Development, under HUD's provisions for low- and middle-income family housing supports. There is ample precedent for this kind of campus-HUD partnership in HUD's Joint Community Development Program, which awards five grants annually to universities nationwide (see "HUD Helping Yale" 23).

All of the reconceptualizations and renovations recommended so far adhere to the common ideal of the traditional campus as a haven of learning. It is harder to admit that, to be truly family-friendly, the campus must also become a refuge from violence. As reported in the *Chronicle of Higher Education*, officials at Michigan State, like college administrators across the country, every year "see evidence of domestic violence: Female students drop out or transfer to get away from abusive boyfriends on the campus. First-year students are stalked by the high-school sweethearts they left behind. Foreign women who came to campus when their husbands enrolled suffer beatings from their spouses rather than risk having to return to their home countries." In 1994, prompted by the concerns of the president's wife, Joanne McPherson, Michigan State responded by "setting up education programs for abusers and their victims, and training volunteers who will work with both." In an even bolder move, according to the *Chronicle's* article, "the university opened a permanent shelter . . . to serve as a temporary refuge for battered women who are affiliated with Michigan State." In the view of McPherson, the campus shelter was not simply a reaction to the fact that the women's shelter in nearby Lansing was always filled. For her, the shelter and its associated programs represented both a needed intervention to curtail the escalation of violence to "the point where a woman gets killed," and, just as important, a valuable educational enterprise "for students in counseling, nursing, medicine, and criminal justice" (Leatherman A5).

Unfortunately, the majority of college administrators view Michigan State's shelter as an unaffordable luxury, however much it might be needed, and admit that, when they think of "violence," they think of the violence being done to their annual budgets. The dramatic cuts in federal and state support for higher education that I discussed in earlier chapters have forced schools to curtail campus services, not improve them. Instead of constructing shelters for the battered, most colleges and universities are barely able to afford the maintenance for buildings that already exist. For students, staff, and faculty, the quality of campus life suffers accordingly.

But one ironic outcome of the current economic squeeze is that schools are now more willing to experiment with a number of family-friendly policies, not only because those policies respond to the real needs of otherwise restive faculty, staff, and students, but also because they are either revenue neutral or may even bring savings. The cost of establishing and staffing a shelter for battered women and children may seem prohibitive, but rescheduling department meetings to accommodate individuals with children in school or allowing for delays in the tenure clock to accommodate parenting responsibilities are generally without economic consequence. Even policies that permit employees to leave work, without any loss in pay, in order to attend parent-teacher conferences or their children's school performances are proving cost effective, because most employees—grateful for that opportunity—are making up the lost work on their own time. Also, significant savings in salary (and savings in benefits payments, as well) can be achieved by instituting policies for half-time or shared tenure track appointments for faculty, combined with flex-time, part-time, or flex-year schedules for staff. A 1994 headline in a University of Arizona campus newspaper, for example, boasted that the "Flex-year option aids budgets and burnout," with the article itself explaining how staff employees benefited from extra time with their families, while departments welcomed the option as "the answer to budgetary woes" (Kayler 1).[3]

Those same "budgetary woes," however, are making it increasingly difficult for any administrator anywhere to advocate introducing paid family care leaves for faculty and staff. As one member of the Arizona Board of Regents said to me when I tried to raise the issue with him, "that's the whole enchilada," meaning such a policy would break the school's budget. In Arizona, the problem is compounded by the fact that university personnel are governed by state policies for all state employees, and the state has no provisions for such leaves. Nonetheless, as dean, one of my highest priorities was to initiate a process that might eventually lead to enhanced leave policies on a statewide basis, and certainly for the three state universities. As demonstrated by the continuing disappointing national statistics for women in initial promotion and tenure reviews (see Noble 25, and Rohter 9), I knew that the professoriate was still losing too many bright young women to the conflict between career imperatives and the desire for family. And staff women confided that they put off the completion of a degree or additional skills training because they actually *feared* the increased responsibility of a promotion, even when they desperately needed the money. The combination of job, home, and childrearing was already too demanding, they said. Happily, the majority of department heads and program directors in the College of Humanities were sensitive to these dilemmas and shared my eagerness to *do something.*

By the end of my first year as dean, therefore, the department heads, program directors, and I agreed to experiment with granting any faculty member who was to become a parent (by birth or by adoption) up to a semester of "adjusted workload" at full salary. This generally meant a semester free of formal teaching assignments *in addition* to the university's paid maternity leave. Adjusted workloads of up to a semester were also to be extended to faculty with responsibility for an ailing family member. Faculty could request an unpaid leave either in lieu of this arrangement or in addition to it. In most cases, the semester's release from classroom teaching coincided with delays in the tenure clock. Similar workload adjustments were to be developed for staff, and I urged supervisors to try to accommodate staff wherever family responsibilities were at issue.

When I discussed this experiment with other administrators or with members of the Arizona Board of Regents, I generally began by pointing to parallel policies at peer public institutions. The University of California at Berkeley, I noted, offers six weeks of paid maternity leave with the additional option of a semester's "modified duties" at full salary, while Indiana University at Bloomington offers six weeks of paid maternity leave followed by modified duties at half salary for the remainder of the semester. I then pointed to private institutions that were taking a leadership role in this area. Faculty members in the arts and sciences at Harvard, for one, "may request six months of relief from teaching with full pay for each child they have, up to two children"; and "for each child they have, junior faculty members at Harvard can put off the review for their next promotion for a year" (Robin Wilson, "Colleges Help Professors," A24). Despite examples like these, I was always confronted with the same set of objections: such a policy would be unduly costly because hordes of absent faculty would have to be replaced in the classroom; I was providing an incentive for staff and faculty to have more children (and, thereby, take off more time from work); and male faculty would cheat by staying home and writing their books, whereas women on adjusted workload assignments would "really" be caring for their infants. As it turned out, none of this proved true.

During my five years as dean, only four faculty women requested nonteaching semesters, while a few female staff members requested workload adjustments for limited periods only. Each of them also utilized the university's standard paid maternity leave. A woman caring for her critically ill mother was offered the opportunity for a teaching reduction, but she declined; and no other employee with a sick relative was brought to my attention. No men, whether faculty or staff, requested adjusted workloads related to family responsibilities (though male faculty were rarely shy about requesting teaching reductions when involved in a research project or completing a book before tenure review).

My observations over those years led me to speculate that caring for a sick relative was still not regarded as a circumstance for which people believed they deserved accommodation—in contrast to attitudes about infant and child care. And I was aware that, as the second largest city in a major retirement state, Tucson provided a vast array of senior care services, for those who could afford them. Thus the local environment itself encouraged care outside the home, rather than within the home, at least for older people with means. I also concluded that very few employees in the College of Humanities were having large families (with three or more children) and that, overall, this was a relatively low-birth-rate population. Taken as a whole, our 300-plus employees were far from even reproducing their own numbers. At least in part, this explained why so few individuals were taking advantage of our experiment. At the same time, our relatively low rates for birth and adoption among both faculty and staff coincided with the findings of population studies around the globe: regardless of nationality, ethnicity, or race, as people experience themselves more securely anchored in the middle class, their birth rate declines proportionately.

Of the four faculty women who requested nonteaching semesters, all were untenured assistant professors, two from the same large department of about seventy full-time tenure-eligible faculty; but the two took their workload adjustments in different years. Another faculty woman was from a medium-sized department of about twenty-five; and the fourth was from a small department of fewer than fifteen members. At no point did the dean's office provide the departments with additional funding to hire replacement faculty, nor did the departments have the funding to do this on their own. Instead, with some advance planning and the minimal rearrangement of course assignments and class sizes, we were able to sustain majors, graduate programs, and general education offerings alike, with no loss in student enrollment numbers. In other words, neither our students nor our FTEs (the "full-time equivalents" on which funding is determined) suffered from the loss of any faculty member's two or three courses for a single semester. Considering that, during tight budget times, faculty routinely enjoy sabbatical or fellowship leaves without being replaced, this was hardly surprising. Even so, to compensate the departments for whatever hardship might have accrued, I asked department heads to come up with a formula, appropriate to their unit, by which faculty on family care adjusted workloads would teach an additional course and/or a summer school offering within three years. Unfortunately, this was not pursued in any consistent manner, and in retrospect I regret that we did not formalize such a procedure, so that it would be applied to everyone fairly. After all, as family-sensitive policies are put in place, it is crucial to protect the rights and privileges of faculty and staff who will never utilize those policies. *Their* revised work schedules, *their* adjusted meeting times, and any additional workloads that they occasionally shoulder in order to accommodate a colleague must also be recognized and rewarded.

To the best of my knowledge, only two male assistant professors (and no male staff) became fathers during the years of my deanship. I have continued to wonder why neither requested the available semester's reassignment of duties. On the one hand, I suspect that their male department heads may not have been aggressive in making clear to these men what was now possible, whereas women were informed more consistently. And the women themselves activated a network through which they informed one another. On the other hand, for both the department heads and the prospective fathers, the idea of a work adjustment that allowed *men* time for parenting may still have seemed unusual, inappropriate, and even demasculinizing. Such attitudes would echo those of men nationwide regarding the Family and Medical Leave Act signed into law by President Clinton. According to an item in the 27 December 1993 issue of *U.S. News and World Report,* only 7 percent of the men surveyed said they "would take all 12 weeks of unpaid leave allowed after the birth of a child," while 43 percent of women expressed their intention to take full advantage of the new act ("Baby Makes Three" 106). Clearly, *unpaid* leaves will do little to change such entrenched asymmetries. But *paid* leaves, or at least adjusted work assignments, accompanied by assiduous encouragement to utilize them, certainly should make it easier for more men to take on the full partnership of parenting.

Indeed, the argument could be made that schools soon will have little choice but to accommodate the increasing participation of men in all family care responsibilities. There is growing evidence in the private sector that women employees are no longer the only ones to refuse travel assignments and to defer promotions or relocations for the sake of family. In 1995, a study of "more than 6,000 employees in professional and manufacturing jobs . . . found that many—and only slightly more women than men—have made career trade-offs to try to balance their work and family life." At large corporations like Du Pont, "one of the first large companies to develop extensive work-family programs," men as well as women are taking advantage of "flexible work hours, job sharing, subsidized emergency child care, and referrals for care for elderly relatives or children, or for other family needs" (Lewin 14). With the continued restructuring of the American family, changing social mores, and hard economic realities that require two full-time working adults to sustain a middle-class household—and whether in heterosexual or same-sex relationships—men are more and more often finding themselves expected to perform as caregivers and co-parents. It is a shift that the campuses of the twenty-first century will feel in force. If a few men on paid family leaves or adjusted workloads cheat, as some university regents are certain they will—so what? Most will not, and those few who try, we may hope, will be pressed by their partners to remain at home at least some of the time, writing their books with one hand while rocking the cradle with the other (as women academics have always done . . . while also teaching full time and running the house).

That said, my commitment to beginning a process that could lead to instituting paid family care leaves stems only secondarily from my conviction that this is the best available means for involving men in an altered orientation toward family responsibilities. Even more important, in my view, is the fact that gender equity on campus has progressed very unevenly—for women themselves. As Alison Bernstein and Jacklyn Cock put it, "Life is improving for the most advantaged women on the campus, but the basic structure and the inequities of non-professional women's lives have barely changed in the last 20 years" (Bernstein and Cock B3). The Family and Medical Leave Act is itself a case in point, extending its benefits only to the few who can afford them. On my campus, the overworked and poorly paid custodial worker who had no other option but the student union ladies' room as a shelter for her daughter could hardly take advantage of an unpaid leave if her daughter became seriously ill. Without salary, she could not pay the rent, and there would be no food on the table. Although the situation might not be quite so dire for a young assistant professor, if she were in the arts or humanities (where academic salaries remain comparatively low), a semester without salary could also prove an impossible hardship—especially if she were a single parent with no other source of income.

Admittedly, while providing paid family care leaves for faculty might have minimal impact on an institution's budget, providing such leaves for all regular employees *will* cost money. In order to maintain vital campus operations, at least some of these employees will have to be replaced during their absence; or other employees will have to be paid overtime. My brief experience with adjusting staff and faculty workloads at the University of Arizona, however, suggests that most predictions of just how costly such a policy would be are grossly exaggerated. In a related situation at Stanford University, for example, the initial financial objections to "health benefits [for] gay and lesbian couples and unmarried heterosexual couples who are in committed, marriage-like relationships" proved groundless. Once the policy was instituted in 1994, only twenty-nine people (and not the projected sixty) actually "registered for medical coverage." As one official of the College and University Personnel Association (CUPA) commented then, "Contrary to what people might say, there won't be this ground swell of thousands and thousands of people signing up" ("In Box" A19).[4] A 1995 survey by CUPA revealed that although more schools were offering benefits to domestic partners—in the attempt "to attract and retain top-notch faculty and to comply with faculty policies that sometimes prohibit discrimination on the basis of sexual orientation"—the actual "number of recipients receiving such benefits was small" ("Domestic Partner" 3). And the additional cost to institutions was accordingly modest.

Similarly, with regard to paid family care leaves, until colleges and universities begin monitored case studies—experimenting within a single unit for three years, for example—and gather hard data on how many leaves are anticipated during any fiscal period, objections based primarily on cost can have no weight. Only when realistic cost projections are in hand can campuses assess their resources, determine what kinds of paid leaves are feasible (three months instead of a semester, perhaps, or some other form of paid workload adjustment), and begin the campus dialogue over priorities. As part of that dialogue, administrators need to examine national studies showing that employees will regularly accept smaller salary increases or even a lower wage scale if the workplace is supportive in other ways. Moreover, as the Du Pont corporation found, employees who had utilized the company's family-friendly programs "were more likely than others to say they would 'go the extra mile' to assure Du Pont's success." Commenting on Du Pont's experience, one corporate analyst said, "It's striking evidence that if you do something to meet the employees' needs, they return the favor" (Lewin 14). Indeed, it just might be the case that a family-friendly environment reaps higher quality work from all its employees and, in the end, proves tangibly and intangibly cost effective.

Even so, the objections to my particular mapping of the family-friendly campus have never been exclusively financial. When I was dean, a few faculty complained that my emphasis on affirmative action hiring, my activism on behalf of child care, and the new workload adjustments for family care were all evidence that I was attempting to use the campus to correct the ills of society and practicing "social engineering" in the process. But the fact is that schools *do* carry a range of societal responsibilities, among them responsibilities for the health and well-being of students and employees. Even in a state as politically conservative as Arizona, the Board of Regents accepted the view of the Commission on the Status of Women that universities must acknowledge "the importance of home, family, and community in a balanced life. By promoting the value of a balanced life for both men and women, university policies and university human resource programs provide the opportunity and climate in which women, along with men, can succeed" (*Reaching the Vision* 11). Most of the Commission members went even further, arguing that family-friendly innovations could significantly reduce the currently high drop-out rates among minority students, shorten the time to completion of degrees, increase the retention of women faculty, reduce staff turnover, and generally initiate a new climate of cooperation and community among students, staff, and faculty alike. As one of our members liked to point out, surprising new friendships were often formed at the child care center.

iii.

"We are the least child-oriented society in the
world—10 years behind every other civilized
country in backing up families. Our kids are
suffering in ways no one wants to face. . . .
We have got to change our systems."
—T. Berry Brazelton, M.D. (qtd. in Kinkead 34).

Alison Bernstein and Jacklyn Cock are correct when they say
"it doesn't cost the colleges much financially to make decrees about
sexual harassment and sexist speech. Changing a family-leave policy,
however, can be expensive. . . . Child care costs money" (Bernstein
and Cock B3). As a result, in the present climate of diminishing budgets and rising costs within higher education, discussions of family-
friendly initiatives easily become mired in competing agendas: child
care is played off against upgrading the library's computer system, and
paid family care leaves compete with the renovation of undergraduate classrooms. In such a climate, there is always the temptation to
dismiss family issues as catering *only* to some small "special interest
group" and to continue with business as usual. But business as usual
will serve neither the newly emerging workforce nor the anticipated
student cohorts of the twenty-first century; nor will business as usual
help us to understand that funding in academe is not necessarily a
zero-sum game. Creative approaches to funding challenges are available.

At the University of Arizona, for example, we established a permanent "Child Care Endowment" within the university's private
fundraising foundation. When I first proposed this to the Council of
Academic Deans in 1988, I argued that, unlike endowments to fund
chaired professorships for a privileged few and unlike endowments
to equip the laboratory of a single scientist, an endowment for child
care was both comprehensible and necessary to large numbers of faculty, staff, and students alike. Thus, as the university moved into a
new phase of its capital campaign, child care could represent an endowment category capable of attracting substantial and sustained on-
campus support.

When I proposed the new endowment, I hoped that it might some day provide the funding for an on-campus cooperative child care center. But my fellow deans raised the thorny problem of utilizing a tax-supported institution's facilities for an activity that might compete with the private sector, which is against the law in Arizona; and it became increasingly clear that some kind of partnership between the university and private child care providers was inevitable. In the short term, therefore, I hoped the earnings from a Child Care Endowment might subsidize private off-campus child care services. After all, where —as in Arizona—local laws prohibit a school from developing an independent child care center, and where schools cannot be granted a legal exemption by embedding child care within a College of Education or a School of Social Work (or the like), there is no alternative but partnership with qualified private providers. Still, this need not be a problem since, even with private providers, cooperative agreements can be reached that assure parental oversight, parental involvement, and quality services.

Ideally, the uses of a child care endowment fund should be flexible, determined by local circumstances. On one campus, endowment earnings might be used to help furnish an on-site facility, with user fees covering the costs of staffing. On another campus, endowment earnings could supply an ongoing source of income by which to subsidize the costs of private child care for college and university students and employees. In this way, where a private provider is involved, that provider receives its full negotiated fee per child, but the actual cost of child care to the student or employee is tied to a sliding scale based on ability to pay. On a campus where no private provider is involved, the school simply devises its own sliding fee scale and dips into endowment earnings to make up any shortfall. In every case, the full professor, presumably, would pay more than the groundskeeper or student— but all would receive the same high quality care for their children.

Elder care offers still other opportunities for innovative funding. As the population ages and more healthy and vital people find themselves in retirement, educational programs for this population will be in great demand. As it is, Elderhostels—four- and six-week educational residence programs for seniors—have proved enormously successful and generally profitable for the schools that have hosted them. But while

Elderhostel programs can certainly be expanded, other equally attractive educational options for retired seniors must also be developed. Good management and the use of facilities not otherwise employed (like empty dormitories and classrooms during the summers or midyear breaks) can turn such programs into what schools like to call "revenue centers," or profit-makers, even when the program fees are modest. There may even be ways to combine educational opportunities for seniors with specialized elder care "wellness" programs, especially at universities with nursing schools or medical centers. But the most intriguing possibility, to my mind, is the potential coordination of elder care with child care. Here one can imagine a variation on the surrogate grandparent volunteer programs that many local communities have devised to pair retired seniors with lonely latchkey kids. The only essential difference is that the campus facility would bring both groups together in a safe and professionally supervised setting, all of it supported by fees, by associated educational programs, and by endowment earnings.

Clearly, none of the challenges posed by the changing structures of the American family need prove insurmountable. A fee-based elder care "wellness" program can be self-supporting or even generate profits. And a Child Care Endowment, relatively easy to start, can eventually bring in continuing earnings. Nor did it require any large commitment of resources to move the University of Arizona onto a list of the nation's "most 'family-friendly' . . . institutions" (Robin Wilson, "A Report," A13). In 1994 the university hired its first full-time Child Care Coordinator to head "the newly created Office of Child Care Initiatives" (Leibold 3). The coordinator and her office were charged to work with the already established Child Care Steering Committee— made up of faculty, staff, and students—to develop goals and priorities for enhancing child care services and to assess all related needs in this area. That same year, the university began the Sick Child Program, "designed to support the working parent who has a mildly ill child unable to attend school or child care." Under this program, "a trained provider will come to the employee's home and stay with a child while the employee is at work. . . . Parents are charged $1 an hour and the UA picks up the remaining charges" ("Employees Can" 8). Beginning in 1996 with an initial outlay of $50,000 from the provost and from the vice president for Business Affairs, the university launched an income-based subsidy program to help eligible employees with job-related child care costs. Depending on income, an employee could receive "up to 50 percent" of such costs as long as s/he utilized a state-regulated licensed provider (Blackwell 1). Student parents were aided by a $5,000 commitment from the Department of Student Programs and by an additional $2,000 outlay from student government. Like the employee program, the Student Child Care Subsidy is need-based and covers costs for licensed providers only (see Ginis 6).

Good as these programs are, however, they do not yet meet the campus community's needs. The financial commitments cannot cover everyone eligible for child care subsidies, and there are waiting lists for both the employee and student programs. Current policies that govern the assignment of adjusted workloads in the case of employees affected by the birth and care of a newborn, or the adoption or foster care placement of a new child, are still woefully inadequate, as are provisions for stopping the tenure clock. And elder care issues are not even on the table. Like most schools around the country, despite good intentions, the University of Arizona is still trying to deal piecemeal with family care demands and financing its responses on an ad hoc year-to-year basis. What is required, instead, is a long-term comprehensive analysis of the full panoply of family-related needs and a long-term financial plan—comprising both private and public funding—to meet those needs.

One possible tool for prompting colleges and universities to embark on a comprehensive needs assessment is the "Summary Checklist of Selected Family-Friendly Initiatives and Programs," which appears as an appendix at the end of this book. If schools will utilize this and other tools to begin that needs assessment now, then by the end of the first decade of the twenty-first century, colleges and universities should have had ample opportunity to transform benefits and selected family services into a constellation of options that cater to changing family configurations and also allow the institution to anticipate reasonable and stable funding levels for those benefits and services. One approach entails a virtual "menu" of variable options. Taking into account such factors as salary level, years of service, and full- or part-time status, schools would generate a formula for assigning annual "benefits credits" to all employees. After deducting required credits for mandatory minimal levels of health care and retirement contributions, employees would then enjoy the option of utilizing their remaining credits for benefits most useful to them at the time. A family with young children, for example, might utilize remaining credits to enhance their health care benefits and to subsidize child care costs, while a family whose children had already left the nest might require services to help care for a sick grandparent; or they could invest those same optional credits in additional retirement contributions. Individuals would have the opportunity to reassign their optional benefits credits at least once a year. In this way, as family needs change, so too do the benefits that respond to those needs. And from the point of view of the institution, overall costs remain relatively stable.

My point here is simple: solutions and funding sources can be identified, but only when a school chooses to focus on the changing family and its multiple requirements. The difficulties in creating a family-friendly campus do not derive entirely from a paucity of financial resources. Instead, the real problem is our long-term failure of commitment and imagination, a failure that we can no longer tolerate.

iv.

"We must do the things we think we cannot do."
—Eleanor Roosevelt (qtd. in Mitchell x).

In pursuing the initiatives I have outlined here, colleges and universities do not have to act in isolation. Socially responsible charitable organizations like the United Way are available for alliances in opening shelters for battered women and children. Government agencies, like the U.S. Department of Housing and Urban Development, can be approached as partners in building innovative on-campus housing that responds to the needs of poor and middle-income students with families. Private research foundations like the Carnegie Corporation, which issued a report in April 1994 that calls for paid leaves of up to six months for all wage-earning new parents, can provide the necessary data to justify family-friendly policies (see Kinkead 36). And sympathetic players in the nation's capital can be called upon as lobbyists. Attorney General Janet Reno has already "spoken out for a workday ending at 3 p.m. so that parents can be home when their kids return from school" (Kinkead 34).

Most important, as a group, college and university presidents and chancellors must stop closing their eyes to the impossible burdens facing the contemporary single-parent or two-wage-earner family. It is time for these senior administrators to risk (and perhaps thereby re-invigorate) their waning public prestige by confronting a government that does not provide adequate family supports and by challenging what the *New York Times* termed "a cultural ethos that has degraded" family roles, "rewarding only competition and wealth" (Kinkead 32). In other words, the leaders of institutions entrusted with the education and training of future generations must now insist that politicians forgo the empty rhetoric of "traditional family values" and, in its place, return realistic family supports to the top of the national agenda. I would have these positions articulated not solely on the grounds of necessity or social justice, however, but also on the firmer ground of *educational mission*. Let us be clear: classrooms are not the only places in which learning occurs. We teach our students not simply by "professing" but, even more powerfully, by example.

As every educator knows, the structures and policies of institutions are themselves telling signifiers, teaching students (however silently and indirectly) what is and is not prized. Because neither students nor their teachers dissociate intellectual inquiry from the material conditions in which that inquiry is conducted, it *signifies* that, on some campuses, the Business College is housed in the newest and best-equipped building, centrally located, while Fine Arts are taught in out-of-the-way, outdated facilities, much in need of repair. Similarly, it *signifies* that colleges and universities regularly grant paid research leaves to faculty. And these same institutions grant paid administrative leaves to faculty and senior administrators when they work on projects for local, state, or federal agencies. At the same time, it *signifies* sadly that those who care for young children or sick parents must take unpaid leaves, or no leaves at all. In this society, where (for good or for ill) we pay for what we value, there is a terrible lesson in those facts.

6 Teaching and Learning in a World of Cognitive Diversity

"Equality! Where is it, if not in education! Equal rights!
They cannot exist without equality of instruction."
—Frances Wright, "Of Free Enquiry," *Course
of Popular Lectures* (1829).

"How we learn is what we learn."
—Bonnie Friedman, *Writing Past Dark* (1993).

In order to head off any misunderstanding that this chapter assumes a simple one-to-one correlation between intellectual styles and ethnicity, race, or cultural background, I begin with some family history. I am the oldest of three daughters, each of us two years apart in age. When we were young, my sisters and I all scored significantly above average on national standardized tests. Both our parents had earned postgraduate professional degrees; they encouraged our intellectual curiosities; and the importance of education was stressed in our home. Little surprise, then, that in school, my sisters and I were always achievers.

As the oldest, I developed a proprietary interest in my younger sisters' successes. A favorite weekend activity was "playing school," complete with a portable blackboard and miniature school desks that my parents had purchased, and with me always in the role of teacher. Until I tired of the game sometime in junior high, I regularly explained geography, arithmetic, and poetry in ways I was certain that my sisters would understand—because those were the ways in which *I* understood those subjects. Not until I witnessed the methods by which my two sisters prepared themselves for the national College Board exams did it begin to dawn on me that, however similar our academic records, we three were remarkably individual in how we approached learning. My sisters' methods were radically different from my own earlier preparations for the College Boards, and their methods were also different from one another's.

Of course, each of us reviewed the booklet of sample questions provided by the College Board, and we attended the brief weekend sessions on the exam's requirements offered by our high school. After that, every two years, we each proceeded on a very different path. Taking advantage of the considerable library resources at Brooklyn's Erasmus Hall High School, I located prior years' versions of the College Board's sample questions booklet and pored over them. By examining years of sample questions, I hoped to understand what kind of knowledge (or skills) were being tested—so I could study accordingly. In effect, I was looking for the exam's grand plan or motivation.

Although I cannot recall every detail of my second sister's exertions two years later, I can never forget what struck me at the time as both inventive and crazy. Having reviewed the sample words listed for the vocabulary section of the exam, she went to the dictionary, looked up the meanings she was uncertain of, and began to construct—alphabetically—sentences that utilized these words correctly. She then memorized each sentence in order. The first sentence was, "I abhor and abominate all abortive abettors of criminals"—and so on through the z words. It was a complex form of rote memorization, structured not around abstract dictionary definitions but, instead, around an orderly progression of statements that cued my sister to the words' meaning by providing a context for their usage. I was flabbergasted—both by the originality of the device and by my sister's ability to remember all those alphabetized sentences.

My youngest sister followed my advice to review questions from previous years' sample booklets, in order to get a better feel for the overall shape of the exam, but she concentrated on something else. This sister calculated and recalculated the relative advantage (or disadvantage) of guessing at or skipping questions to which she didn't know the answer. How would it affect her score, she pondered, to take time to puzzle over questions she found difficult, to skip them altogether in order to complete a larger number of questions she was sure of, or to take a chance with a raw guess? Unlike me and unlike my second sister—who had, albeit differently, attended to the kinds of information demanded by the exam—my youngest sister put her main energy into devising a strategy for *taking* the exam.

In the end, we all received high scores on the College Boards. I completed a Ph.D. in American literature and became a college professor. My second sister, who learned words by putting them into sentences, studied art, working with strong shapes and vivid colors on large canvasses. My youngest sister, the test-taking strategist, majored in criminology as an undergraduate and then went on to become a corporate lawyer specializing in international contracts.

For years, I puzzled over the implications of this sibling experience and many other family occurrences just like it. Clearly, despite the same home environment and despite attending the same schools (often taking courses with the same teachers), my sisters and I grew up with radically different intellectual and conceptual styles. We were, I now like to say, *cognitively diverse.* And what allowed us our academic achievements was that, somehow, even before there was a name for such a concept, we had each intuited our particular cognitive style and, whenever possible, we had played to it.

It took me years to articulate this understanding because, during the 1960s, when I first began to teach in earnest as a graduate student at the Berkeley campus of the University of California, such musings were taboo. If misapplied, they could harm our students irrevocably. Those were exciting years in higher education, let us recall. Inspired by the social justice movements of the period, progressive faculty and administrators at Berkeley—along with colleagues on other campuses across the country—worked assiduously to open doors to women and other underrepresented groups. In 1967, Kingman Brewster, president of Yale, perfectly captured the mood of the decade when he memoed his director of Admissions that "[a]n excessively homogeneous class will not learn anywhere as much from each other as a class whose background and interests and values have something new to contribute to the common experience" (Paul 39). In that spirit, colleges, universities, and professional schools did away with exclusionary admissions quotas and experimented with everything from open admissions policies to summer enrichment programs for targeted segments of the school-age population.

At Berkeley during the summers, advanced graduate students in math and English were recruited for one of the nation's first Upward Bound programs. Paired with experienced high school teachers from local public schools, we developed our own curriculum and team-taught these subjects to junior high and senior high students who had been identified to us as "talented" but "at risk." Most of our students came from the poorer neighborhoods in Oakland, and they were predominantly African American; but my sections also enrolled two Native Americans, three Chinese Americans, and one white student. All had been in some kind of trouble, but in each case, a teacher, a school counselor, a parole officer, or a social worker had intervened to insist that, whatever the problems, these students had the potential for college. Our goal in Upward Bound was to turn that potential into meaningful possibility.

The catchphrase for those of us teaching in such early experimental outreach programs was "every student is capable of learning." What we rarely said out loud back then was that every student doesn't learn in the same way. To be sure, instructors talked among ourselves about "difficult" or "inappropriate" classroom behaviors. The African-American student who responded to every classroom question as though it were a personal conversational opening directed only at her, answering immediately without first raising her hand and waiting to be called on, would be misread as rude or arrogant by teachers and classmates when she matriculated into college, we feared. By contrast, we fretted over what kinds of classroom signals would be sent to college professors by Native American students reluctant to raise their hands and volunteer an answer, even when they knew the material cold, because they were unwilling to risk humiliating peers who didn't know the answer and couldn't raise their hands. And we worried that the Chinese American student from a traditional Chinese home, trained in the rules for showing respect, would continue to avoid making direct eye contact with her revered instructors and thus unintentionally suggest that she wasn't prepared, despite her mastery of the subject. Our response to these dilemmas was to pour added energy into our teaching, hoping to make our students academically unassailable, whatever their behavior. We invented new curricula that reflected the varied cultural backgrounds of our "nontraditional" students, and we added endless office hours for individual tutoring.

For all our eagerness to introduce culturally diverse materials into our syllabi and for all our shared agonies over unexpected classroom behaviors, however, most of the Upward Bound instructors recognized that although our students were extraordinarily bright, their processes for assimilating new knowledge—when we could observe them—were often new and unfamiliar to us. Still, we remained stubbornly reluctant to even discuss the possibility that we might be teaching a cohort whose *cognitive* styles—not just classroom behaviors—had also been culturally inflected. At the time, our reticence was justified.

Throughout the 1940s and 1950s, untested assumptions about intellectual differences based on gender or race (or ethnicity or cultural background) were regularly cited as rationalizations for tracking some groups into one educational specialization over another. Middle-class white boys took "shop" and were encouraged to pursue math and science, while girls took sewing and cooking and were expected to do well in literature and arts courses. And even in racially integrated schools, African-American students, especially if they were poor, were placed in vocational or commercial tracks in high school (usually typing and filing for girls), whereas white students, even when their academic performance was mediocre, were more often tracked into the college-prep curriculum. Racial stereotypes, gender-role expectations, and learned cultural inflections, we knew, could too easily be turned into biological imperatives. Thus, in the mid-1960s, even to introduce the notion of cognitive diversity ran the risk of revitalizing outdated and retrograde educational policies. At the end of the 1990s, by contrast, more than a third of the students in the nation's schools (K–12) are minorities, and the number rises daily. With the approach of the demographic changes of the twenty-first century, it may therefore prove an even greater risk to continue ignoring differences in learning styles and thereby bar talented individuals from fields where they are vitally needed.

As I hope my opening family reminiscence demonstrated, in any population, however homogeneous, there is always evidence of a multiplicity of intellectual talents and cognitive patternings. But it is also the case that different cultural groups can privilege certain cognitive styles over others. For example, a culture or cultural subgroup may purposefully (or even unintentionally) emphasize assimilating new knowledge by various means: listening to instruction about a skill rather than watching it performed by those already adept; reasoning by analogy instead of a strict linear logic; taking an inductive approach to problem-solving instead of a deductive; favoring empathetic identification with human agency as a means of understanding a situation over analysis by abstract principles. Among certain Pueblo peoples here in the Southwest, parents prefer to teach their children basket-weaving and pottery by means of a hands-on apprenticeship of performing discrete tasks repeatedly as opposed to receiving any verbal introduction to the intended goal. The children thus learn these arts less through words than through practiced imitation. Many other examples come to mind, of course, but the point to be made is this: as teachers at all levels of our educational system face the demographic shifts of the twenty-first century, their most pressing challenge will be an adequate response to these many facets of cognitive diversity.

In spurts and tremors, the challenge has been addressed differently on different campuses and across the disciplines. Efforts to internationalize the undergraduate curriculum by enhancing students' fluency in more than one language have pushed foreign language departments into the forefront of experimentation. Many are now developing complex learning assessment tools that can alert an instructor as to how any individual student most effectively processes information. Guided by the results of such learning assessments, instructors can then work with a variety of interactive technologies that permit students not only to learn a new language at their own pace but, more important, to learn more efficiently by means of strategies tailored to their individual needs, abilities, and cognitive styles. By updating and revising these learning assessments throughout a student's career, moreover, teachers can adjust their pedagogy accordingly and thus treat each individual student as unique, no matter how perfectly or imperfectly she or he conforms to the norms of some larger group. And, as full participants in the learning assessment process, students come away with a current personalized profile that can help them make better decisions about how to study *any* subject.

When I was dean, for example, the director of the basic language program in the Department of German Studies worked with the director of the Language Research Center to refine and improve a "learning mode profile" that was already being used with some success on other campuses. When completed, the new Language Learner Profile indicated whether a student requires a large conceptual framework at the outset or, conversely, builds linguistic competence from the aggregate of details. In other words, will the student learn German more easily if she is first introduced to the theory and structure of an inflected language, or will she do better with some basic grammar rules and vocabulary-building? Assessment procedures for the profile also determine whether a student learns best through auditory, visual, or written cues—or some combination. Even common personality traits are taken into account insofar as they affect language learning. Extroverts prefer to gain speaking competence as quickly as possible in a new language and don't mind being corrected, whereas more introverted personalities prefer to listen, write, and read as the primary means of gaining competence. Obviously, these are preferences that a German instructor needs to take into account as he prepares his lesson plans.

In a related project in the Department of Russian and Slavic Languages, another faculty member began assembling a "Russian Cultural Data Base." Utilizing microcomputers, CD-ROMs, and interactive video, this project promises to enhance instruction by giving professors a new method of presenting text, sound, still pictures, and motion pictures in the traditional classroom. Among other things, this data base will offer instructors both synchronic and diachronic options for classroom presentation, as well as the capacity to concentrate on any combination of textual, graphic, or auditory informational units. An instructor could thus take students on a visual stroll through the Hermitage while simultaneously cuing them to appropriately related musical selections or poetry texts. An accompanying student module, which can be used outside the classroom in any multimedia language laboratory, gives students the ability to access the same kind of assorted textual, visual, and auditory information, alone or in combination, and thereby permits students to select those learner cues they find most congenial. The students themselves report that Cyrillic script and Russian grammar become less daunting when these kinds of tools are made available.

Technology that can accommodate cognitive diversity and the development of learning mode profiles do not benefit only students, however. When faculty examine our own learning styles, we are reminded that we all tend to teach in the modes through which we ourselves learn best. Like the students, teachers too need the opportunity to branch out and experiment with instructional strategies that appeal to cognitive styles other than our own. A personalized learner mode profile is thus just as valuable for helping a teacher enhance her instructional repertoire as it is for helping a student improve his learning skills. By engaging students and faculty together in the development and constant updating of their individualized learner profiles and by encouraging faculty to creatively appropriate the new instructional technologies, projects like the two I have just described turn students and teachers alike into joint participants in a teaching/learning community that values difference, plurality, and change. Faculty can design learning programs, software, and classroom strategies tailored to respond to a full spectrum of cognitive styles. And students who enjoy a clear understanding of their cognitive style or learning personality can thereby take full advantage of current strengths or even explore the option of adding alternative learning strategies to their repertoires.

Anecdotal evidence suggests that science and engineering—which traditionally have been unable to attract minorities and women and are now seeing significant declines in the enrollments of all U.S. citizens—are also taking advantage of the new research on cognitive diversity. When I taught at Rensselaer Polytechnic Institute in the 1980s, the need was urgent. It was a campus commonplace, for example, that the biomedical engineering major was one of the few engineering majors to attract women students in large numbers. Yet, to everyone's dismay, women's attrition rates were always high. If one listened to the women, it wasn't the difficulty of the major or any loss of interest that caused them to withdraw but, rather, the ways in which most classes were taught. When presented with the detailed medical history of a specific patient, the women generally excelled in the problem-solving abilities required to develop a biomedical engineering solution. They quickly grasped what kind of polymer might best coat a new joint replacement apparatus or what kind of spring mechanism might enhance the mobility of some other prosthetic device. In effect, the women responded to what they understood to be a particular patient's specific needs. Though they didn't name it as such, these young women were utilizing empathy as a learning strategy. What frustrated them was that specific case histories were rarely introduced and, instead, raw data abstracted from the human matrix represented the bulk of classroom instruction. Instead of a human face with a human problem, the women mostly confronted engineering problems devoid of context. In that learning situation, the men performed better. And the women switched majors.

In her 1990 *Female-Friendly Science,* an appeal for fundamental change, Sue Rosser examined why science pedagogy is so often alienating for women and minorities and recommended participatory teaching methodologies derived from the women's studies classroom. That same year, in *They're Not Dumb, They're Different,* Sheila Tobias also made a compelling argument for rethinking how we teach science. After following a group of humanities specialists through selected science courses, Tobias discovered that many of her subjects demonstrated outstanding abilities in science and math (two had earlier declared majors in those areas), but all were put off by the ethos and design of science instruction. Summarizing her findings in an article in *Change* magazine, Tobias reported that one student complained about a physics professor who neglected to explain "how the concepts were related" (Tobias 21). That same professor, continued this student, also omitted any "indication of a linear movement through a group of concepts" (Tobias 21). Another student attributed his boredom to the large lecture format and a science curriculum without "personal expression" (Tobias 19). For him, math and science courses were marked by "their lack of community" (Tobias 19). Learner profiles on these two might have indicated that the first required repeated conceptual linkages rather than the constant presentation of discrete problems and their solutions; while the second required the reinforcement of shared group exchanges. For the second student, understandably, the small literature seminar provided the most congenial learning situation and, hence, his choice of major. Even so, as Tobias makes clear, both had the potential to do well in science; yet science never became a real option for either.

To be sure, Rosser and Tobias were not the first to raise questions about pedagogy in the science disciplines; nor were they the first to suggest linkages between that pedagogy and its impacts on the very different kinds of students who might want to study science. In 1989, building on earlier work by scientists and education specialists, two sociologists, Gabriel Bar-Haim of Tel Aviv University in Israel and John M. Wilkes of Worcester Polytechnic Institute, disputed the contention that cultural prejudice and sex-role stereotyping, by themselves, adequately explained "the underrepresentation and marginal position of women in science." Instead, speculated Bar-Haim and Wilkes, "at least one of the crucial differences between men and women who choose scientific careers is their cognitive styles" (Bar-Haim and Wilkes 371, 377).

Eager to attract large numbers of students to their majors—and at least vaguely aware of the kinds of observations being made by Rosser, Tobias, Bar-Haim and Wilkes, and others—a number of science departments have been, for several years, thoughtfully experimenting with new course designs. And even where responsiveness to cognitive diversity was not cited explicitly, many of these experiments did, in fact, offer the student significant choice in learning strategies. With the stated goal of conveying "the spirit of biology as an investigative science," for example, in 1989 Worcester Polytechnic Institute redesigned its introductory biology course by eliminating lectures and replacing them, among other things, with "literature review, brainstorming, and group discussion" (Miller and Cheetham 388). The University of Arizona established the Biology Learning Center, an instructional computing laboratory designed to supplement the classroom experience by offering students a hands-on self-paced selection of computer-based tutorials, interactive multimedia, courseware, and laboratory simulations. And, as a result of these efforts, incrementally—year by year— the numbers of women and minorities drawn to the sciences have slowly been climbing.

Clearly, there is no lack of good intentions. What is lacking is any systematic attentiveness, *across the disciplines and across the nation's campuses*, to the very fact of cognitive diversity. That lack of attentiveness makes progress slow and piecemeal. Faculty members ready to begin the pedagogical and curricular retooling that I am recommending here require incentives and support. To begin with, college and university faculty will want to establish new partnerships between all educational levels so that responsiveness to cognitive diversity can inform teaching and learning practices from preschool onward. At our research institutions, deans and provosts need to place cognitive diversity on the campus-wide agenda with a modest redistribution of research support. Some of my own attempts in this area may prove suggestive. As always during my years as dean, I began with incentives.

With the initial outlay of only $4,500, I funded Project RUTH (Research on Utilizing Technology in the Humanities), a cross-departmental collaborative effort to explore changing technologies for the purpose of designing new instructional formats. Participating faculty and graduate students attended a one-day brainstorming retreat, enjoyed frequent demonstration sessions arranged by the director of our Language Research Center, and all were encouraged to seek external funding for projects first seeded by RUTH. No one had to be a technical whiz-kid to get something out of Project RUTH. Its focus was always on the pedagogical ramifications of the available technological media rather than how it gets turned on or plugged in.

In addition to Project RUTH, I offered an annual competitive $5,000 grant to any humanities department or program that wanted to re-conceptualize its curriculum for the twenty-first century. In part, we defined twenty-first century curriculum revision as coming to terms with the fact of changing demographics, thus imposing on faculty an obligation to think about not only *what* they will be teaching but *who* they will be teaching and *how*. That $5,000 grant could be used in a variety of ways, including inviting consultants from other institutions, supporting a group retreat with consultants, or funding the development of new teaching tools. Finally, in a cooperative effort embracing all humanities programs, departments, and the dean's office, a committee of faculty and graduate students designed a two-year series of interrelated symposia, guest lectures, and workshops on "Humanities Education in the 21st Century." The object here was to involve all faculty and graduate students in an ongoing dialogue about both curricula and pedagogical change. The happy outcome was that specialists in cultural studies, literature, and critical theory began talking with specialists in linguistics and language pedagogy. New cross-disciplinary links were forged and some old boundaries began to be eliminated.

Now that I am no longer a dean but back in the classroom, I have tried to incorporate the concept of cognitive diversity into the design of my courses. In the absence of learner profiles, I often begin a semester by asking undergraduates to write out answers to a few key questions. The first questions are intended to gauge students' familiarity (or lack thereof) with the course's subject matter, while the second set of questions asks about learning styles. In my course on the literature of the American frontiers, for example, I ask students to list all the words and phrases that come to mind when they hear or read the word "frontier"; then I ask them to identify the sources of those associations. This proves a useful tool for opening discussion about the competing and changing cultural images of the frontier. And it gives students a chance to compare and analyze the ways in which they themselves have been introduced to shared cultural images—from movies, television series, novels, comic books, family histories, and oral narratives. In classes that routinely enroll Native Americans, Mexican Americans, and Euro-Americans (who usually identify as "Anglos" in the Southwest), these discussions are always lively and sometimes contentious. Students leave the room understanding that this course is not a museum piece. The way we image the frontiers of the past tells us a great deal about how we construct ourselves as "Americans" today.

If the first questions alert me to students' sophistication about the course materials, so that I can link new information to prior levels of knowledge and thus choose the readings more wisely, a second set of questions helps me assess the students' range of cognitive styles, so that I can present the readings more effectively. The second set of questions consists of three parts. Students are initially asked to give specific details about their best learning experience (including their age at the time and the particular circumstances); and they are asked to identify what made this learning experience distinctive or unique. Finally, they are asked "what features or elements best describe those classes at this university in which you feel you learn the most—and with pleasure?" Not surprisingly, students write about teachers who loved their subject matter and conveyed that enthusiasm to the class. But in addition to such general observations, many students reveal a great deal about their individual learning preferences. Some require a class in which there is a "sense of trust"; some learn easily from lectures, especially when the teacher "draws graphs and tables on the chalkboard to illustrate the lecture." Other students happily remember courses in which there was "much manual and visual activity" or those in which "I was always permitted to 'try on my own.'" One student felt she had finally learned how to learn when she signed up for a Mock United Nations project "in the 6th grade—age 11." This experience was remembered as distinctive because "it was a participatory learning experience as opposed to passive." As this student further explained, the Mock UN "forced me to use knowledge that I got from outside the classroom. I loved reading newspapers, fiction, and biography and I was able to apply all my 'outside' interests to a classroom situation."

Taking my cues from responses like these, I have changed my classroom practice. I now punctuate my lectures with visual materials—slides, film clips, graphic handouts—and put key words or outline concepts on the chalkboard. I assign all students to small-group projects in which they independently research a topic related to the course materials (a topic of their choosing) and then present their research to the entire class. When appropriate to the readings, I sometimes ask students to role-play. After studying Puritan captivity narratives and the native cultures of New England, for example, I may ask students to compose an entry in Mary Rowlandson's private diary after her return from eleven weeks of captivity among the Naragansett Indians in 1676. And whether in a small seminar or a large lecture class, I try to ask questions that invite students to call upon a variety of learning strategies, including analysis, synthesis, rote memory of facts or texts, and even that catch-all category that I call "creative guessing." I think it is working because I find myself learning even more from my students than I used to.

The tired debates over "canon wars" or introducing "cultural diversity" into the curriculum are already beside the point. Today's graduate students have assimilated the impact of three decades of scholarship in women's studies, African-American studies, ethnic studies, and the like. And, whatever the discipline, they are already embarked on professional careers in which gender, class, race, and ethnicity constitute legitimate categories of analysis. What these graduate students desperately need from the faculty now is training in classroom skills that will help them become effective teachers for the increasingly diverse student body they will encounter in freshman composition and Math 101. Appropriate responses to culturally inflected, and perhaps unexpected, student behaviors and some familiarity with the recent research on cognitive diversity thus constitute a vital part of their graduate education. The next generation of Ph.D.s, in short, must be prepared to teach a more inclusive *everyone,* and they must be prepared to teach everyone *well.*

1   Setting an Agenda for Change

"We live in an age of continuous change. The only constant we
have at this point in our national development is change. And
change is threatening. It creates apprehension. It makes us nervous.
Fear brings about protectionism: economic protectionism, moral
protectionism, demographic protectionism, political protectionism,
academic and intellectual protectionism. The progress we have
made in creating a democratic multicultural and multi-racial society
is in doubt and further progress is threatened by fear: fear of change."
—Arturo Madrid, "Less Is Not More . . . in the Case of Education,"
Brooklyn College commencement address, 4 June 1997.

i.

Whenever I am confronted by individuals eager to declare the
imminent demise of the public research university, I always ask which
of the nation's major established institutions have really done better.
After decades of withdrawing investment from their own infrastructure, exchanging long-term growth for short-term profits, the business
and manufacturing sectors found themselves losing markets domes-
tically and unable to compete abroad. In order to recover lost profit-
ability, U.S. corporations now ship manufacturing jobs overseas while
deskilling and downsizing the labor force at home. This is hardly a success story. At the same time, the nation's political institutions—especially at the federal level—appear increasingly enfeebled and incapable
of meaningful leadership. In larger and larger numbers, Americans are
not even bothering to vote. Again, not my idea of a success story. By
comparison, American research universities are the envy of the world,
with scholars from every nation flocking to them. As Robert Blackburn and Janet Lawrence observed in 1995, "no other segment of the
U.S. economy has the foreign trade balance that approaches that of
higher education" (Blackburn and Lawrence 294). And despite attacks
from the right, all polls indicate that colleges and universities have
generally maintained the public's confidence because they continue

to produce a steady stream of educated graduates, while they make possible research breakthroughs that markedly enhance the quality of daily life.

With their unique tripartite commitment to teaching, research, and service, the public universities established after the Civil War by the 1862 Morrill Act have always demonstrated a capacity for responsive innovation. From the first, the public universities experimented with everything from the design of the academic year calendar to the design of courses. Neither European nor older U.S. models were systematically imitated. Novel agricultural extension services turned farmers and ranchers into partners with the science faculty in the land-grant colleges of agriculture, thus significantly expanding agricultural output by the end of the nineteenth century. On the same campuses, business and engineering curricula were developed to serve the needs of an expanding corporate sector, while courses in Sanskrit, Chinese, and classical archeology were also available, even when enrollments were small. In effect, the evolving public universities of the late nineteenth and twentieth centuries not only made all areas of learning available, but they made that learning increasingly available "to social strata whose members had not previously imagined the university was intended for them or their children" (Graubard 365). Combined with already established private colleges and universities, the new public universities resulted in a mix of higher educational institutions unlike any of their European predecessors.

If all these prior changes in structure and transformations in curriculum were appreciated, the current calls for change and innovation in the university might be better understood as part of an ongoing and inevitable process with long historical roots. Rather than being labeled as a failing enterprise, the public research university would stand as an incredible success story, especially in comparison with the current state of our governmental and business institutions. And critics who now predict its demise would grasp that the capacity to innovate in the face of challenge has been the modern research university's most salient feature.

But as every administrator and faculty member is quick to point out, change always comes hard—and never without a price. Even where there is general agreement that change is long overdue, there is rarely any consensus about what kind of change might be desirable or how change should take place. This chapter, therefore, is constructed as a loosely organized meditation on change. The first three sections summarize some of the changes we put in place during my years as dean. I concentrate on changes that impacted pedagogy, personnel decisions, and governance, and I outline the creation of an environment that made those changes possible. The rest of this chapter contemplates the changes that I'd be grappling with today if I were still an administrator. A laundry list of *all* the changes with which administrators are now dealing doesn't fit the meditative mode, however, and so I've chosen to concentrate only on those I consider crucial: the training of graduate students, the culture of decision-making on campus, new patterns for academic leadership, shared governance, student advising, the potentially positive implications of a growing union movement, and the need for incentives and rewards. What may not always be evident in the pages that follow, unfortunately, is something that I only slowly learned as dean: while change is hard and bumpy, sometimes it can also be fun.

ii.

"We are all multiculturalists now."
—Nathan Glazer, from his book of that title (1997).

The easiest changes to effect when I was dean were curricular changes that responded in practical ways to current opportunities. Acknowledging demographic shifts was the obvious place to start.

In seven states today, 25 percent or more of K–12 public school students speak a language other than English at home, and nationwide the schools enroll over 3.5 million children from non-English-speaking backgrounds. While the popular media emphasize the approximately 73 percent of these children who are Hispanic, teachers are aware of well over 150 languages spoken in the public schools. Additionally, more than five million children of immigrants are entering our public schools during the current decade, with most demographers projecting that in the first quarter of the twenty-first century almost half the students in our colleges and universities will be the children of parents who have only recently arrived on our shores.

Because the University of Arizona is a public land-grant research institution located in Tucson, just sixty miles from the border with Mexico, in many ways the situation there anticipates that of the rest of the nation. As in California, the majority of students in Arizona currently enrolled in public schools are members of groups that traditionally have been considered minorities, and significantly more than half of these students are bilingual. As a result, for the past three years at the University of Arizona, over 20 percent of the entering students have been members of previously underrepresented ethnic, cultural, and racial groups. Older students are also increasingly conspicuous in every class, and the vast majority of the undergraduates work at least part time throughout their college years. Given the fact that the College of Humanities carries a major responsibility for instructing *all* of these undergraduates—through required first-year English composition courses, foreign language instruction, and interdisciplinary general education offerings—it was a relatively simple task to consider the implications of our changing student body and collectively identify literacy, language learning, and cross-cultural understanding as the critical goals for a meaningful humanities education. In all of our public documents, this is how we characterized ourselves to the rest of the campus and to the local community.

Literacy was an obvious goal. In the abstract, it is universally approved and applauded in the United States, because basic reading and writing skills are considered central to the active functioning of an informed citizenry in a democracy. Even so, the great wave of immigration in the 1980s that swept even more foreign-born people to our country than the 8.8 million who came between 1901 and 1910 has posed a challenge to our previously comfortable conceptions of what literacy entails. The College of Humanities saw this as an opportunity for reconceiving our curriculum. In a nation forged from a continuing mix of linguistic diversity, with many communities retaining their original languages, and in the face of an increasingly interdependent global economy with its own demands for multiple language competencies, we asked ourselves what should literacy mean and include, and how should it be developed?

By the mid-1980s, public school educators in Arizona determined that literacy must encompass more than the ability to read and write

English at the fifth-grade level, the minimum goal set by the Coalition for Literacy, which estimates that thirty million Americans now fall below its definition of skills required to complete even a simple job application (Robert L. Jacobson A16).[1] In multilingual and culturally mixed Arizona, there was statewide recognition that literacy cannot be limited to facility in a single language or to an understanding of a single cultural tradition. Accordingly, the Arizona Department of Education adopted a requirement that all elementary and middle schools, grades 1–8, would provide foreign language instruction in at least one grade level by 1993–94. In each year thereafter, the schools were asked to provide an additional grade of foreign language instruction, so that by the targeted year of 1998–99 children would be gaining foreign language proficiency throughout the elementary and middle school years.[2] In adopting this policy, the Department of Education unequivocally declared that the goal of literacy must now be the preparation of students "to communicate better with native speakers in this state" as well as with those from "other nations" (*Foreign Language Essential Skills* 4).

Although a Republican governor and a Republican majority state legislature have yet to fund this ambitious project, the College of Humanities acted to ensure that the needed instructors would be available to those school districts that implemented the policy on their own (as many have). Using existing faculty resources, we created a new interdisciplinary Ph.D. program in Second Language Acquisition and Teaching (SLAT) that prepares individuals to research and analyze the language education needs within diverse multicultural environments. SLAT students learn how to prepare innovative curricula that meet those needs, and they learn to train teachers and administrators in implementing these new language programs at every grade level. Because it is essential that grade school and middle school teachers be prepared to go beyond teaching only basic proficiency skills, the SLAT curriculum recognizes that language is deeply embedded within complex cultural contexts and that these cultural contexts must also become a focus of instruction. In other words, in future years Arizona schoolchildren will come to appreciate how languages represent doorways to different cultures, and they will understand, for example, that Spanish reflects and constitutes one set of cultural meanings when spoken in the barrios of Tucson and another when spoken in the streets of Seville.[3]

Worthy goal though it is, however, second language proficiency *by itself* will never adequately prepare students for the culturally diverse mosaic that has become the U.S. workplace; and it does not confer the skills required of an increasingly interdependent global citizenry of the twenty-first century. Within the College of Humanities at the University of Arizona, therefore, we took the goal of the Arizona Department of Education one step further. We committed ourselves to the view that cultural differences need not be barriers as long as different cultural traditions are taught in their dynamic relations to one another—and those relations are acknowledged as often hostile, sometimes friendly, at other times mixed. We thus redirected our curriculum toward what we came to term *cross-cultural literacy.* Implicit in that phrase is the requirement that students master more than one language and explore multiple cultural continuities within radically comparativist contexts. If our efforts prove successful, cross-cultural literacy should nurture our students' capacities to understand and respond to important differences in social customs, verbal cues, rhetorical patterns, aesthetic norms, and intellectual paradigms and traditions across cultures and across human history.

In order to establish cross-cultural literacy as an anchor of our curriculum, we introduced, in addition to the SLAT program, a second independent interdisciplinary program called Comparative Cultural and Literary Studies (CCLS). As the catalog copy for this new program indicates, CCLS was designed to teach students how to "explore the similarities and differences within and among national cultures and literatures" through a sequence of courses focusing "on the production, circulation, and interpretation of meaning and value in all cultural activity" ("Comparative Cultural and Literary Studies," 174). Drawing on theoretical approaches and critical methods from both the humanities and the social sciences, this is a curriculum committed to examining the intersections of disciplinary knowledge, a curriculum that aims at dialogic understanding.[4]

Our aims were never merely local, however. We understood that if comparativist pedagogies were to become a permanent feature of humanities education nationwide, and if cross-cultural literacy was to develop as a meaningful concept beyond our own campus, then graduate students had to become invested in their elaboration and survival. Today's graduate students, after all, will be designing tomorrow's curriculum as faculty members at other institutions. To ensure that these kinds of curricular changes would be ongoing and widely dispersed, between 1990 and 1993, the dean's office sponsored a cross-disciplinary series of discussion groups, colloquia, and workshops called "Humanities Education in the 21st Century"—which I mentioned in the previous chapter. These activities brought together faculty and graduate students from every department and program in the college, and they engaged faculty and graduate students together in rethinking what would be required of humanities educators in the decades ahead.

iii.

"Before this dean came aboard, this was just
an office building; now it's a community."
—Reference to me by a faculty member
unaware of my being able to overhear him.

The intellectual catalyst for almost every college initiative during my years as dean was our ability to succinctly define our shared mission as cross-cultural literacy. But an intellectual catalyst does not, by itself, create a climate congenial to change. To have successfully received authorization and funding for two new academic programs; to have secured substantial faculty interest in curricular innovation; and to have engaged graduate student leadership throughout the process—and all within five years—required something more than a catchy mission statement. It required a sea change in culture and attitudes, so that, first and foremost, the College of Humanities could become a welcoming environment for curricular renewal and experimentation. In order to create that environment, the dean's office worked closely with faculty, staff, and graduate students to develop workable practical strategies for fostering and rewarding scholarly and pedagogical risk-taking. We also sought to create a sense of community and an inclusive approach to problem-solving. Where we could, we borrowed what seemed to work on other campuses; where there were no available models, we invented freely. If there was any key to our success, it was that we implemented most of our changes within a concentrated time span so that—through a kind of synergy—they had a cumulative and mutually reinforcing effect.

Although individually each new policy and strategy enjoyed widespread support from staff and faculty, there was decided unease about both the speed of change and its expanding implications. But despite pockets of sometimes vocal resistance, the majority of faculty—and almost all of the support staff—took seriously the need to respond boldly to altered economic conditions and rapidly diversifying student cohorts. As a result, if any one concept characterizes the assemblage of strategies and policies that worked for us, it is this: our avowed commitment to cross-cultural literacy implied a responsibility to acknowledge—and expand—the diversity on our own campus and within our own ranks.

Here, then, are some of the practical strategies that helped us create an environment supportive of and responsive to change:

• As discussed in chapter 3, a Faculty Planning and Policies Advisory Committee, working with department heads and program directors, designed a new Promotion and Tenure Criteria document that recognizes and rewards current forms of scholarship related to teaching. This includes the development of computer-assisted language pedagogies as well as publication of innovative textbooks, inter- and cross-disciplinary teaching approaches, and instructional participation in programs like Women's Studies, Mexican-American Studies, African-American Studies, American Indian Studies, etc.

• Also as discussed in chapter 3, a new Promotion and Tenure Procedures document ensures fair evaluation of cutting-edge or unfamiliar areas of scholarship and research activity; and it creates a level playing field for women and minority scholars who often face a variety of unacknowledged obstacles in the promotion and tenure process.

• The dean's office regularly funded retreats so that all the faculty, staff, and elected graduate student representatives in a program or department could go off-campus for two days in order to examine their current course offerings and, where needed, redesign their curriculum with an eye to the twenty-first century. In some cases, these retreats proved so energizing that departments continued to schedule them annually, even when the dean's office was no longer providing the money.

• The dean's office also instituted twice-yearly two-day retreats—always held off-campus in a congenial setting—which included all members of the dean's office and administrative staff, all department heads and program directors, and the members of the Faculty Planning and Policies Advisory Committee. While the first day was usually devoted to immediate concerns such as budget cuts, personnel matters, and the like, on the second day an outside facilitator (someone with no ties to the university) took us through a process of reflection and looking to the future. In essence, we envisioned where we wanted to be in five years and in ten years; critically examined the programs already in place in terms of our shared visions for the future and measured the progress already made in achieving our future goals; and set short-term and long-term agendas for change. Among other benefits, these retreats helped reestablish the college as an integrated and coherent unit as opposed to a collection of independent and sometimes warring departments. And in everything from equipment purchases to cross-disciplinary course development, the retreats fostered increasing levels of cooperation across departments and disciplines.

• As mentioned in the last chapter, the dean's office sponsored an annual competitive $5000 "21st-Century Curriculum Development Grant" for any program, department, or cross-departmental faculty group that developed a plan for reviewing its curriculum in light of both the latest scholarship and research in the field and the need to prepare for a rapidly changing student body. The annual announcement of this competition explained that the goal was to foster development of "curriculum that will be responsive to the ethnic, racial, and cultural diversity that we may expect in the student body of the twenty-first century. This implies a rethinking of curricular matters as well as pedagogical approaches." Experience proved that a number of people were usually involved in putting together the grant proposal, and so the very process of submitting the application had ongoing positive benefits for a unit, whether the application was funded or not. Few faculty wanted to abandon the momentum that the proposal process had generated, and several departments, when they were not funded, either resubmitted their proposals again in a future year or proceeded to make changes on their own, even without dean's office funding.

• With support from the vice president for research, we instituted an annual blind-submission "Faculty Research Mini-Grants" competition designed to fund outstanding original research and creative projects in as wide a spectrum as possible. A three-person committee, composed of individuals from the three professorial ranks, evaluated the applications solely on the basis of their quality and without regard to the applicant's rank, department, or reputation—all of which were unknown to the committee. The outcome of the blind submission process was that, each year, half or more of the successful applicants were untenured faculty; and at least half were women (across the ranks). Almost everyone in the college applauded the wide distribution of the grants to junior faculty and the grants' support for women and minority faculty especially. Equally gratifying was the fact that much of this newly supported research was quickly translated to the classroom, thereby reinforcing the college's efforts at curricular renewal.

• Because the dean's office support staff (secretaries, administrative assistants, business managers, etc.) are also professionals, and because they function as essential components of the larger administrative team, we instituted formal development opportunities for them as well, including an annual $1,000 competitive scholarship. In addition, by application to the dean's office, support staff from any College of Humanities program or department could secure funding to attend workshops, conferences, seminars, or classes—as long as these would prove helpful in enhancing the individual's job performance. And because we viewed personal development and skills enhancement as equivalently valuable, there was wide latitude in the kinds of activities thus funded. Some staff members chose to take workshops in relaxation techniques and stress management, while others wanted only further training on the computer. Within my own office, I annually provided a full scholarship for three support staff members to join me in attending an out-of-town professional or scholarly conference—the annual meeting of the Modern Language Association, for example, or that of the National Women's Studies Association. With these rewards in place, staff morale remained relatively high, despite the university's chronically low wage scales. And those who joined me at professional conferences experienced an enhanced appreciation of their vital role in the research-and-teaching enterprise; an increased level of comfort with the technical vocabularies associated with language pedagogy and literary criticism; and a more acute understanding of national issues and debates affecting the humanities. In one happy instance, energized and inspired by the sessions she had attended at the National Women's Studies Association meeting, a talented administrative assistant decided to return to school, part time, in order to complete a long-delayed bachelor's degree and become an educator herself.

• In order to enhance contacts and collegiality across departmental and programmatic barriers, we instituted "buddy groups." Each fall, a volunteer committee of faculty and staff assigned all new incoming faculty members two "buddies." Those who served as buddies were also all volunteers. New untenured assistant professors were assigned faculty buddies for three years; new tenured associate or full professors were assigned faculty buddies for one year only. One buddy was male, the other female. One buddy came from the new faculty member's home department, though never from the same area of specialization, while the other buddy came from another department within the College of Humanities. Additionally, all new department heads were assigned two buddies for one year (usually current or former heads from other units), and new administrative assistants were assigned one buddy for a year (usually a seasoned administrative assistant from another unit); in some cases, departments extended this to include secretaries, too. To enhance the attraction of becoming a buddy for a new faculty or staff member, each buddy group enjoyed two free lunches every semester on the dean's budget at the Union Club (a comfortable but inexpensive dining room in the Student Union).

The purpose of these buddy groups was never formal mentoring. Faculty and staff were not assigned to one another on the basis of mutual scholarly or job-related interests—at least not primarily. I had seen too many well-intentioned mentoring programs at other institutions fail when senior faculty were assigned as mentors to the new hire in their own field. Too often, the senior expected the junior colleague to become a disciple, following the senior's theories or methodologies rather than branching out on his own. Exclusively field-specific mentoring relationships, I knew, were rife with the potential for rivalry and hurt feelings. Instead, the purpose of our college's buddy groups was to provide supportive *personal* contacts for faculty and staff alike. Senior faculty who volunteered as buddies were tacitly being asked to guide their junior colleagues through the first three years in order to prepare them for the crucial fourth-year pretenure review. Buddies were asked to introduce new faculty to promotion and tenure expectations, as well as to introduce them to friends, colleagues, and the institution as a whole. Buddies were also expected to help the new person get acquainted with the greater Tucson area.

In some instances, we grouped individuals who were recent parents, so that they might exchange information on child care facilities, pediatricians, and so on. In other instances, we matched individuals known to be golf enthusiasts or rock climbers. So positive was the response that, as I was leaving my position as dean, everyone who had completed a one- or three-year buddy assignment volunteered to buddy again, or, if the individual was herself "buddied," to buddy yet another newcomer. In 1994, with the blessing of the dean who succeeded me, faculty in the Buddy Program initiated a brown bag luncheon series. The series offers an informal occasion for faculty, graduate students, and staff to exchange ideas and to share research projects and creative accomplishments. In retrospect, the benefits of the buddy groups have been wide-ranging: collaborative research projects that cross discipline lines; initiatives for group- or team-taught courses; improved morale and a stronger sense of "belonging" among staff and junior faculty; and, most important, a deeper commitment from the senior faculty to the career success of junior colleagues.

• Recognizing that only a widely diversified faculty would provide the intellectual scope required for the curricular and pedagogical innovations in which we were engaged; and recognizing, further, that faculty from many different cultural backgrounds would provide supportive role models for our changing undergraduate population, the department heads and I experimented with new approaches to faculty recruitment. During my first year as dean, we designated all our searches for new faculty as "affirmative action searches," and the college invited the university's affirmative action director to give a workshop on appropriate search procedures. The workshop was open to all interested faculty, but it was required for those who would be serving on search committees. With guidance from the Affirmative Action Office and the university's legal staff, we began to advertise position openings in a wider variety of venues, and we rewrote our advertisements to emphasize the College of Humanities' commitments to diversity and interdisciplinarity, highlighting Tucson itself as a multicultural community. The department heads and I agreed that all of our search committees would be gender-balanced, with one-third minority participation—even if this meant that a department would have to "borrow" faculty from another humanities department or program.[5] If a search was aimed at a specific area—say, premodern Chinese poetry or English Renaissance drama—area specialists were always appointed to the search committee; but gender balance and minority participation ensured that narrowly parochial interests could no longer dominate the search process. Our purpose, after all, was to build for the future and avoid, out of habit, merely replicating a department's prior emphases or traditional configuration.

In addition to affirmative action considerations on available open budget lines, when a department identified a specific woman or minority scholar whose expertise would enhance their programs, we initiated what the University of Arizona termed "Target of Opportunity" procedures and aggressively recruited these specific "targeted" individuals. Because Target of Opportunity lines came from the provost's office, they always represented additional funding for an entirely new faculty line, even if a department had no available openings. In some instances, the promise of a new faculty line through the Target of Opportunity process proved sufficient incentive for otherwise resisting departments to actively seek out qualified women and minority candidates. With our burgeoning enrollments, every new faculty line was a boon.

As a result of the new search procedures and the Target of Opportunity process, finalist candidates began to emerge from very different groupings. To increase our chances of attracting these highly sought-after people to the University of Arizona, finalists invited for campus interviews were always given the opportunity to meet others from their community at a scheduled lunch or dinner. Thus, if a candidate were African American, at least one lunch or dinner was scheduled with other African-American faculty from all across campus. Similarly, if the candidate were Chicano, he would enjoy at least one meal with other Mexican-American faculty. When resources permitted, we invited candidates to bring their children or partners for the visit so that they could, as a family, visit schools and residential neighborhoods. For some candidates, this demonstrated sensitivity to work *and* family issues proved the deciding factor, and we were able to hire individuals who would otherwise have gone to more prestigious institutions. By arranging such visits for a Saturday night sleep-over, we saved considerably on airfares and thus were able to afford the additional travel and hotel expenses.

As negotiations went forward and offers were made, department heads saw to it that candidates with equivalent credentials received identical salaries and start-up packages within a department. We did this even when candidates themselves had omitted requests for computer equipment or research funding, as was often the case with new women hires. We thus compensated for the apparent reluctance of junior women faculty to bargain as assertively as their male peers and, in the process, maintained the principle of equal treatment.

Finally, in designing our annual recruitment plans and in making the hiring decisions, we took into account not only our instructional needs but also our rejection of merely "token" hiring. Instead, whenever possible, we adhered to the goal of "cluster hiring": *several* new women faculty hired both within and across departments in the same year and two African scholars recruited for the Department of French and Italian. Our purpose was to create and solidify a diversified community, so that new faculty would put down firm roots in a welcoming environment.

• The administrator who claims to exemplify the kinds of behaviors she seeks to nurture in others may have to become pro-active herself. When a cross-college Arts and Sciences faculty curriculum review committee repeatedly raised nonacademic questions about a proposed new undergraduate English Department course to be called Introduction to Gay and Lesbian Literature (the first such course offered in the state of Arizona) and withheld its usually pro forma approval, I intervened immediately. First, in order to communicate that the course had the full support of the dean's office, I secured its funding. In addition, I offered not only to serve as professor of record but also to team-teach the course with the advanced graduate students who had first designed it. My professional stature as a nationally known literary scholar and my willingness to take formal responsibility for the course gave its subject matter a new legitimacy. The course was then speedily approved. After two successful semesters, with enthusiastic responses from the students and surprisingly supportive statewide press coverage, Introduction to Gay and Lesbian Literature moved from an experimental offering to the permanent catalog. And a group of faculty and graduate students from various departments now meet regularly to develop a series of gay and lesbian studies offerings.

I do not exaggerate when I say that our successes were many. By building on past accomplishments and pursuing goals that the faculty itself had identified, we diversified our faculty, our student body, and our curriculum. In 1988, for example, there were only forty-one women on the faculty, concentrated almost exclusively in the junior ranks, and representing 29.9 percent of the total. Because of our changed approach to hiring, by 1992 there were seventy-seven women on the faculty, visible across all ranks, and representing half (49.9 percent) of the total College of Humanities. Similarly, in 1988, there were only ten minority faculty, representing 7.3 percent of the total. By 1992 there were thirty minority faculty, representing 19.2 percent of the total faculty.

By diversifying the faculty, we provided role models who helped open up the pipeline into higher education for previously underrepresented groups. In 1988, only twenty-two graduate students in humanities departments or programs were from minority backgrounds. By 1991, the number was forty-three, representing an increase of 95.5 percent in only three years. No less significant, minority students were not routinely tracked into ethnic or identity-related area studies exclusively. African-American students were regularly enrolled in the graduate programs in the Department of Russian and Slavic Languages; a Chinese immigrant earned her doctorate in Spanish; and several Chicano/a students completed master's degrees in classical archeology.

In 1992, when departments and programs within the College of Humanities submitted new copy for the university's next two-year course catalog, the many textual changes amply demonstrated the massive curricular renewal taking place. At the same time, the rewritten course descriptions easily explained the attractions of these curricular innovations for students from every background. Clearly, our successes in expanding and diversifying the faculty had allowed us to expand and diversify our educational offerings.

Additionally, five years of intensive support for pedagogical research also had its impact. The Department of German Studies and the Department of Russian and Slavic Languages—as highlighted in the previous chapter—were not the only units to host innovative experiments with technology. To offset the problems of overcrowded classes and expand the opportunities for conversation practice, the director of Basic Languages in the Department of Spanish and Portuguese introduced computer conferencing to supplement second-year Spanish courses. Careful monitoring of the results demonstrated that, in the computer-supplemented sections, students' levels of oral and written proficiency far exceeded those achieved in only face-to-face classroom situations. Students who used this computer-mediated communication were not limited to contacts with their immediate peers, however. International "pen pal" contacts were readily available, and these helped students to become more aware of cultural differences on a global scale. Routinely, instructors reported that "students became addicted to conferencing and were reluctant to leave their classes at the end of the semester, for they had become more personally attached to their classmates than they had in any other course" (Smith and Maginnis 114). Not coincidentally, success with computer conferencing led to implementation of Macintosh-based interactive reading and listening programs that also had impressive outcomes: students increased their receptive skills in Spanish by 30 percent on standardized tests (as compared with those receiving only traditional forms of instruction).

While computer-assisted instruction was being explored in the foreign languages, a "non-tech" experiment in selected sections of freshman composition proved successful in introducing students to the concept of ethnographic research. After assigned readings on the theory and practice of ethnography, students were asked to go into a community of their choice—their own or some other that they identified and defined—and produce an ethnographic study of an individual life, a group, or the community as a whole. Because the students in these experimental sections shared and critiqued one another's work as it progressed, not only did they refine their research skills and improve their writing, but they also had the opportunity to learn about and appreciate the complexity of communities with which they might otherwise never have had contact. Students who examined their own ethnic neighborhood or cultural community, moreover, developed a more informed sense of pride in membership. When, toward the end of the semester, these first-year classes applied their new-found ethnographic skills to an examination of the university, they saw the campus from a wholly new perspective: no longer did it appear an impersonal monolith. Instead, so their instructors reported, the students recognized the many different communities and the interconnected diversity that now surrounded and invited them.

Although none of the experiments and innovations discussed in this or in earlier chapters resemble one another in technique or technology, each in its way contributed to the shared goal of cross-cultural literacy. And that expanded concept of literacy helped to generate what one former faculty member has termed a "highly creative and interactive environment for learning, thus opening the way for an educational revolution that promotes individuality, creativity, and originality" (Smith 77).

iv.

"Since the provost isn't going to listen to us anyway,
let's get this meeting over with quickly and give him
recommendations he can *really* ignore."
—A disgruntled faculty member on a newly formed
campus-wide budget policy committee.

Despite five years of steady advances in curriculum and pedagogy, despite successful new hiring strategies and new promotion and tenure policies, and despite our continuingly exciting research activities, soon after I left the dean's office in 1993, the College of Humanities faced a new round of crises. In subsequent years, an unexpected downturn in the university's enrollment and even deeper budget cuts at the state level threatened to gut established academic programs and undermine the security of new ones. The College of Humanities was not alone in this: the crisis was campus-wide. Still, for a unit whose funding base had never matched its enrollments, all new cuts were potentially devastating. From the comfortable distance of the research sabbatical year that followed my tenure as dean, what troubled me more than the possible threats to the academic integrity of the College of Humanities was the manner in which central administration was attempting to manage the crisis. Wary of playing bully by deciding, on its own, where cuts would be made, the provost's office sought the laudable goal of cross-campus consultation and advice. Tenured faculty from several different colleges and departments were appointed to a committee charged with reviewing all academic programs and recommending places for downsizing or even elimination. The problem was that the committee members were appointed without considering whether every affected constituency was represented and without considering what vested interests or relevant expertise those who were appointed might (or might not) bring to the table. And they were provided no training of any kind—only an overwhelming amount of raw information. As a consequence, faculty, program directors, and department heads in the College of Humanities—as in every other college on campus—expended enormous amounts of time and energy in trying to justify their existence in what was perceived as an adversarial process. In our college especially, innovative new programs that had only recently survived the myriad hurdles of the approval mechanisms— programs that we had once been so proud to develop—were now in the demoralizing situation of having to explain, yet again, the rationale for their innovations. Happily, in the end, no College of Humanities program or department was slated for elimination, but the entire process bred campus-wide mistrust of both central administration and the process itself. This was then exacerbated by a number of recommendations for cuts or program consolidations in other units that caused much turmoil and resistance—recommendations from which, in some cases, central administration finally backed away.

While this scenario is familiar nowadays in academe, to me it seemed dangerous and unnecessary. And it crystallized for me an underlying problem no less critical than the budget cuts and enrollment contractions that had precipitated this latest round of crises. In a nutshell, the underlying problem was the inadequate decision-making structure on campus. In fact, in my view, this underlying problem was ultimately responsible for turning a bad situation into a crisis, because outdated governance patterns were now magnifying the traditions of autonomy, self-interest, and independent constituency interest that characterize the complex modern university. As Nannerl O. Keohane, the president of Duke University, has noted, the high degree of autonomy enjoyed by the tenured faculty, as well as by individual departments and research centers, makes it "difficult to chart a course and arrange the incentive structure . . . so as to encourage semiautonomous actors to converge around common goals" (Keohane 153). With the advent of electronic communication, moreover, the difficulty of "converg[ing] around common goals" has become even more pronounced: university faculty can easily "exchange ideas along lines of disciplinary interest [across the globe] with almost total disregard for national or institutional affiliation" (Keohane 175). Thus, *except in times of crisis*, large numbers of faculty and even entire departments may be far more attentive to developments in their discipline around the world than to political or economic events on their own campus. This can make it very difficult for faculty to take an effective role as participants in any policy-making process.

Yet faculty *must* become the indispensable participants in policy-making, bringing all aspects of their disciplinary expertise to the multiple challenges of guiding the research university into the coming century. But this will only happen when graduate students are appropriately trained, when faculty understand that their role now encompasses yet another set of responsibilities, and when the patterns of decision-making on most campuses have changed radically. In place of the current relatively rigid hierarchical structures that are more usually top-down rather than bottom-up—especially at the larger comprehensive and research universities—what will be required in the future are horizontally inclusive patterns that are both flexible and goal-oriented. To survive as a viable institution into the twenty-first century, the modern university must reconceptualize decision-making and policy development as forms of creative problem-solving; and creative problem-solving must be understood as a species of integrated systems teamwork. As I argued in my preface, this means that large complex campuses must deal with specific problems and face defined challenges in a manner that includes all constituents and addresses the part as an integral component of the larger whole. The hard choices regarding the best use of diminishing resources—choices about admissions standards, teaching loads, class size, faculty salary increases, etc.—should no longer be made within autonomous units that do not communicate with one another; nor should they be made exclusively by vice presidents or provosts. Staff, students, and faculty must become full and knowledgeable partners in making these decisions. They must *own* the solutions, or there will be no real solutions.

v.

> "Mission statement?—I never heard of such a thing.
> They never taught us this is graduate school."
> —A first-year assistant professor appointed to a task
> force to revise her university's mission statement.

If I were still a dean, I would begin the process of changing decision-making procedures on campuses by asking the faculty—and the students themselves—to rethink the training of graduate students. At the moment, we do these students a grave disservice by omitting from their training preparation for tasks that will constitute a full third (or more) of their future professional responsibilities. Who, as a graduate student, was encouraged to think about committee obligations, administration, departmental management, scheduling, curricular reform, or any of the other details that make up the dailiness of university life? And how many graduate students learn anything about the history of higher education in this country or understand the distinctions between different types of higher educational institutions? Clearly, we need to develop opportunities for training graduate students—or at least those who indicate their wish to become the faculty of the future—to understand not only their fields of expertise and the skills of teaching for cultural and cognitive diversity but also to understand university budgets, institutional goals, and the different governance models available within academe. Even as graduate students, these future members of the professoriate ought to develop a fuller appreciation of the complex interface between campus, community, and nation.

Before they embark on the academic job market, advanced graduate students should be offered at least one course that introduces them to the history of higher education in the United States and that clearly explains the differences between kinds of institutions, from the community college to the research university. In addition to learning about administrative, funding, and governance patterns at different institutions, graduate students would also gain an understanding of the varied expectations for faculty performance at a small private liberal arts college as opposed to a community college or an AAU Research-I public university. Complementing this general overview, symposia offered by colleges or departments could focus on the history and role of specific disciplines within the different kinds of institutions. In this way, graduate students would seek academic employment with a firmer grasp of which institutions will demand that they bring in significant external funding for their research in biochemistry or which institutions will expect their tenure-track faculty to teach freshman composition on a regular basis.

Ideally, when hired, the incoming assistant professor then would be given some form of analogous orientation to her or his new campus. A series of informal seminars could explain to new hires how things work at *this* institution and alert newcomers to particular problems or challenges facing the school. Not only would such a seminar series afford the opportunity for new faculty from different departments and disciplines to meet one another; but, if administrators were to participate in teaching the seminars, the seminar series also could give new faculty and administrators an opportunity to better understand one another's concerns. At the very least, the lines of communication would *feel* more open.

Admittedly, this kind of training might add some time to the completion of a graduate degree; and it might require colleges and universities temporarily to lighten the teaching loads or committee assignments of new hires in order to give them time to attend the orientation seminar series. But both investments have the potential to pay off handsomely. A new generation of faculty with revitalized training of this kind would surely help to diminish the current adversarial relations between faculty and administrators on campuses; such a generation would also provide new models of leadership, both as faculty and as a potential pool of future administrators. Today, we suffer

as a community nationwide because too few faculty have any historical perspective on current educational issues and even fewer have had
any opportunity to develop an adequate understanding of the political
and economic constraints within which their schools must function.

vi.

"Administration is too important to be left to the
administrators. Especially *our* administrators."
—A professor to his supporters after having been elected
to the Faculty Senate of a large eastern university.

The large and complex research university that I have limned
in these pages is as multifaceted as a city. The larger and more complex
an institution, the greater the autonomy granted each of its constitu-
ent units. In other words, the task of defining and solving problems
is assigned to discrete segments of the campus that may or may not
interact with one another, and decision-making becomes increasingly
atomized. Each unit exercises its authority and allocates its resources
within the parameters of what it takes to be its areas of responsibility
and in terms of its unique understanding of institutional needs. Thus,
the dean of Arts and Sciences receives data, reports, and recommendations from a variety of sources—individual department heads and
program directors, a faculty governance group, an assistant dean for
advising, an associate dean for personnel, and so on—not all of whom
consult with one another in any regular fashion, and few of whom
have time to consult with entities outside of Arts and Sciences—like
Room Scheduling or the Office of Minority Student Affairs. The dean is
then expected to organize this disparate material, absorb its meaning,
find a way through the tangle of sometimes conflicting recommendations, and make decisions that will maximally benefit students, staff,
and faculty.

The situation is not dissimilar at the provost's and vice presidents'
levels where, presumably, no campus-wide policy is put in place and
no major budgetary reallocation made without their prior approval. To
be sure, senior administrators routinely turn to the Faculty Senate and
to their councils of deans for the shared evaluation of pressing problems and the generation of policy or budget recommendations. Even

so, those on whom they rely are themselves captives of piecemeal data and limited perspectives. Everyone is trying to do their best for the institution within the confines of their area of responsibility; and because each group and each administrator knows how necessary their own unit is to the institution's functioning, part of their role is to protect their turf from budget cuts or reorganization, even if that turf protection is purchased at the price of some other unit's survival.

This familiar pattern of hierarchical reporting lines combined with the fact of semi-autonomous units, each with its own complex infrastructure, places an impossible decision-making burden on deans, provosts, and presidents. And it all but paralyzes the evolution of campus-wide organic institutional perspectives. Moreover, in the current budgetary crises affecting most public universities, this pattern has contributed substantially to adversarial relationships between staff, faculty, and central administration.

In my view, one way out of the dilemma—and perhaps the only way for a campus to converge around common goals—is for a strong, risk-taking administrator to distribute problem-solving horizontally by developing an inclusive team approach. By "a strong, risk-taking administrator," I refer to a dean, vice president, or president willing to clearly articulate the problem, even if that risks temporarily polarizing the campus; willing to lay out the facts of the case candidly, no matter what constituency may be discomfited or offended; willing to provide all the relevant information and hard data, no matter how contradictory; willing to explore all possibilities, and willing to engage—as an equal team member—in the search for solutions, putting the resources of her/his staff and office at the team's disposal. In this model, the most valued administrator will not be the one who functions best without restraints, but the administrator who can work best under multiple (and often frustrating) constraints and still convey both a personal and an institutional vision, all the while facilitating concrete progress toward implementing that vision.

By "inclusive team," I refer to a team that brings together diverse representatives from every group or unit implicated in the problem in its broadest definition along with members of every constituency potentially impacted by a budget reallocation or pending policy recommendation. Representatives from Room Scheduling would thus necessarily serve on a team charged to improve the delivery of general education courses, and the Office of Minority Student Affairs would send members to any team considering budget cuts in Career Counseling Services. The team should be given as specific a charge as possible by the initiating administrator;[6] and, rather than requesting a single solution, in some instances the administrator would do well to invite a series of options, with analyses of the advantages and disadvantages of each. In most situations, at least at the outset, the team will benefit from a professional facilitator guiding the group to a clearer definition of its goal and the process for reaching it and, at the same time, ensuring that no individual or faction comes to dominate the verbal space. Depending on the nature of the problems to be addressed, the team will also benefit from an orientation and training period in which those with relevant expertise (from on-campus, off-campus, and from other institutions) prepare the team members for the scope and complexity of their task.

Once the team has produced a preliminary report or set of recommendations, that draft should be widely circulated to invite input from all concerned parties as well as from the initiating administrator and her staff. The team then redrafts, sends out another version, and, this time, holds open meetings for information-sharing, discussion, and feedback. The team repeats this process until the majority of team members are satisfied that they have received meaningful input from all affected parties. Not until the majority of team members feel confident that they have publicly explained the rationale for the recommendations they are considering, and responded adequately to feedback, do they generate their final document. Because the initiating administrator not only had her own representatives functioning as team participants but, as well, met with the team and offered input on the prior drafts, the recommendations in the final document *should* be recommendations the administrator feels comfortable implementing immediately.

Speedy and effective implementation is essential. When for some reason that proves impossible, it is incumbent upon the initiating administrator to meet with the team quickly and explain the situation fully, seeking the team's further advice to resolve the obstacles to implementation. The inclusive team approach only works if those willing to participate see the demonstrable fruits of their considerable labors. Nothing will more profoundly alienate staff, faculty, and students from administration than the perception that their time and energies have been wasted.

The objections to introducing an inclusive team approach to problem-solving are that some teams may become so large as to appear unwieldy; and the very fact of inclusivity—coupled with a mandate that the team repeatedly reach out for additional feedback—may mean that solutions to pressing problems will not always be speedily forthcoming. These objections are well founded. Until faculty, staff, students, and administrators become habituated to team problem-solving as part of a new institutional culture; until they learn through practice to work effectively in teams; and until they view team-generated recommendations as influential in planning, policy, and budget decisions, this approach to problem-solving will be relatively slow and cumbersome and may even be regarded with mistrust.

The alternative, however, no longer works. Individual administrators and their staffs cannot endlessly sift through multiplying sets of interpreted data and the competing agendas of those who report to them and still be expected to come up with policies that benefit the institution as a whole. Small committees hastily put together, with no special training for the task at hand, cannot do the job either. Only inclusive problem-solving teams brought together to utilize all the relevant talents on a campus can adequately grasp the complexity of the modern research university. In this environment, the administrator's role is to consult widely in order to facilitate the appointment of appropriate team members; make certain that he himself—or some of his staff—are part of the team; offer powerful incentives for teamwork that encompasses multiobjective institutional thinking; give the team its charge and objectives as clearly as possible; provide all the data relevant to the team's concerns; provide the resources needed for the team to do its job thoroughly; encourage creative thinking; and then work with the team on speedy implementation once their recommendations have been accepted.

During my own tenure as dean, I experimented with the team approach by appointing a variety of task forces to examine several problem areas, from the training and compensation of graduate student teaching assistants to the development of an academic program in Multicultural Technical Communication. Routinely, these task forces included faculty, staff, students, and administrators (department heads, program directors, and/or an assistant or associate dean from my office). I provided some task forces with funds for technical or secretarial assistance; or I assigned a support staff member from the dean's office to assist as needed. Whenever I could, I supplied the task forces with relevant reading and background materials, as well as hard data. I also encouraged them to add members as they deemed necessary or to seek out those who might serve as expert consultants.

To counter the potential slowness of an inclusive team process, I set deadlines for preliminary draft reports, and, to a large extent, this worked. Larger teams handled their unwieldy numbers by breaking themselves into subgroups, later reconvening as a committee of the whole when substantive matters warranted review. The requirement to send out preliminary drafts for feedback, coupled with the scheduling of open meetings for further discussion, inevitably slowed each group's progress. But the benefits were enormous. Useful feedback strengthened a number of policy documents, including—most notably—both our new Promotion and Tenure Criteria document *and* our new Promotion and Tenure Procedures document. And although each document took two years to complete (a year longer than I had hoped), when sent out for faculty ballot they each enjoyed strong and informed support. By continuing to reach out to the affected constituency for help in developing these documents, the team had generated a faculty-wide sense of agency and ownership.

The most compelling argument for the inclusive teach approach, however, is its educative function. Within the College of Humanities, teams made up of staff from different kinds of units, faculty from all ranks and from large and small departments alike, department heads and program directors, dean's office personnel, and graduate and undergraduate students at different stages of their academic careers allowed for a very different kind of problem-solving conversation. In order to grasp the problem, each member of the team had to learn to analyze the data in terms of her unique perspective and situation; at the same time, in order to generate solutions, each team member had to come to terms with understandings, needs, and expectations other

than his own. In this situation, faculty members gain new appreciation for the constraints within which administrators must function;
students come to understand the many-faceted roles of support staff;
and everyone gains a new appreciation of the difficulties facing the
undergraduate who works part time or the graduate student who is
raising a family while completing a Ph.D. Above all else, if proffered
solutions were to be accepted and workable, teams had to understand
how the component units and constituencies interrelated so as to constitute the whole of the College of Humanities. With that, segmented
approaches to problem-solving gradually gave way to organic models
and integrative thinking.

Rather than resulting in a superficial consensus or in diluted com-
promises that neither satisfy nor offend, the inclusive team conversation benefits from the synergy of the group. Because its solutions are
the result of several varied intelligences working together both to overcome *and* to take advantage of each individual's necessarily limited
but unique insight and expertise, the inclusive team produces results
that are creative and holistic. Indeed, the inclusive team approach
often can be visionary in its complex understanding of a problem. The
inclusive team is thus the seedbed for generating an integrated institutional vision and a campus-wide sense of institutional participation. It
is the only mechanism I know that successfully disposes faculty, staff,
and students to take responsibility for an active and ongoing role in
the shared governance of the institution.

vii.

> "We share too damn much with them now. . . .
> I'm sick and tired of the faculty thinking we're
> supposed to roll over and play dead."
> —Ward Connerly, a University of California
> regent (qtd. in Scott B1).

As universities restructure themselves for the new century,
the willingness of students, faculty, and staff to participate in shared
governance will prove decisive in determining the shape of that restructuring process. But shared governance has been in jeopardy for
some time now. When, in July 1995, the Board of Regents of the Uni-

versity of California voted to abolish affirmative action considerations in admissions, hiring, and contracting, it did so against the express advice of the university's president, the system's nine chancellors, faculty representatives, and organized student groups. Similarly, when in 1996 the regents of the University of Minnesota initially attempted to revise the tenure code, they did so without consulting faculty. Both incidents made headlines, alerting the academic community to the inherent fragility of both the principle and the practice of shared governance. It should not have required examples like these to make that point, however. Coincident with diminishing funding supports for higher education, especially at public institutions, governing boards increasingly began to micromanage everything from budget distributions on campus to the appointment of administrators to decisions about curriculum and tenure policy. What happened in California and Minnesota were only extreme outcomes of a developing trend.

To be sure, on some campuses, what I am calling trustee micromanagement has worn what appears to be a benign face. University presidents desperate to compensate for dwindling state and federal funding have promoted industrial parks, real estate investments, and increased contract research for the private sector. Understandably, they called on the expertise and contacts of prominent trustees to help accomplish these goals; and the trustees, in their turn, confident in their mastery of private business practices, have written institutional policy in these areas without first seeking significant faculty or campus-wide input. On other campuses, trustee micromanagement is more obviously troubling. Apparently without any understanding of the concept of academic freedom, a member of the Christian Coalition newly appointed to the board of James Madison University in January 1996 told a reporter for the *Chronicle of Higher Education:* "I'm planning to go course by course in the James Madison manual to see what I don't like and what I think doesn't have a place on our campus" (qtd. in Scott B1).

Although the example from James Madison University is the kind that more often attracts attention, both instances of trustee intervention can be equally threatening to quality education and the concept of academic freedom. Clearly, the impulses of the James Madison trustee threaten to abrogate students' rights to confront controversial knowledge and ignore faculty responsibilities to utilize their research and disciplinary expertise in the design of courses. Just as clearly, the writing of campus-corporate sector policy documents by trustees can also present problems. With only an imperfect understanding of faculty obligations to disseminate research results widely, to avoid conflicts of interest in the training and mentoring of graduate students, and to pursue free and open inquiry wherever it may lead, trustee policy-makers inevitably run the risk of turning the campus into a dependent research arm of the private sector and thus transforming campus-based knowledge creation into a profit-oriented activity *only*. In many areas, this would spell the end of basic research. Shared governance was instituted precisely to protect universities against such distortions of their mission.

Historian Joan Wallach Scott, a professor of social sciences in the Institute for Advanced Study at Princeton University, makes the point that "shared governance developed in the first decades of this century as a way to take into account the varied skills needed to run an institution of higher education: fiscal, administrative, and educational." Whether the method of selecting regents for public institutions was through "election or appointment by governors," she continues, boards were traditionally expected to protect the university "from partisan political interference"; and they were expected to respect the right of faculty members and administrators "to participate in decisions that affect them." In recent years, avers Scott, "boards of regents all over the country are bypassing established practices of governance," abdicating their traditional role and becoming "instead an agent of political intervention." When this occurs, renegade boards force faculty and administrators into an oppositional posture in order to "defend their right to participate in decisions that affect them" (Scott B1–B3).

The model of inclusive team decision-making that I have advocated here goes a long way toward strengthening such defenses when they are needed. The examples of California and Minnesota notwithstanding, few governing boards relish contravening policy decisions that have undergone deliberative consideration from a variety of constituencies and enjoy campus-wide support. In other words, even those boards that, as Scott describes them, "care little and know less about education" (Scott B1) tend to shy away from adversarial confrontations when students, staff, faculty, and administrators share an institutional vision and speak with one voice. Perhaps even more important, however, the inclusive team model invites the participation of board members in the deliberative process by which the campus is now governing itself. While the individual regents or trustees who participate in any inclusive team may bring essential expertise to the table, like the rest of the team, they will also have to acknowledge the expertise, concerns, and special perspectives of all the other team members. And if these trustees and regents can engage in the team process in good faith, there is hope that they can come to a fuller understanding of the complexities of running a modern research university. What trustees may come to learn, in other words, is that universities can certainly retool and be restructured where needed. But because of universities' primary commitments to educate students, serve the public, and seek new knowledge—all within the framework of academic freedom and open inquiry—they cannot, like a private business, easily be streamlined, simplify their operations, or precipitously shift funds from one area to another. At least they cannot do these things without seriously jeopardizing one or more of their missions.

As a former academic dean, however, I want regents—and even state legislators—to participate in campus-based decision-making teams, so that they can see, firsthand, the devastating consequences of the timing and nature of the fiscal decisions they impose on public universities. In order to manage change effectively, to innovate, and to plan cogently, administrators need to project their budgets for future years with reasonable accuracy. Unfortunately, too many regents and state legislators demand that universities employ the latest in corporate strategies for conserving and maximizing fiscal resources, while these same regents and legislators simultaneously withhold the crucial tool upon which they themselves depend in their own private business enterprises: firm funding expectations over the next several years. When I was dean, I sometimes didn't know what my budget might be from one semester to the next. And, like other administrators, I struggled to put in place innovative (even cost-saving) strategies, only to witness the next semester's rescission or the next year's lower enrollment derail the new project before the desired change could be effected. As I recall in my preface, this ended up wasting human resources and fiscal resources alike.

viii.

"I'm still in shock—one of my best students last semester
committed suicide. I had no idea she was having problems."
—Overheard in a faculty lounge.

I do not wish to leave the case in the negative, however. That
is, I don't want to conclude the argument for inclusive team decision-
making by recommending such teams merely as a defense mechanism against intrusive governing boards. Instead, I want to return to
my earlier point about the possibility of a campus converging around
common goals. Ask almost anyone employed on a campus—whether
a groundskeeper or a faculty member—and he or she will generally
agree that everyone's ultimate shared common goal is to help the students to succeed. How to go about doing that is not always in common
agreement. But it is my conviction that a campus habituated to team
approaches would solve one of the current major obstacles to student
success by breaking down the barriers between academic advising and
student services.

The development of sprawling high-enrollment public research universities—which nowadays train more than half of the college population—has contained costs for quality education while putting significant numbers of undergraduates into direct contact with cutting-edge
research. But it has also led to a situation in which more and more students fall too easily through larger and larger cracks. Especially at risk
are those who are the first in their families to go to college. These students often don't know where to turn when they get into trouble; and
there is rarely anyone watching when they do falter. At best, an academic adviser notices a cumulative pattern of low grades and informs
the student that he is no longer eligible to remain in his chosen major.
This kind of intervention is too little too late. And it allows for the
currently alarming dropout rate among talented minority students.

To redress this trend, the great divide between the academic side of
the house and what is euphemistically labeled "support" or "student
services" must be bridged. What I am calling for is not simply closer
cooperation, coordination, and information-sharing between faculty,
academic advisers, and student services personnel but a true partnership that links everyone in a single coherent effort. As everyone

readily admits, the most glaring problem on most public campuses today is student advising—whether that entails advising undergraduate majors, preparing graduate students to plan out their Ph.D. course of study, guiding students in financial aid applications, presenting career choices, or offering psychological counseling. The fact is that the student who is being advised on courses for her major is also tacitly being prepared for a certain set of career options. And the student who seeks advice on choosing a career inevitably translates what he hears into course selections. Analogously, the student who is labeled "at risk" because of poor grades generally is not at risk *only* academically: there are usually other factors—emotional, psychological, or financial.[7] A family member may be dying; or a student is exhausted from having to work 30 hours per week while going to school full-time. Poor grades are as often a signal that the student is undergoing some kind of personal stress as they are a signal that the student is academically unprepared.

In order to reverse spiraling student dropout rates, student advising must become a coordinated team effort. No one can expect the academic faculty adviser to have the expertise of a career counselor; and neither of them should be asked to do financial aid advising or psychological counseling. But while each adviser will not have the expertise of the others, they can all share certain kinds of joint- and cross-training in order to enhance their skills; together they can regularly review the status of the students assigned to them. Where appropriate—but only with the student's consent—someone from the advising team can alert professors that the student is experiencing some kind of serious problem; and reasonable accommodations can be sought. In this way, teams of advisers working together can move students through the system with a caring knowledge of the uniqueness of each individual and with a multiplicity of options for responding to any problems that arise.

The objection to implementing this proposal is that it will be impossibly labor-intensive and hence prohibitively expensive. The charge is an accurate one—but only at the beginning, when the retraining of advisers and the reassembling of advising activities take place. Once established and running smoothly, the team approach actually will allow larger numbers of students to move efficiently toward graduation in a more timely fashion because obstacles and risk areas are identified at an early stage, when solutions are less costly and have a greater impact. In terms of our shared societal investment, it is far more cost effective for a student to graduate than to delay completion of the degree or to drop out altogether.

ix.

> "These are ordinary, everyday folks in graduate
> school who . . . have the same kinds of interests
> and concerns as other workers."
> —A graduate student at the University of Michigan
> (qtd. in Schneider A14).

In making the case for an inclusive team ethos in everything from policy-making to student advising, I have neglected one emerging constituency: unions. Admittedly, college and university faculty have traditionally been reluctant to join unions out of a studied unwillingness to blur the boundaries between blue-collar wage earning and salaried professional status, combined with a view of themselves as a largely self-governing core within higher education. But at the end of the twentieth century, with intellectual and professional training transformed into just another marketable commodity (indistinguishable from the sale of physical labor), all that is changing. Medical doctors and college professors alike are looking at collective bargaining arrangements. While managed health care under the control of for-profit insurance megacorporations has driven doctors and nurses to join unions, analogous pressures are driving union activity on the nation's campuses.

To begin with, even once-relatively secure tenured and full-time faculty are getting nervous as administrators and governing boards dismantle tenure and tinker with other academic freedom protections. Salary scales have flattened, but class sizes continue to increase while the resources that aid instruction—like library book purchases and journal subscriptions, xeroxing budgets, secretarial help, audio-visual equipment, and even computer access—are disappearing or sorely limited. Research is also threatened as federal and foundation dollars dwindle, as more and more schools do away with sabbatical leaves, and

as governing boards and local politicians utter louder and louder statements about what kinds of research—and what subjects or creative
activities—they consider worthy of support. But even as these circumstances spur tenured full-time faculty to reconsider their habitual reluctance to unionize, the tenured full-time faculty do not make up the
movement's critical mass. At the moment, that critical mass is composed of nontenured part-timers and graduate student activists.

According to Ernst Benjamin, associate general secretary of the
American Association of University Professors, about 25 percent of
faculty in community colleges, four-year colleges, and universities
were part-time employees at the end of the 1970s. By the end of the
1980s, one-third of the nation's faculty members were employed part
time. And "in 1993, the last year for which he's seen figures, the number was officially 42 percent, but Benjamin thinks it's really closer to
45 percent or perhaps more" (see Tomasky 46). Exploited and underpaid, their employment always precarious, part-timers recognized the
strength in their growing numbers and were among the first faculty
actively to unionize. But they have not been alone. New York's SUNY
and CUNY systems are unionized, as are the California State system, the Washington and Oregon systems, and many community colleges. In 1996, faculty at the Carbondale campus of the University of
Southern Illinois voted to unionize, as did faculty at the University of
Alaska. As a result, about 40 percent of all faculty (part time and full
time) in public colleges and universities are unionized, with community colleges in the lead (see Tomasky 46).

Today's graduate students—the next generation to enter the professoriate—share little of their mentors' suspicion of unions. Especially
in the humanities and social sciences, graduate teaching assistants
justly complain that they are poorly paid for a twenty-hour week,
while they actually devote many more unpaid hours to teaching, preparing instructional materials, and meeting with students. When these
new Ph.D.s encounter a drastically downsized job market, part-time
and one-year temporary appointments at unlivable salary levels, and
classes overcrowded with students (even when they enjoy the rare
good fortune of a full-time tenure-track job), they have few compunc-
tions about seeing themselves as exploited labor. Across the country,
graduate assistants have organized around issues of salary and health

benefits (which few receive) and have asked for more reasonable teaching assignments.

In November 1996, a day-long conference at New York University, "Between Classes: A Conference on Academic Labor," brought together 250 students, professors, and union activists who, according to the *Chronicle of Higher Education*, planned "strategies for organizing in the face of what they called the 'corporatization' of the university" (Leatherman and Magner A12). In February 1997, thousands of graduate students on more than thirty campuses participated in a "National Day of Action," organizing "marches, picketing, rallies, and teach-ins . . . to underscore their demand for union representation"; and during the 1996–97 academic year, "graduate students at more than 20 universities . . . contacted the council of graduate-student unions, asking how to unionize" (Schneider, "Graduate Students," A13–A14). As a graduate student organizer at the University of Iowa commented, "One of the things we've realized is that we *are* workers. We share a lot in common with machine operators who over the past 10 years have been working harder for less pay—the same thing we're facing in academia now" (qtd. in Schneider, "Graduate Students," A14).

Clearly, what fuels this activism are the steadily deteriorating conditions of employment on most public campuses. But the flames are also being fanned by legislators and regents who make no effort to disguise their contempt for faculty and who loudly insist that, like their own private business operations, campuses must become "lean and mean." Indeed, it is the rare trustee nowadays who does not secretly believe that, given the reins, he could get his institution into competitive shape in months. Added to this is the fact that, as presidents and vice presidents in higher education attend to the escalating demands of boards of trustees engaged in micromanagement, the same trustees at whose pleasure they serve, it is the trustees—rather than faculty, staff, or students—who become their most influential constituency. Power thus shifts incrementally upward to the board, while faculty, staff, and students experience themselves "lagging a distant second or third as a presidential concern" (Lazerson 14). That sense of disempowerment inevitably translates into alienation, not only from the president and central administration but from the institution itself.

I have advocated inclusive teams—teams that include, among

others, faculty, staff, students, administrators, trustees, and even elected officials and community leaders, where appropriate—as one means toward stemming the alienation and allowing all constituencies to become, in effect, stakeholders. Together, they *own* the process, and they know they have to live together with the outcome. At least in part, the impetus for unionization has also been driven by faculty, staff, and graduate students' shared desire to gain an enhanced sense of control over their workplace and learning environment. As a former administrator, I am persuaded that, if they choose, unions could play a vital role in moderating the growing divides on the nation's campuses by actively supporting the radical transformation of the culture of decision-making that I've been describing in these pages.

Few administrators support the idea of unions. Signaling how little they any longer identify *with* or *as* faculty (out of whose ranks they usually come), the majority of senior administrators see themselves as informed managers who may share, but must never lose control of, decision-making to uninformed faculty and staff. Trustees often express this same attitude toward both faculty and administrators. But if more administrators would see the wisdom of inclusive team decision-making, then they might also see how useful unions could be in preparing faculty, staff, trustees, and students for their roles in that process. After all, with their national (and often international) resources and affiliations, unions are better equipped than are the administrators on a single campus to develop and maintain the kinds of training programs and informational databases that could help trustees, faculty, staff, and students to understand complex issues related to shared governance. For example, financial and strategic planning, budget management, and capital goods allocation are all areas in which faculty and staff vaguely know they have an interest; yet almost no faculty and staff today can claim sufficient acquaintance with these areas to offer useful advice. Trustees may claim more expertise in these areas, but only from the perspective of the private business or corporate world in which they work. And so, usually begrudgingly, they all allow administrators to take full responsibility, only to complain bitterly when administrative decisions have consequences that faculty and staff did not anticipate or trustees do not approve.

All this could change if unions worked collaboratively with the

staffs of boards of regents and with administrators to gather and disseminate the requisite information and if unions shared their considerable resources to cosponsor, with administration, local and regional forums and training seminars with experts brought in from all
over the country (or even the world). Surely this is the best way to
keep faculty, staff, and students prepared for inclusive team decision-
making. The burden on administrators to provide all the data and
devise appropriate training for each and every problem-solving team
would be lifted. Trustees, faculty, staff, and students would gradually
develop national and even global perspectives on what had once been
perceived as only local issues. Union leaders, trustees, and administrators alike could shed the enervating role of adversaries, and shared
governance might finally become a lived reality.

This is a very different role for unions, I admit. In the past, most
campus unions have concentrated on due process and academic freedom protections and on collective bargaining for wages and benefits.
All that must continue, of course. But to be viable in the twenty-first
century, unions on campus must do much more. They must become
full and knowledgeable partners in redesigning the campus for the
internationalization of higher education. They must acknowledge the
value of distance-learning opportunities for those who might otherwise be deprived of an education, but they must also work with fac
ulty and administration to ensure quality in such outreach and to
ensure the intellectual property rights of faculty who develop video
courses and computer programs. They must lobby for family-friendly
policies and extend their members' expertise in helping to implement
those policies. They must press for reasonable class sizes, teaching
loads consistent with quality education, chalk on the blackboards, and
colored markers on the whiteboards. In short, at every level, campus-
based unions in the next century must attend to the quality of life on
a campus as well as to the conditions of employment. Union leaders
must take responsibility for educating their membership to assume
the sometimes heavy burden of shared governance.

For their part, trustees and administrators should welcome the crucial services that unions can offer, especially in the arenas of public
relations and politics. Because unions have ready access to national
media, and the means to buy expensive airtime, they can become

another vehicle through which to give the general public the facts about higher education, thus countering the right wing's avalanche of distortions. The ability of unions to involve themselves in political campaigns in ways not open to administrators at most public institutions also enables unions to support the bids of proeducation candidates. In the twenty-first century, only those trustees and administrators trying to hold on to outmoded governance practices will waste precious resources in fighting unionization. A savvy administration and governing board will be seeking partnerships everywhere and inviting the unions in.

X.

"Don't expect anyone to say 'thank you.'"
—Advice from the provost who hired me as dean.

Finally, if the future I have sketched in these chapters is ever to become a reality, we need to address the most vexing problem currently facing academe. Not only are there fewer rewards for doing the jobs we already know, but—even more alarming—there are no reward systems for change and no incentives to be bold, visionary, or experimental. The problem is acute at public universities, on which state legislatures regularly impose bare-bones budgets but offer a campus no opportunity to respond creatively. Everyone *claims* that they want universities to move forward boldly. But, as yet, there are only threats of more budget cuts and increased micromanagement by legislatures and governing boards if change does not take place. In this atmosphere, academic leaders become more cautious—avoiding risks and risk-taking for fear of losing their jobs—while faculty and staff dig in their heels to protect the status quo. Everyone suffers, most especially the students.

Significant change *is* possible, but only if two conditions prevail. First, institutions of higher education require a breathing space in which to ascertain what will be required of them in the next century and a further period of budgetary stability in which to devise radically new mechanisms for visionary restructuring. Second, institutions willing to embark on this difficult process must be offered concrete incentives to begin and meaningful rewards for succeeding. The need for incentives and rewards cannot be overemphasized. If faculty, staff, and administrators are to participate in good faith, then they must be assured of positive rewards because, essentially, they are being asked to facilitate a set of coordinated activities across campus that may well redefine or even wholly eliminate their areas of traditional responsibility. Individuals can be expected to participate honestly in such a process only if they have confidence, from the outset, that their recommendations are to receive serious consideration. And, even more important, they must be reassured that the entire process is not simply a ruse for getting them to collaborate in eliminating their own employment. My experience as dean taught me that faculty and staff are capable of exercising great ingenuity and creativity in restructuring and consolidating services and programs—but only when they know that they will have a secure place in the new order of things, even if that place requires retraining, retooling, or even some reorientation of teaching and research areas.

If the quality of education is not to be sacrificed, the savings that can be realized in the near term from collaborative campus-wide restructuring fall mainly into the categories of better utilization of the physical plant and equipment; more efficient monitoring of equipment purchases and maintenance; better coordination of academic programs across departments and colleges to reduce redundancy or overlap; streamlining cooperation between academic programs and the various offices for student services; phasing out and redefining some positions as retirements and vacancies occur; and redefining selected jobs into flex-time or part-time positions. Several institutions can also begin to work together to share resources, either electronically or through other kinds of cooperative programs. Such savings can be considerable. Over the long term, moreover, these initial transitions can lay the foundation for more comprehensive moves toward intra- and intercampus interdisciplinarity; and some portion of the ongoing savings can be earmarked for reinvestment in a variety of curricular innovations and in incentives for continued restructuring. In order to make the restructuring process work, however, those responsible for making the changes must be guaranteed both continued employment and continued incentives. The will to make the needed changes, in other words, is dependent on the participants' sense of reward, empowerment, and security.

Tangible rewards are not all that hard to come by. Whether written or spoken, a few words of "thank you" from the president, the board of trustees, the legislature, or the governor can have significant impact. "A job well done" is a magic formula for ensuring that the job will be done even better in the future. It's no secret, after all, that people go the extra mile if they know it will benefit them in the end and that their efforts are meanwhile greeted with gratitude. But over time, words are emptied of meaning if they are not accompanied by concrete actions.

Ideally, faculty, staff, and administrative salaries should be maintained at competitive levels, with extra compensation for special merit, and bonuses for cost-saving innovations. But during periods of severe cutbacks, even small salary increments can act as positive reinforcements; so, too, salary incentives for curricular redesign, extra money for course development or research, a new copier for a department, additional funding to allow untenured faculty and graduate students to attend conferences, even refurbishing a faculty-staff lounge. What is paramount is some concrete and demonstrable expression of appreciation to let an individual or a group know that their efforts at restructuring have been noted.

Above all else, however, it must be made clear that, at some specified point, a portion of the realized savings will be plowed back into the institution's annual budget as a permanent add-on. Administrators and faculty must also have a reasonable expectation that, eventually, the institution will receive funding levels required to meet the challenges of the next century. As I argued in chapter 1, those challenges will be considerable—and quality education will not come cheap. But consider what we are purchasing with our education dollars, especially at research universities. Not only are the faculties of these universities providing us with better treatments for cancer, tools for redeeming our deteriorating environment, and a better understanding of our human condition; they also provide undergraduates with a unique learning opportunity. Professors who are at the cutting edge of research in their fields do more than just pass on to their students a settled body of knowledge. They engage their students in the knowledge that is *not* settled, sharing with undergraduates the processes by which new evidence is evaluated and accepted ideas reconsidered. As Adrienne Jamieson and Nelson Polsby—both of whom developed innovative interdisciplinary courses for undergraduates at the University of California at Berkeley—state the case, "undergraduates in a research setting can become privileged witnesses . . . to the formulation and reformulation of problems and to the data gathering, analysis, discussion, and criticism that takes place incident to the expansion of knowledge" (Jamieson and Polsby 226). In the twenty-first century, even more important than their amassing bodies of knowledge will be our citizens' abilities to embrace precisely these competencies. As "privileged witnesses" to "the expansion of knowledge" in action, the undergraduates trained at research universities in the next century will enjoy a decided advantage.

8 Failing the Future; or, How to Commit National
Suicide at the End of the Twentieth Century

"You can't escape the responsibility of
tomorrow by evading it today."
—Abraham Lincoln.

i.

On 19 April 1996, I flew back to Tucson, Arizona, from South
Carolina, where the day before I had delivered the Academic Convocation Address at the University of South Carolina's Aiken campus. The
one-year anniversary of the bombing of the Murrah Federal Building
in Oklahoma City, 19 April was an inauspicious day to fly. Passengers
and airline personnel spoke quietly of increased security measures,
and recorded warnings about unattended vehicles and luggage were
piped frequently into the airport waiting areas.

Not wanting to add to my habitual unease about flying, I settled
into my seat with a handful of outdated magazines snatched hastily
from an overhead bin. I would lose myself in old news stories and the
kind of reading I only have time for on airplanes or in doctors' and
dentists' offices. As I turned to an article boldly titled "Busting the Big
Blob," about "beat[ing] back the educrats," in the 8 April issue of *Newsweek* (Alter 40), I could feel the woman next to me looking over my
shoulder. "Why do they always blame the teachers?" she asked. A large
white-haired woman, she was now retired as a third-grade teacher in
the Middle West, but her only son had followed in her professional
footsteps and become a high school science teacher. She was clearly
proud of his choice and her own.

She had read the *Newsweek* article when it first came out, she told
me, and it made her angry. "That article calls us a 'wall' and an 'estab-
lishment' that resists change, but what kind of help did we ever get?"
She continued, sensing she had a willing listener. "When different

schools wanted to experiment with a new curriculum or find better ways to use teacher's aides, we were stopped by state regulations. That article blames us for poor test scores, but how often do we get small enough class sizes to work with students individually? Some years, in some schools, I didn't even have enough textbooks to go around; the kids had to share. That article calls for more teacher accountability, but when did we get any help in dealing with parents who don't seem to care if their children complete their homework or even come to school regularly?"

Following her husband's job changes, she had taught in both rural and urban school districts, some of them poor, some of them affluent. "One year, while I was teaching in the city, I moved to a school just a mile from my previous school—and what a difference!" she exclaimed. "It was like a different world. The classrooms were bright and cheery, the school grounds were lovely, we had all the latest textbooks, and there were ten computers just in my classroom. All the third-grade classes were capped at twenty-five, and for two years, I had only twenty-two students in my class *and* a teacher's aide to work with individuals or small groups. And, oh yes," she added, "when that school recruited me, they also offered me a salary increase." The school from which she had transferred, by contrast, had no computers and classes of forty or more. Funding for teacher's aides had been cut from that school district's budget. The textbooks were old and worn, and the ceiling paint was peeling. "That's what you see when you move from a poor school district to a rich one," she added.

Turbulence briefly interrupted our conversation, as my flight companion turned away and closed her eyes until we were through it. When she opened her eyes, she seemed to have remembered something important. "I hate to admit it," she said, "but I was a better teacher at the second school." What she meant by that, she explained, was that she had more time to give children the individual attention they needed, and she could make sure that no one fell behind. And because, with smaller class sizes, she was less exhausted at the end of the school day and took home fewer exercises to grade, she had more time to put together the weekly lesson plans and more energy to experiment with innovations and creative pedagogy. "Those children learned more, I think, because I had the time to make learning fun for them."

Then, musing over the children she had taught at different schools, she warmed to particular memories—of the child with the beautiful voice who turned reading assignments into songs, of third-grade holiday pageants that she and her students had written together, of successes she had enjoyed by introducing drawing into the arithmetic curriculum. The more she talked, the more I liked her. Teaching had been her life, and she had loved it.

I asked what she thought about various reforms that were being recommended by politicians and business leaders. She agreed that changes were overdue and that schools needed to become more rigorous in their expectations for promotion and graduation. She wanted more programs that involved parents in their children's education, and she was particularly enthusiastic about the possibilities of team-teaching and self-paced computer learning programs for basic math skills. But she feared that proposals for standardized testing would lead only to a bland homogenization of curriculum and textbooks—thereby thwarting teacher creativity—and that national standards would inevitably degenerate into minimum achievement standards. "If the textbooks are only geared to training kids for passing some national test," she complained, "then the chapters certainly won't deal with anything very complex; and kids may learn facts and dates, but they may not learn how to think and analyze. And, anyway," she added, "I'm partial to teaching children about their local area. I'm not sure that national testing would leave us room in the curriculum for projects on the Indian nations of the Midwest or on local environmental issues. And would the kids in Boston still learn about the Revolutionary War sites in their neighborhoods?" The use that would be made of the scores on standardized national achievement tests also concerned her. "You can just bet some politician will want to use low scores as an excuse for cutting funds, penalizing schools with poor test scores"—the very schools, she said, that needed the most help. "Talk to those of us who are in the trenches everyday. *We* know what's needed and what will make things better, at least in our own school."

The plane entered an extended area of turbulence, and all conversation subsided. Jolted as I was by the bumpiness, I was even more jolted by the conversation. The most common complaint that I hear from colleagues in higher education is that they routinely confront poorly prepared students who matriculate into colleges and universities from defective secondary school systems. As more and more college teaching thus becomes compensatory and remedial, professors complain of the "dumbing down" of the college classroom, and they bemoan the waste of their own training. Often enough, this woman and her son are blamed as the source of the problem: lazy or unimaginative public school teachers, accountable to no one. Yet this warm and articulate woman was telling me a very different story. She had been engaged, creative, devoted to her pupils. She believed teaching to be the most important job in the world, and she had encouraged her son to become a teacher too.

Although we tend to speak of our educational system as a series of fragments—daycare, preschool, primary school, middle and high school, with some form of higher education at the apex—in fact, education is a linked continuum, with student success (or failure) at one level presaging success (or failure) at the next. If we don't offer quality education at every level, then all subsequent levels suffer. The former third-grade teacher sitting next to me had reminded me of that fact profoundly. As I thought about what she said, I realized that I couldn't end a book on higher education without some consideration of the education that comes before. She and I are colleagues in a shared enterprise, after all.

Sadly, part of what we share is the struggle to provide quality education to students from very different communities at a time when funding for all levels of education is both inequitably distributed and quickly diminishing. The uneven funding of higher education has its analogue in the systems of funding that characterize most public primary and secondary school districts. When the woman on the plane described moving only a mile from one district into another—like entering a "different world"—she was describing a national pattern. As Howard Glickstein, who follows school finance issues, observed in 1995, "Pennsylvania's highest-spending district spends three times the amount of its poorest district—$9,504 per pupil compared with $3,148 per pupil. In Illinois, the disparity is even greater, with a per-pupil expenditure of $14,316 in the wealthiest district and $2,253 in the poorest district." To give such numbers concrete meaning, Glickstein cites Ohio where, "in 1990, there were school districts that could not afford to install indoor toilets or have running water in the buildings, while other districts had $1 million sports fields and Olympic-size swimming pools" (Glickstein 723, 724).

As with higher education, "federal assistance to elementary and secondary education," too, has been declining steadily; "adjusted for inflation," such assistance "was reduced by 12 percent" between 1980 and 1988 (Callan 8). This put an increased burden on state and local tax bases—but at precisely the time when those monies were also being called on to finance the ever-increasing costs of Medicaid, law enforcement, and the building of prisons. But the increased competition for state and county dollars does not explain the inequalities that Glickstein describes. The real problem, as he sees it, is that "local funds, derived almost exclusively from the real property tax, provide nearly one-half the revenue for elementary and secondary education in the nation as a whole." Glickstein explains the implications of that fact: "The amount that can be obtained through a property tax is a function of the tax rate employed and the value of the property taxed. Use of the property tax, therefore, subjects educational financing to the massive disparities in tax base that characterize local governments throughout the United States. Consequently, the richer a district, the less severely it need tax itself to raise funds. In other words, a person in a poor district must pay higher local taxes than a person in a rich district for the same or lower per-pupil expenditures." The disturbing inequity that results from this method of school financing, continues Glickstein, "is that variations in per-pupil expenditures among school districts tend to be inversely related to educational need. City students, with greater-than-average educational deficiencies, consistently have less money spent on their education and have higher pupil/teacher ratios than do their higher-income counterparts in the favored schools of suburbia" (Glickstein 722, 723). To be sure, larger expenditures do not always translate into significantly improved educational quality; but additional funding surely helps to secure more and better-trained teachers, smaller class sizes, up-to-date textbooks, computers, and maybe even a music or fine arts program. Thus my concern in earlier chapters with funding policies that are turning higher education into a "have" and "have not" system is deeply connected to my fear that most of our public primary and secondary schools are already irrevocably entrenched in such a system.

Admittedly, I am no expert on preschool and primary or secondary school educational issues, and so I offer here only random ruminations, pieces of a larger whole. I share what I have learned from my reading and from those who, like the woman on the airplane, took the time to try to educate me. I claim to offer neither a comprehensive overview of the problems nor any comprehensive set of solutions. Instead, I seek to make the problems palpable and to grasp at possible causes and connections.

As the products of overcrowded classes, poorly equipped schools, low teacher morale, and peer group attitudes that distrust excellence as subversive and creativity as un-American, too many young people are now graduating from (or dropping out of) high school without the skills needed to survive in a fluid and changing twenty-first-century workplace. As I flew home from South Carolina, it struck me that this fact was as disturbing as everything else transpiring on that particular 19 April.

ii.

My friend Marianna is a full professor of English at a public university in the rural south. She has lately begun to complain that she cannot afford to retire for another eight years, but she is already counting the days. Her litany of grievances is familiar. Due to severe budget cuts, faculty who leave or retire are not replaced, thus increasing the numbers of students taught each semester by the remaining faculty. With fewer faculty available, students have fewer courses from which to choose, and those courses are inevitably overenrolled and overcrowded. Some popular required courses for English majors can be scheduled only once every other year. Student frustration at this state of affairs occasionally boils over into disruptive classroom behavior. Even worse, says Marianna, the students are less well prepared for college-level work than they were a decade ago. Grading essays has become torture because, with the rarest exceptions, the undergraduates she now encounters can neither think clearly nor express themselves grammatically. Most don't even see this as a problem. And no matter how many office hours she adds to her day, Marianna knows she will never have enough time to give her students the kind of intensive individual attention they need.

Under the stress of increasing student numbers, poorly prepared students, and the disappearance of money for research, secretarial support, conference attendance, or even copying course materials, Marianna's colleagues have become fractious, their accustomed southern civility fraying jagged. Marianna dreads department meetings and avoids them when she can. And even though she's taken on large numbers of additional students, continued to serve on committees whenever asked, and still managed to publish a prize-winning book, she received only one 3 percent raise in the last seven years.

A gifted teacher, Marianna no longer finds the classroom satisfying enough to make up for shabby buildings, increasing class sizes, edgy colleagues, and a stagnant salary. The approach of each new school year brings on headaches and depression, which Marianna "treats" by scaling back her expectations for how much this year's crop of students will be willing to read and write.

In a recent letter, Marianna sent me a local newspaper article about a third-grade teacher in a neighboring township who threatened the school board with a one-woman walkout when her class size was doubled while the number of textbooks remained unchanged. Other teachers interviewed in the article complained of similar conditions throughout the school, citing increased stress levels among the teachers and unruly behavior among the children. Members of the school board, though sympathetic, insisted that they had no more money to disburse. "If I don't retire in time," Marianna wrote along the margins of the newspaper clipping, "those will be my students, and I will become that teacher."

In the same letter, ever more impatient to retire, Marianna tells me she has now taken to playing the lottery.

iii.

When I first told my cousin Jeffrey that I was finishing a book about the future of higher education in the twenty-first century, he laughed and asked if I were writing science fiction. Jeffrey teaches at a small alternative public high school in one of the poorest neighborhoods in New York City, and he works with teachers in surrounding areas on curriculum development. In the schools he now visits, there is nothing remarkable about "a second-grade class [held] on a stairway landing," a middle school science class conducted in a hallway, or a school administrator who, for lack of any other space, sets up his "office in a boys' lavatory" ("Students without Desks" 16). As the *New York Times* protested in 1995, "city schools are now so overcrowded that 1 out of every 11 students does not have a desk or chair. Gymnasiums, auditoriums, even closets have been converted to classrooms" ("Students without Desks" 16). These are not circumstances that prepare anyone for higher education, Jeffrey reminds me.

It is not only the physical circumstances that anger Jeffrey. In a school system that once gave the two of us the opportunity to participate in student-produced light opera productions in junior high and to study Latin in high school, it is the packed classrooms and the steady erosion of academic programs that most upset him. Not only in the poorest neighborhoods but all across the city, music and fine arts classes have been eliminated in many high schools and foreign language offerings pared to the bone. Only a few magnet schools can now offer the advanced science classes that he and I once enjoyed in seventh grade. The problems are particularly acute at schools like his, schools that try to serve the educational needs of children from chronically underserved communities. "To make up for everything else that's missing in their lives, these kids need small classes and individual attention," Jeffrey insists. "And they sure as hell shouldn't be getting the message that it's okay for them to go to school on a stairway landing!"

Long after it would do any good, he tells me, even the *New York Times* finally editorialized against the city's habit of repeatedly slashing the public school system's operating and capital budgets "to help balance the city budget" ("Students without Desks" 16). But the editorial was too little too late, says Jeffrey, because New York City expects public school enrollments to increase by 250,000 between 1996 and 2003. "And nobody has even begun to plan for the schools or the teachers that these students will need," he finishes.

From the vantage point of a high school teacher in the South Bronx, the future is not to be found in a book by me on higher education but, instead, in the dismal model of California, the national precursor for "a slow but dramatic decline" in the quality of public schools. "In the mid-1960's," according to James Sterngold of the *New York Times*, "California had the fifth-highest rate of spending per pupil in the country and an envied education system." Like the New York City schools that Jeffrey and I knew as children, this was a public school system that set national standards. Today, by contrast, after almost two decades of the tax revolt that began with Proposition 13, California "is 42d in spending; it has one of the highest school dropout rates in the country (only two states are worse)," and in 1994, "its fourth graders tied for last place in an educational assessment test that was given in 39 states" (Sterngold 3). As a billion well-trained and talented new workers enter the global workforce in Asia, Latin America, and Central Europe, too many American children are being educated for failure, Jeffrey believes.

My friends who teach secondary school in Tucson tell me the same thing. Echoing Jeffrey and the woman on the plane, they describe resource-rich school districts where student achievement is high, and they contrast these with the overcrowded classrooms and underpaid teachers in poorer districts, where student test scores remain low. When test scores are simply averaged statewide, without regard to the wide divergence in funding and quality from district to district, complain my Tucson friends, the results suggest that the public education system, as a whole, is failing. By way of example, an English teacher at a downtown middle school gave me the results of the 1991 International Assessment of Educational Progress (IAEP), in which participating countries tested nationally representative populations of nine- and thirteen-year-olds for achievement in a variety of subject areas. Except for reading levels among nine-year-olds, students from the United States were routinely outperformed. Comparisons of the mathematics skills of nine-year-olds showed that "students from Korea, Hungary, Taiwan, the former Soviet Union, and Israel all had average test scores that were significantly higher than those from the United States"; in the math assessment of thirteen-year-olds, Americans fared even worse: "15 nations tested nationally representative populations, [and] the average test scores of U.S. students were higher than only one country, Jordan" (Snyder and Hoffman 410). "If the American kids in that sample all came from the wealthy foothills school district," my friend assured me, "the results would have been very different."

Her point was compelling. In the well-funded, well-equipped school district, expectations for student achievement were high; the community thought well of its schools and its teachers; and parents actively participated in their children's learning. When such circumstances prevailed, students thrived, and American public schools were the best in the world. (Even the children bussed in to maintain "racial diversity" performed well in these schools, my friend emphasized.) But in her own chronically underfunded middle school—in the face of classes of forty-five students or more, with only ancient dog-eared textbooks to teach from, and working parents too exhausted or too poorly educated themselves to help with their children's homework—even dedicated teachers, like my friend, felt stretched to the limit, and it was difficult to maintain either enthusiasm or high expectations. At her school, the situation was exacerbated by the fact that fully one-quarter of the children enrolled at any given time had no permanent home address, and the school had no resources to reach out to—or even track— the homeless when they stopped attending. For my friend, this was the most wrenching frustration of all.

Sadly, the friend who supplied the IAEP test results has now left teaching. Exhausted by years of arguing for smaller class sizes, up-to-date textbooks—she despaired of ever seeing a computer in her classroom—and frustrated by the lack of support services for at-risk children and their families, she has resigned from a profession she once loved. In her opinion, public school teachers are asked to do the impossible: society expects them to compensate for poverty and inadequate social services, conduct science labs under leaky roofs, and patrol the hallways when everyone knows the students might be carrying weapons. "And then, to add insult to injury," she asserts, "every three years, when our contract expires, we have to fight for a lousy cost-of-living increase or a decent health plan."

My friend admits she's burned out, but that's not the only reason she's stopped teaching. The decision was also financial. She and her husband are both teachers, but they've calculated that even with their combined income they can't afford the costs if any of their three children chooses to go to college outside Arizona. So, in an attempt to protect their children and themselves from years of crushing debt in repaying large tuition loans, they have decided that her husband will continue to teach high school mathematics in the Tucson Unified School District while my friend takes courses to become a real estate agent.

Too many of my students at the University of Arizona have gotten the same message. Repeatedly, I hear bright young women and men tell me they'd love to become teachers in kindergarten, primary, middle, or high school (K–12), but they've rejected the idea because almost any other career path will offer them better working conditions and prove more lucrative. These students know all too well that the average annual salary of public elementary and secondary teachers, in 1994 constant dollars, barely inched up from $35,270 in 1973 to $36,495 in 1994; and they know that average salaries in Arizona always fall below the national averages (see the *Condition of Education, 1995* 410–11). Understandably, despite their real desire to teach, college students decide that they owe it to their own children to earn a better income.

The net result is that we drive away gifted young people from a profession that, "over the next 10 years, will need to hire more than two million new teachers" to handle expected enrollment increases (Nicklin A12).[1] Trip Gabriel reports that "Every year since 1989, according to the Census Bureau, there has been a bumper crop of more than four million births in the United States"; as his 1995 front page story in the *New York Times* noted, "the last time the birth rate climbed above four million was in the baby boom" (Gabriel 1). Instead of preparing the teachers needed to educate what Gabriel calls "a boomlet," however, we push college graduates into fields—like law, business, and engineering—that are already overcrowded. Without public policies that make teacher education and the profession of teaching more attractive, this is a form of "brain drain" that we will be unable to staunch. Therefore, while the case must be made that we cannot delay implementing more equitable formulas for funding the physical and academic infrastructure of K–12 public schools, just as pressing is the need to attract and retain the best and the brightest as teachers. From

Scandinavia to Japan, the other industrialized nations seem already to have figured this out; and we might consider some of their models.

We might, for example, want to position the U.S. Department of Education to function like the Japanese National Personnel Authority, which recommends standards for teachers' salaries.[2] In Japan, this has meant, as Stephen M. Barro has noted, "that the average [K–12] teacher's salary buys a significantly larger share of the nation's goods and services than does the average teacher's salary in the United States." With annual cost-of-living adjustments as well as adjustments for further educational attainment and years of service, moreover, "senior Japanese teachers enjoy a relative standard of living beyond the reach of equally senior teachers in the United States." As of 1986, the last year in which the U.S. Department of Education commissioned a comparative statistical analysis, "the relative economic status of Japanese and U.S. teachers" was strongly dependent on seniority: "At the outset, the Japanese teacher's salary is only slightly higher, relative to national per capita income or output, than that of the U.S. teacher. After 35 years of teaching, however, the Japanese teacher's relative advantage is in the range of 80 to 100 percent" (Barro 6, 7). In analyzing those same data, professor of education Willis D. Hawley noted that "the certainty of reaching a secure well above average income is a clear benefit of teaching not enjoyed by other Japanese white collar workers" (Hawley 3). Thus, as a profession, primary and secondary school teaching in Japan is not only respected and rewarded; it is also extremely attractive.[3]

If the U.S. Department of Education followed the lead of the Japanese National Personnel Authority in monitoring the wage levels of teachers relative to other workers in their geographical region with comparable levels of education and professional responsibility, Americans might finally be disabused of the delusion that public school teachers are wildly overpaid, and teachers might finally earn a decent wage. While it is true that in some states and in wealthier school districts teachers are appropriately compensated, the vast majority of teachers are not. In Tucson, for example, a middle school mathematics teacher of my acquaintance, with a master's degree in bilingual education, is earning three thousand dollars less each year than a friend's son who dropped out of college last year and now works as an assistant manager of a medium-sized discount department store. The bully pulpit of the U.S. Department of Education could surely help to advertise such inequities.

The motivating principle behind Japan's formula for funding education is also worth examining. Because they maintain modern, well-equipped K–12 facilities and attract (and keep) talented teachers through generous salary and pension packages, more so than is done in the United States, the Japanese invest at the front end of the educational process. In 1990–91, as a percentage of their total public expenditures, the Japanese devoted to the support of elementary and secondary schools eight times the amount allocated to higher education. In that same year, by contrast, the U.S. formula was closer to three-to-one.[4] To be sure, Japanese universities do not fund major scientific research laboratories on the same scale as their American counterparts; most do not have dormitories (a significant savings); and Ph.D. degrees are not required for faculty membership (thereby lowering the cost of wages). The two countries' different ratios thus make for an imperfect comparison.

I cite the Japanese funding ratio neither as a model nor as an argument for defunding higher education in order to increase expenditures for K–12. On the contrary, I am arguing for a national recommitment to increased funding for *all* levels of education. I introduce the Japanese formula not as a paradigm for ourselves, therefore, but, rather, to point out that if we spend the money required to ensure excellence in K–12, then the additional funding required to maintain excellence in higher education will be that much less. After all, given the diversity of learners and the wider array of social problems facing the U.S. educational system—especially when compared to the relative economic and cultural homogeneity of the Japanese school population—the different spending ratios ought to make us take a second look at our own formula. When we do, we may decide that our current formula is out of balance. And we may discover, further, that some of the public's anger at what are perceived to be the failures of large universities in providing undergraduate education may actually represent a displacement of an underlying anxiety that we have failed to provide adequate K–12 preparation first.

Let us remember that one of the major reasons for the rising costs of academic programs at colleges and universities today is the need to offer underprepared entering students training in skills and subjects that should have been mastered by the end of high school. But our K–12 public schools don't always have the resources they need to get the job done. When the Arizona Board of Regents voted in 1995 to raise entrance requirements for the state's three public universities, for example, public school districts across the state protested that they could not afford to hire the additional teachers for the newly mandated two years of foreign language instruction or the basic mathematics courses. Still, the requirements held, even though the state has yet to allocate any additional monies to meet them. This leaves some public high schools with only two bad choices: they can ignore the new university requirements entirely, or they can assign faculty with expertise in literature or physical education to pick up an additional class in French or math, subjects they have never been trained to teach. Either way, the students suffer.

When the talented graduates of underfunded school districts enter a university—as, against all odds, they often do—they find they need a year or more of compensatory coursework in key areas like English composition, mathematics, and foreign languages. Whether that coursework is provided by the university itself or by a local community college, it imposes an unnecessary additional financial burden on the post-secondary system, where instruction is generally more costly. And it delays the student from proceeding expeditiously toward fulfilling degree requirements. The more prudent model for allocating educational resources, therefore, would seem to be Japan's, investing in quality at the outset, where the payoff is greatest and the costs lower.

As I completed the last draft of this book, I telephoned my cousin in New York to tell him he'd become part of a new chapter on improving K–12 public education. "It'll never happen," he responded. "The population is aging, and less than 25 percent of potential voters have children in school. For most voters, education just isn't a priority anymore. Think about it," he continued: "Senior citizens on fixed or limited incomes can't afford higher taxes, and the wealthy leave the snow and cold to retire in Florida and Arizona. They don't feel any connection to the local schools, so why should they support them?

As far as they're concerned, they already paid their children's school taxes back home" (see Glickstein 726). My cousin caught me up short, but he went on, relentless. "Besides, Annette, in hopes of attracting a few more jobs to their area, state and local governments are competing to lure corporations and big businesses with huge tax breaks. That means even less tax revenue to help pay for the local schools. And don't forget how the executives and CEOs of those corporations are choosing to live nowadays. The power and wealth in this country are barricading themselves in the suburbs or in gated communities, and more and more of them are sending their kids to private schools. They're not interested in paying for the education of anybody else's kids. Our generation—maybe my daughter's—will see the last of the middle class." He paused, but only briefly. "And the middle class isn't feeling very generous, either. Wracked by downsizing, forced into overtime and work speed-ups, and anxious about how little time they have to spend with their kids, the middle class is full of exhausted people who are fast losing any sense of connection to those poorer than themselves. They resent taxes, they resent government, and they resent anyone telling them they have a responsibility for others. So, Annette, who's gonna spend money on public education in the twenty-first century?"

I protested, but he insisted that I was naive. "I hope your publisher is planning to market your book as science fiction," he said again before hanging up.

iv.

Struggling all these years to find funding for his alternative school, my cousin has turned cynical, I tell myself. I don't want to accept his vision of corporate greed and a society so fractured that we would condone vast inequalities in educational opportunity. I don't want to believe that any group, especially the affluent, could see it as in their self-interest to continue accumulating private wealth while public schools are permitted to deteriorate. I don't want to contemplate the disappearance of high-quality education that allowed my maternal grandparents, who immigrated to this country as penniless teenagers from Eastern Europe, to become "Americans" and to educate their own children into proud citizenship and middle class stability. I want to reject Jeffrey's scenarios of class and generational warfare.

But I can't. I live in Arizona, where the wealthiest voters from the most expensive retirement communities routinely block bond issues for new schools and vote down every tax initiative for education. I live in a state that prides itself on its tax incentives for corporations and businesses, even though the state's three tax-supported universities and an educated workforce are part of what attracts these profit-making enterprises in the first place. If, as former secretary of labor Robert Reich estimates, "the overall corporate share of local property tax revenues declined 'from 45% in 1957 to around 16%' in 1990" (Berliner and Biddle, The Manufactured Crisis, *85), the corporations and big businesses in Arizona have managed even to surpass the national averages in evading their civic responsibilities.*

When I read the Letters column of the March 1996 Desert Leaf, *my neighborhood's monthly tabloid of local news and advertising, I heard my cousin's voice all over again. The lead letter was from Clifford Altfeld, a member of the Catalina Foothills School District board. In Altfeld's view, school board members face so "hostile" an "attitude to public education" that he felt compelled to publish an "S.O.S.", hoping someone would care that "issues like academic achievement . . . and even small class sizes, have been totally lost in the fray" (Altfeld 3). What occasioned Altfeld's letter was the school board's recent "meeting on school financing with state legislators." Exposing what he termed "'open season' on students," Altfeld used his letter to report on the meeting in Phoenix:*

- *There will be a $200 million property tax cut, the benefits of which will go primarily to commercial and industrial property owners, not homeowners. This will make it much more difficult to pass school bonds. [In Arizona, property taxes on private homes provide the major source for school financing.]*
- *Teachers are considered freeloaders "feeding at the public trough."*
- *There will be no inflation funding for the next two years. We asked how to explain to school principals that we cannot cover*

the increased cost of paper and how to explain to teachers that they will not be getting increased pay for greater experience or the cost of living. The head of an education committee laughed and answered, "That's why we created school boards."

• Arizona ranks 45th in expenditures per student in the U.S. But, according to one senator, "If the state keeps on trying, we can get to 50 in no time." (Altfeld 3)

When I quote this letter to friends in other states, at first they don't believe me. It couldn't be that bad, they want to say. But then they share anecdotes from their own area, and the similarities are inescapable. It *is* that bad, and it's getting to be this bad everywhere.

v.

Of the five provosts to whom I reported during my years as dean, one responded to insupportable state budget cuts by telling faculty that mathematics was more central to the university's mission than classics. At another meeting, he recommended eliminating all foreign language requirements because, in his view, the important people in the rest of the world speak English. I walked away from such pronouncements appalled at the provost's ignorance and chilled by his jingoistic arrogance.

My distress derived not simply from the fact that, as dean of the College of Humanities, I saw that it was departments and programs in my college that this man was targeting for downsizing or termination. Even more powerful was my sense of frustration that this man could not grasp the intrinsic linkages within a liberal arts education. If a basic understanding of mathematics is central to undergraduate education, went my reasoning, then so too must be some understanding of the ancient world that gave rise to Euclidean geometry or some grasp of the intellectual ferment of post-Renaissance western Europe in which René Descartes invented coordinates to express geometrical relations in algebraic form. The various branches of mathematics, after all, have historical and cultural roots. It was also inconceivable to me that this man could not understand how fluency in the language, literature, and arts of another culture represented a doorway to understanding more about the human condition. And, at the most

practical level, such fluency is the mark of respect that clinches busi-
ness deals and trading partnerships with those from other countries.

But it's unfair to single out this particular administrator. Under the
stress of successive budget cuts, almost every vice president in central
administration was looking to find some academic program expend-
able. The fine arts were said to be too labor intensive—too many paint-
ing and music instructors for too few students—and, at one point, a
president even suggested doing away with the marching band.

My profound resistance to central administration's easy willingness
to gut our liberal arts programs as cost-saving measures came not just
from my position as dean, however, or from my commitment to cross-
disciplinary learning. It dates back to what I had come to take for
granted as requisite to any educational experience during my years
at Erasmus Hall High School in Brooklyn. On that elm-shaded en-
closed campus, an entire world of learning had opened up for me—
from physics to classics to glee club. And, somehow, there were always
connections.

So now, to make certain that nostalgia has not exaggerated how
much we were offered, I browse through the Arch *of 1958, my senior*
class yearbook. Instead of exaggeration, I find many more clubs, many
more extracurricular activities, and even more academic programs
than I had remembered. I am reminded that "the Classics Depart-
ment has for some time been publishing Orbis Latinus, *a prize win-*
ning magazine dealing with the whole body of Roman civilization." I
am reminded of required courses in art history and electives in paint-
ing. I remember devouring all of Don Quixote, *unexpurgated, in the*
original Spanish. And following the pages of pictures of the Boys' Glee
Club, the women's Cantata singers, and the Choral Club, I read about
"the instrumental side," the band and the orchestra. "Music has been
and will continue to be a fundamental part of life at Erasmus Hall,"
predicts the 1958 yearbook. "Is it ever possible to walk across campus
without some strain of music reaching after you, beckoning you to
join in the song?" (Arch 23, 38).

Unfortunately, not everyone had been invited through the school's
arched entryway to join in that song. The yearbook faces that still
look so familiar to me are overwhelmingly white and mostly Jewish,
even though the neighborhoods around the school were far more eth-

nically and religiously diverse. But in the Brooklyn of the 1950s that I knew, most of our Irish and Italian Catholic neighbors sent their sons and daughters to parochial schools, while the few remaining wealthy WASP families in the area enrolled their children in private schools in Manhattan. Of course, I had classmates with Greek, Italian, Irish, Scotch, Dutch, Armenian, and Hispanic surnames; and the faculty was very mixed. Still, the feel of Erasmus Hall was middle-class Jewish, although the actual socioeconomic compass of the student body was far more varied. Among my closest friends were those who lived in public housing projects and whose families received public assistance. My school friends—both Jewish and non-Jewish—included the sons and daughters of small shopkeepers, doctors and lawyers, successful clothing manufacturers and poor tailors, Holocaust survivors, recent immigrants, and working-class parents like the sales clerk from the local five-and-dime and the man who drove the Good Humor truck. If anything, social class and economic diversity was the diversity that marked us.

Almost wholly absent are black faces. Yet I remember solidly middle-class and working-class African-American enclaves within walking distance of Erasmus Hall. Some of their children, I was aware, attended local church schools. But the vast majority found themselves outside Erasmus Hall's district boundaries and were assigned by the Board of Education to other high schools. My nostalgia shrinks before the recognition that, while we were not rigidly segregated by economic class and ethnicity, my high school classmates and I certainly had been segregated by race. My nostalgia altogether disappears before the suspicion that the high schools attended by our African-American neighbors may not have offered the same academic opportunities as did Erasmus Hall. Those were the years, after all, when "separate but equal" really meant only separate.

As a society, we continue to pay a high price for the racially segregated and inherently unequal K–12 education of the past. But we now continue equally disastrous patterns through school funding policies that segregate the children of property-rich districts into well-maintained schools with relatively low teacher-student ratios, while the children of property-poor districts, in the main, are segregated into poorly equipped schools with too few teachers and crowded classes.

In certain urban areas, where Native Americans, Hispanic Americans, Asian Americans, and African Americans are disproportionately overrepresented in poorer school districts, the school funding patterns effectively reinscribe what had once been racial segregation by policy. As a result, in the intricate cross-hatching of race and economic status that marks the new educational apartheid, we sow even more ominous seeds for the future. Education, this society's most dependable equalizer, is about to be rationed, with those most in need receiving the least.

The rationing will not stop with high school but will extend to higher education, too. The young men and women who enter college from school systems too poor to afford programs in classics, physics, music, fine arts, and the like, will force universities to offer those subjects in ever more introductory and elementary versions—if the students enroll in them at all. The more probable outcome is that students in college will shy away from areas of knowledge that had been unavailable to them throughout K–12. For their part, in efforts at further cost-savings, universities will be tempted to close down departments that represent disciplines in which students are unprepared to study, citing falling enrollments as their rationale. The net result is that certain fields of study—if they survive at all—will devolve into isolated graduate school specialties. And, except at those colleges and universities with the wealth to maintain broad-based undergraduate liberal arts offerings, students will encounter progressively impoverished educational choices as they enter higher education. Higher education, in other words, will mirror the shrinking artistic and intellectual possibilities of the K–12 systems from which its students matriculate. This could mean that, with the beginning of the next century, an institution like the University of Arizona, one of the nation's top ten public research universities, might find itself unable to provide undergraduates with an education as comprehensive and as rigorous as did my fondly remembered neighborhood high school.

Still, while K–12 schools (except for those in the wealthiest districts) are forced to dismantle anything beyond "reading, writing, and 'rithmetic" as a mere "frill," I stubbornly hold on to the memory of a high school that offered physics and classics courses, even to children from public housing projects. And I want to weep as I read the dedication page of the Arch. *In 1958, the yearbook was dedicated "to the Erasmus Hall of tomorrow," in bright confidence that "the Erasmus Hall of ten, twenty or fifty years from now will surely deserve the title 'great,' and will deserve it in even more fields of endeavor than our present-day school"* (Arch 5). *I wish I could believe that we had been prophetic.*[5]

vi.

Although it is not the popularly received image of the 1950s, more often than we imagine women in two-parent, solidly middle-class households were full-time wage earners, working outside the home. My mother was one. While I was still in grade school, she took the Civil Service examination and was assigned to the Brooklyn Naval Yard as a claims investigator, tracking the paper trail of lost inventory. She didn't particularly like the job, nor did she ever think of it as a career, but, as my father's progressive heart disease forced him to limit his dental practice, my mother's salary increasingly represented our family's financial security.

I was in the fourth grade when my mother started working, but I remained barely aware that our home situation was different from that of most of my friends. The only major change was that now my father came to fetch me when I got sick at school. The rest of my life went on as it had before: my mother helped my two sisters and me dress, and she made breakfast for us every weekday morning, leaving for work just before we left for school. By the time I returned at the end of the day, my father had dinner started, and my mother was already in the kitchen, preparing to put food on the table. Because Brooklyn's P.S. 139 had a full complement of after-school activities—all of it free and supervised by school personnel—my school day had been expanded to accommodate my mother's employment. To my delight, my parents signed me up for twice-weekly oil painting classes as well as weekly sessions in folk music and folk dancing. Rarely did any of the children in these programs leave the school grounds before 5 P.M. Junior high and high school offered even richer after-school choices—math club, debate society, and Erasmus Hall High School's celebrated mixed chorus. My parents never had to contemplate the prospect of "latch key" children, letting themselves into an empty apartment.

Today, with "thirty-two percent of all men between 23 and 34 years of age earn[ing] less than the amount necessary to keep a family of four above the poverty line" (Thurow 11), even married women who would prefer to remain at home—like my mother—are forced into the labor market. *Workforce 2000*, a report by the Hudson Institute, predicts that by the year 2000, women will make up 48 percent of the workforce. A mother who works full time outside the home is no longer an anomaly. What *has* changed is that, in poor, working-class, and middle-class families, the children have no place to go after school. Only private schools and the wealthiest public school districts can any longer afford the array of after-school activities that my sisters and I took for granted; and, for most working women, the costs of private childcare are prohibitive. As a result, with both parents putting in longer work hours (overtime is now commonplace) and with most public schools curtailing extra-curricular programs, after three o'clock each weekday the nation's children are effectively abandoned by both their parents and the schools. Lester Thurow, an economist at the Massachusetts Institute of Technology, estimates that "parents are spending 40 percent less time with their children than they did 30 years ago," and he notes that "more than two million children under the age of 13 have no adult supervision either before or after school" (Thurow 11).

This situation exists not because parents or schools *want* to abandon their children. The situation exists, first, because the massive entry of women into the labor pool has produced no commensurate adjustment in either the private or the public sector that accommodates the responsibilities of working parents. For the most part, men and women still inhabit a workplace designed around a single (male) wage-earner with a nonearning spouse at home. Second, the situation exists because the federal government is increasingly shifting the costs of social programs onto the states even as both state and federal governments seek tax cuts. The result is states with insufficient revenues to adequately support mandatory societal obligations—like basic K–12 education.

In terms of increased rates of family stress, juvenile crime, gang membership, and drug abuse, the human costs of this situation are staggering. But employers know that there is also a toll in the workplace. I saw it firsthand during my years as dean. With a large office staff that included several mothers of preschool- and school-age children, I encouraged flex-time schedules to accommodate their needs. But even flexible work hours could not compensate for the lack of a larger societal support system. Ad hoc childcare arrangements would fall through at the last minute when a neighbor became ill or a play-mate's mother suddenly canceled; or a father was transferred to a later shift, so he could no longer watch the children after school. The con-sequences were predictable: repeated absences, disrupted workdays, a gnawing anxiety that robbed a secretary of her ability to concentrate on the job at hand, and, on several occasions, the office full of small children as I described in chapter 5. Had I ever totaled the hours of compromised concentration and lost worktime, I could have added to a growing body of evidence that worker productivity in this coun-try has been limited, at least in part, by the lack of quality afford-able preschool child care and free after-school activities. Writing about the decline of American affluence, Jeff Madrick has even suggested that in order "to increase the productivity of the work force, govern-ment can . . . support high-quality day care to help working parents" (Madrick 17).

It is a timely suggestion, but it doesn't go far enough. Madrick should have suggested, as well, that worker productivity in this coun-try could be increased dramatically if government would support qual-ity educational facilities at *all* levels, *beginning* with "high-quality day care to help working parents." After all, we need to attend both to today's workers and to tomorrow's.

In order to do that adequately, we need to keep reminding ourselves that education is a continuum, a set of linked developmental processes that begins in infancy. Preschool child care—like the highly success-ful, federally funded Head Start Program—prepares young children for the learning environment of kindergarten and first grade, just as high school lays the foundation for success (or failure) in college, voca-tional school, or on-the-job training. After-school activities—whether sports, a poetry club, or the school orchestra—reinforce what has been learned in the classroom, promote additional learning, and contribute both to social skills and to personal development. When any compo-nent of the continuum is not of high quality, or is not available, suc-cess at all following stages is jeopardized—including success in the workplace.

It is conventional wisdom among economists that investment in education fosters economic growth (see Bradsher 6). Thurow's remedy for the nation's "falling real wages" is "major public and private investments in research and development and in creating skilled workers to insure that tomorrow's high-wage, brain-power industries generate much of their employment in the United States" (Thurow 11). In 1995 Treasury Secretary Robert E. Rubin made much the same point when he told the *New York Times* that the best response to "the long, slow fall in the nation's median wage . . . lies in maintaining spending on education to produce skilled workers who can compete in the global economy" (Bradsher 6).

But both in terms of real dollars and in terms of percentages, support for all levels of education has gone into apparently permanent decline. In 1970, 20.3 percent of the government's total expenditures went to education, but by 1991 only 18.3 percent was spent on education (Snyder and Hoffman 429, table 400). Translated into real dollars, adjusted for inflation, and with rising transportation costs, expanded school lunch programs, and the costs of accommodating growing numbers of disabled and special-needs students factored in, there is no money left to equip a modern high school chemistry lab, purchase computers and educational software, or raise teachers' salaries. That 2 percent loss is severe. No wonder academic programs have been cut, buildings deteriorate, and after-school activities are eliminated.

In the face of such crises, affluent school districts periodically turn to voters for budget overrides or special bond issues that allow purchase of the latest computer equipment and fund salaries for new teachers. Classes in these few privileged districts remain small, and extracurricular programs offer everything from astronomy club to soccer. The residents of less privileged districts, by contrast, already burdened with higher tax rates than the property-rich districts, are unable to afford additional property taxes to pay for computers or new teachers. Their children's classrooms remain packed, textbooks are out of date and in short supply, teachers burn out, and after-school activities include a sports team or two, at best. Given the fact that there is a demonstrable expansion of the education and skills required for most jobs, even at entry level, how will these children compete in the job market? Where is their level playing field?

The fact is, in pursuit of the dubious goal of rapidly shrinking the federal deficit, while simultaneously providing tax breaks for the top 1 percent of income earners, we are shredding an already fragile social safety net and defunding public education at the very moment that the United States boasts "the most unequal distribution of income in the advanced world" (Madrick 14). According to financial journalist Simon Head, the vast majority of American workers have seen their family income, adjusted for inflation, decline steadily since the early 1970s, with "average weekly earnings, . . . again adjusted for inflation, [falling] by 18 percent between 1973 and 1995." "By contrast," Head goes on to note, "between 1979 and 1989 the real annual pay of corporate chief executives increased by 19 percent, and by 66 percent after taxes." The situation was so alarming that even a fiscal conservative like Alan Greenspan, chair of the Federal Reserve Board, "warned Congress in July 1995 that the growing inequality of income in the United States could become 'a major threat to our society'" (Head 47). That same year, a study released by a nonprofit research institute in Luxembourg found the income gap between poor families with children and affluent families with children to be far greater in the United States than in any other country studied. Sadly, the Luxembourg Income Study "found poor children in the United States to be poorer than the children in 15 other western industrialized nations" (Bradsher 6).

In 1996, on the eve of Stand for Children Day, the June 1st rally in Washington, D.C., the National Priorities Project reported even more dismal statistics. "21.8 percent of children in the United States—15.3 million—live in poverty, three to five times the rate of Western European nations. . . . 10 million children have no health insurance. . . . [And] the United States ranks . . . lowest in preschool/daycare attendance among the fifteen major industrial nations" ("State of the Children" 7). Instead of trying to ameliorate these socially destabilizing conditions by providing quality education to all segments of the population and by offering health insurance, childcare, and comprehensive intervention services to families in crisis, current public policy is increasingly punishing the poor and making quality education available only to those few who can already afford it. Everyone else's children can be warehoused, undereducated, or altogether neglected. If a democracy wanted to commit national suicide, we have certainly found the formula.

vii.

Traditionally, higher education has shouldered the major responsibility for teacher preparation, especially at institutions with Departments or Colleges of Education. In the next century, that role will have to be significantly expanded. College of Education faculty will continue to work with K–12 faculty on developing improved curricula and enhanced pedagogical techniques and, no less important, together the two groups will continue to develop standards for quality instructional materials and guidelines for appropriate class size and reasonable teacher workloads. More so than they do now, however, organized groups of education faculty and K–12 teachers must also find more effective ways of alerting legislators and the general public to the social toll of inequitable school financing policies, deteriorating physical facilities, outdated textbooks, overcrowded classrooms, and burned-out teachers. They need to make clear, for example, the real savings in social service expenditures during the 1970s and early 1980s, when the educational gap between white and black students declined by almost half and the gap between white and Latino students narrowed by almost a third. At the same time, they need to warn about the growing potential for massive social instability since 1992, as "the achievement gap has begun to widen again" (Haycock 14). In other words, K–12 teachers and the professoriate must see themselves not only as educators and as researchers but, in alliance with parents and school boards, as advocates for public policy formation.

During a period when it has become fashionable (if foolhardy) to think only in terms of cost-cutting and downsizing, this will be a difficult role to play. Public policy advocacy requires an honest assessment of the real costs involved in repairing and improving our public schools. At the moment, the general public has little understanding of just how far we have fallen behind. When the U.S. General Accounting Office (GAO) released its 1995 report, "School Facilities: Condition of America's Schools"—"the first study in 30 years detailing the physical condition of America's schools"—few paid attention, despite the massive problems cited. In addition to the thousands of school buildings that had simply reached the end of their life spans, the report listed items like "collapsing ceilings, fire-code violations, exposed electrical wires, and ventilation problems that make the air quality in some school buildings as bad as it is in industrial warehouses"; GAO officials estimated the price tag for improvement at $112 billion ("Education Vital Signs 1995" A22). That same year, an independent private sector survey determined that the public schools were not yet uniformly providing students with access to the latest technology and estimated that "it will cost the nation about $31.5 billion . . . to bring schools up to speed" ("Education Vital Signs 1995" A14).

Unfortunately, having accepted the comforting claim popularized during the Reagan and Bush presidencies that the United States already outspends the rest of the world for education, most Americans are unprepared for the real costs of providing high-quality K–12 instruction to all of the nation's children. But, as David C. Berliner and Bruce J. Biddle argue in their 1995 study, *The Manufactured Crisis*, "when it comes to primary and secondary education, the United States actually spends *less* than the *average* industrialized nation." Using a variety of statistical indicators, Berliner and Biddle demonstrate that "in 1988, the United States ranked only *ninth* among sixteen industrialized nations in per-pupil expenditures for grades K through 12"; and "in the late 1980s twelve other nations found ways to spend more of their Gross Domestic Product on schooling than we did" (Berliner and Biddle, *The Manufactured Crisis* 67, 69). Based on yet another set of economic measures, the latest available comparative international figures from the U.S. Department of Education indicate that out of the twenty-two nations listed, in 1991–92, the United States distributed less of its public expenditures on education to K–12 than did Japan, Norway, Portugal, and Switzerland; expressed as a percentage of the gross domestic product, Canada and the United Kingdom both "expended a larger fraction than the United States for 1st–12th grade education" in 1991–92 (*The Condition of Education, 1995* 152). While different economic measures yield slightly different rankings, in toto they do appear to confirm Berliner and Biddle's contention that "regardless of the technique used to compare educational expenditures for primary and secondary schools, the United States *never* comes out first" (Berliner and Biddle, *The Manufactured Crisis*, 69).

For those who believe otherwise—and who argue, thereby, that no additional funding is required—this will be a bitter pill to swallow; and those who advocate improving our schools will have a difficult time convincing a recalcitrant public of just how much national effort is really required. There are specific places to begin, however, and four initiatives immediately suggest themselves. Indeed, without these initiatives, little else can be accomplished.

1. *Redesign state funding formulas so as to minimize differences in per-pupil expenditures across school districts and create incentives to attract the best-trained and most experienced teachers to underserved and impoverished communities.* Because the economies of the fifty states vary so widely, no single funding formula for education will serve. Some states may develop mechanisms for the redistribution of property tax revenues, while others may opt for establishing special trust funds for education. The federal government could create incentives for such redistribution by offering additional federal aid dollars or by altogether conditioning existing aid monies upon states' efforts to reduce inequalities. Whatever the means, the object should be to raise all schools to the same levels of excellence enjoyed by the wealthiest and most successful districts in the state. Any suggestion that the better school districts will be "leveled down"—either in terms of resources or in terms of educational quality—in order to transfer money to poorer districts will be opposed by powerful and influential voting interests; and progress will be stalled.

While equalizing per-pupil expenditures across school districts should do away with gross disparities in teachers' salaries across a state, more may be required to attract the best teachers to where they are most needed. The fact that some schools and school districts carry the baggage of years of underfunding may make it difficult for them to hire the teachers they want, once funding becomes available. To overcome this obstacle, states should consider developing a menu of incentives to lure teachers to these districts—incentives like salary bonuses or tuition waivers for pursuing a postgraduate degree—as part of their K–12 funding formula.

But even if more equitable policies for school financing were put in place by the states and even if the federal government provided resources to help the states bring all their schools up to reasonable standards for safety and access to technology, there would still be a need for additional funding for those schools serving students from impoverished backgrounds where family and community do not (or cannot) provide, as David C. Berliner and Bruce J. Biddle note, the "levels of home support for education that middle- and upper-class families can provide." In order to ensure more than modest gains in the achievement levels of students from poor and previously underfunded school districts, funding equity will have to be supplemented by additional funding for nontraditional programs—like special tutoring for SAT and ACT examinations (now standard in most well-funded school districts), counseling, guidance, adult mentorship arrangements, or even field trips to college and university campuses. While no one has estimated how much this would cost, some supplemental funding is crucial, according to Berliner and Biddle, "if America is to realize its long-cherished goal of providing equal opportunity for all students through public education" (Berliner and Biddle 1995, 289–92).

2. *Assess the vast array of K–12 reform projects that have proliferated since the 1980s.* The past fifteen years have witnessed an unprecedented climate of innovation and experimentation in K–12 education. Acknowledging that they were in crisis, K–12 providers experimented with interdisciplinary curricula and pedagogical innovations from team-teaching to interactive computer-assisted instruction. School districts across the country tried organizational restructuring, privatization, alternative schools, magnet schools, charter schools, and a variety of partnerships with local universities, business groups, arts organizations, and corporate leaders. In some neighborhoods, parents were brought into the classroom as colearners, alongside their children; in other neighborhoods, parents were given educational materials to use with their children in the home. What we do not yet have is a comprehensive overview of all this activity and a report card on its successes and failures.

To get beyond what Arthur E. Levine, president of Teachers College at Columbia University in New York City, characterizes as "anecdote and advocacy," departments and colleges of education must take the lead in providing "solid research on how the various experiments . . . actually work" (Levine 4) and what they cost. Not only must we know what succeeded, but we must know under what conditions it succeeded—and whether it might be applicable elsewhere. A foreign language unit that works well in a rural area with a relatively homogeneous student body, for example, might not transfer to an urban school district with students from varied cultural and linguistic backgrounds. Thus, we also need to study the failures and disappointments and the specific situations in which some of these experiments faltered.

Once assessments like these can be made, they become part of the curriculum for teaching current and future K–12 educators "which experiments are the most promising and the methods by which they can be most effectively introduced" (Levine 4). Additionally, the assessment report card becomes a centerpiece for policy activism among educators. If written in accessible language, with clear budget charts, the assessment of over fifteen years of innovation and experimentation can help inform legislators, school boards, parents, and the general public of the need to institutionalize successes where they occurred and to initiate innovations where they are needed and where, demonstrably, they can work.

3. *Develop an infrastructure that educates K–12 teachers about new discoveries in their disciplines, in inter- and cross-disciplinary approaches, and in the emergence of wholly new disciplines and subject areas.* The surest way to improve student achievement across the educational spectrum is to improve teacher preparation. This means making it possible for K–12 teachers to remain enthusiastic learners throughout their careers by involving them in the design of programs that will facilitate the constant upgrading of their teaching skills and help them to gain an enhanced mastery of their subject area and related disciplines.

To date, according to Kati Haycock, director of the Education Trust at the American Association for Higher Education, school districts and universities have recognized these needs by sponsoring evening courses and weekend seminars that update teachers on disciplinary advances as well as "the broad range of instructional strategies necessary to succeed with the variety of learners in today's classrooms." A few states and school districts also offer marginal incentives—like small pay raises or assignment to more advanced classes—in order to encourage K–12 teachers to enroll in an occasional graduate seminar at the local university. The problem, Haycock contends, is that "these vehicles don't serve nearly the number of teachers who need them," and "they are often neither intense enough nor sufficiently connected to the school setting to result in enduring changes in classroom practice" (Haycock 16).

The solution is a more focused formal partnership between the colleges and universities and the various school districts in an area—but a partnership in which the K–12 teachers carry the major responsibility for designating what kinds of courses and retraining will be most valuable to them at any given time. In order to maximize resources and reach the largest number of participants, computer-assisted instruction and distance learning might be combined with face-to-face classroom teaching. Whatever the delivery formula, however, the goal is to develop ongoing conveniently scheduled courses designed by teams consisting of university professors and K–12 educators. In addition to pedagogical emphases, such courses would offer intensive overviews of recent research in a discipline and material on related emerging disciplines. Crucial to the success of such programs will be significant incentives (including substantial salary increases) that reward K–12 teachers for rethinking classroom practices and incorporating new disciplinary directions. School districts must give teachers both the flexibility to alter curriculum as well as realistic support structures (like modest funding for new classroom materials) that ensure the continuity of these efforts. The current ad hoc nature of most professional development opportunities for K–12 teachers will thus be replaced by a formalized infrastructure that they themselves help to shape.

4. *Utilize the considerable research on early childhood physical and mental development to design programs for the training of professionals in preschool child care and to set minimum national standards for all infant and early childhood care facilities.* Our current lack of systematic safeguards allows standards for childcare to vary from state to state and even from county to county; and in many places, there are

no standards whatever. A few fortunate workers enjoy quality subsidized child care in the workplace; but unlike most other industrialized nations, the United States has not made this a general practice. The wealthy can afford live-in "nannies" or a quality private preschool. And a tiny fraction of the working and nonworking poor can sometimes enroll their toddlers and preschoolers in early education programs targeted specifically for disadvantaged children and their families. But, for the most part, middle-class and working-class families are left to fend for themselves, along with the poor.

Because we can no longer ignore or merely warehouse the preschool children of working parents, and because we can no longer afford the lost concentration of working parents who worry daily that their children are not well cared for, this dismal situation requires immediate action. A wealth of research on preschool programs for poor and disadvantaged children has demonstrated that, with good nutrition and carefully designed strategies for both physical and intellectual stimulation—often accompanied by educational resources for parents—these children gain in test-measured IQ, learning abilities, physical dexterity, and social skills. The successes of these programs, combined with our more general understanding of early childhood development, ought to spur high schools and colleges to introduce specialized training programs for preschool child care workers. Such programs would train these workers to interact with their young charges in a manner that stimulates all aspects of development—physical, intellectual, and social. Preschool child care workers would also be taught how to help parents further these efforts in the home. Whether they are caregivers for infants, or toddlers or preschoolers, these staffers would be well trained in pediatric first aid, rescue breathing, sanitation, and the prevention and detection of early signs of contagious disease. And, in every facility, the staff member in charge of food service would be trained in the nutritional requirements of early childhood and in the food intolerances of different ethnic and cultural groups. (The children of Native Americans, for example, are often lactose intolerant and require something other than cow's milk.) In other words, like K–12 teachers, preschool child care workers must also be appropriately educated, licensed, supervised, and regularly retrained. And, of course, they will have to be appropriately paid.

In her 1996 book, *It Takes a Village,* Hillary Rodham Clinton cites the French system as one training model that Americans might want to adapt. In order to qualify for employment in government-subsidized child care centers, "preschool teachers and directors have the equivalent of a master's degree in early-childhood and elementary education. Infant-toddler educators have a degree that is roughly equivalent to two years of college in the United States, as well as a two-year professional course in early-childhood education and development." In France, even home providers of day care are licensed, with licensing setting quality and sanitation standards but also ensuring "employee benefits, regular mailings of up-to-date information from the government, and periodic visits from a specially trained pediatric nurse" (Clinton 221–22). As Rodham Clinton further points out, this combination of professional training and professional salaries results in quality care in which parents have confidence. And it eliminates the high turnover of low-wage workers that characterizes so many of the child care centers in the United States (Clinton 233).

Given the persuasive data on the social and educational benefits of quality early child care, the government and the private sector should find it in their common interest to forge a partnership supportive of these initiatives. With that commitment in place, child psychologists and early childhood specialists in a variety of disciplines could then begin to recommend minimum national standards for nutrition, safety, and physical facilities. And they could recommend guidelines for the training of preschool child care workers, publish sample workbooks for play-and-learning activities, and even create take-home resources for stressed and overworked parents.

The point here is that there is no lack of information about how to help preschoolers—whatever their background—develop to their fullest potential. We already know how to design and implement comprehensive early childhood education programs for many different kinds of learning needs and for a variety of populations. What we have lacked is the national will to put our considerable expertise to use. As the twentieth century draws to a close, we have witnessed a frightening lesson from that lack of will. As psychiatrist Robert Coles reminds us, "children who go unheeded are children who are going to turn on the world that neglected them" (qtd. in Clinton 109). We should not have to learn that lesson again in the next century.

viii.

I am not so myopic as to suggest that a subsidized national child care network and greater investment in public K–12 education will, by themselves, solve the nation's social ills or mitigate the economic dislocations of the new global information age. But it must surely be clear that we have more to fear from generations of neglected children and from diminished access to quality education than we do from reasonable levels of national debt or higher taxes.[6] If we want to increase both the rate of growth in the economy and the rates of worker productivity, we simply cannot keep cutting the funding for all levels of public education; nor can we continue to ignore child care and supervised after-school activities as if they were not intrinsic to the entire educational enterprise. Most economists agree that it is the *lack* of opportunity to develop appropriate social skills and the *lack* of access to education and technical training that prevent people from contributing to economic growth.

Writing, as I must, from the perspective of a university faculty member, I cannot understand the nation's stupefied passivity before the fact of undereducated children at one end of the educational spectrum accompanied by escalating rates of functional illiteracy and proliferating expensive remediation at the other. Fully one-third of all college freshmen now enroll in remedial courses—mostly in math and English—and two-thirds of all four-year colleges and universities are forced to expend their slender resources on such courses. It is a terrible waste of the costly training and educational riches that every Ph.D. college professor represents. And it is often a deeply humiliating experience for the students who genuinely thought they had qualified for college-level work. In too many cases, these are enormously talented students from poor and racially diverse neighborhoods. But the shock of their unpreparedness saps their confidence and drives them away. Given the nation's changing demographics and the fact that these so-called minority students are the majority of tomorrow's workforce, these are the students we can least afford to lose.[7]

The rest of the developed world no longer looks at the United States with envy, but, instead, with astonishment. When a friend of mine who is a sociologist gave a series of lectures in Sweden recently, his audience could not believe his scenarios of impoverished and illiterate teenage mothers who could not read to their children. "Don't you have public agencies that help those mothers and children?" he kept being asked. "Wouldn't the government provide helpers to read to the children and teach the mothers?" When Hillary Rodham Clinton spoke with political leaders in France—"from Socialists to Conservatives"—one after another asked her the same question: "How can you not invest in children and expect to have a healthy country?" (Clinton 222–23). To make it through the next century as "a healthy country," this is the most important question we will have to face. And if we face it honestly, then we will understand that renewed investment in public education—from infant care through the university degree—must be part of the answer.

A Closing Refrain: Reflections at a Graduation

"If education is restricted or becomes the exclusive province of
the few, then education will cease to be a leveling or enabling
force. It will become an instrument of power in its worst sense:
power over others. Education for the few will lead to authori-
tarianism as well as to the exclusion and the marginalization of
those who are different or lack privilege."
—Arturo Madrid, "Less Is Not More . . . in the Case of Education,"
Brooklyn College commencement address, 4 June 1997.

i.

On 4 June 1997, at its seventy-second commencement exercises, my undergraduate alma mater, Brooklyn College (now a part of
the City University of New York), honored me with a Distinguished
Alumna Medal. As I sat on the dais and looked out at the assembled
graduates and their guests, I remembered my own graduation on
another sunny afternoon in this same tree-lined quadrangle thirty-
five years before. Much had changed in the intervening decades, but
one thing had not. The campus itself had changed remarkably, now
crowded with more buildings to accommodate a larger student body.
And the students themselves were more boisterous than my own
graduating class. These students enthusiastically cheered the faculty
who marched in the academic procession; they applauded and shouted
their approval of various speakers' remarks; and, in marked contrast to
the polite seriousness with which the class of 1962 greeted the conferring of degrees, the class of 1997 shouted with unabashed glee and let
go helium balloons that floated out over Boylan and Ingersoll Halls.

What had not changed was who these students were. To be sure,
the Brooklyn College class of 1997 was not, like the class of 1962,
overwhelmingly white and predominantly Jewish. Instead, these new
graduates were far more racially and ethnically diverse. Here were children of immigrants from the Middle East, Russia, and the Caribbean,

as well as African Americans, Asian Americans, and Latinos, whose families had moved from Cuba or Puerto Rico. Beneath the academic robes I caught glimpses of chadors and dashikis, and under the mortarboards young men were wearing yarmulkes and crocheted skull caps, sikh turbans and Middle-Eastern head wraps. As an Art Department professor remarked, "In them, you see the whole broad spectrum of the youth of our city" (qtd. in Horowitz 233). But because these students came from families of modest means, they were—like most in my own class—those for whom a college education was possible only because of the financial accessibility of Brooklyn College. In my day, tuition had been free. Everyone I knew had to work during the summers; but not everyone worked during the regular school year, and when they did, it was always part time. It was not so easy for these graduates. Since the imposition of tuition in 1976, increasing tuition fees have forced many more Brooklyn College students to work part or even full time throughout their college years. Still, the tuition remains low enough to make a college degree feasible. And that's what struck me as I choked with gratitude during the morning's ceremony: for those able to take advantage of the opportunity, Brooklyn College was still opening doors that would otherwise have remained closed.[1]

At the formal luncheon that followed graduation, I, like the other honorees, was asked to say a few words. As I walked to the microphone, memories flooded back. In the 1950s, the families of modest means in my neighborhood invested, when they could afford it, in the education of their sons. The only reason that many of the smart, talented women in my graduating class had been able to go to college was because it was free, and we all lived at home. Under no other circumstances could poor and immigrant families have contemplated educating their daughters, no matter how much they might have wanted to.

As though the chance for a college education weren't a sufficient gift, Brooklyn College offered its students something even more precious in the stolid and conservative 1950s. Unlike most coeducational colleges and universities of that era, this municipal public institution employed brilliant and dedicated women professors and, in a few select departments, lots of them. Perhaps that's why I was so drawn to English and classics. In those departments especially, I encountered welcome relief from the Ozzie and Harriet role models that the society was everywhere foisting upon me. For even though many of my class-mates came from families—like mine—in which both parents worked outside the home, nonetheless the society around us seemed to sug-gest that a woman's proper role was always and only in the home. In the popular television series that everyone watched, Harriet Nelson portrayed herself as the serene mistress of a suburban California ranch house, never hinting at her real life as an entertainment producer and busy actress. If we girls had to work, our parents told us, it was only to be temporary, to help our future husbands finish school or estab-lish themselves in business; then, like Harriet Nelson, we too could retreat to a well-furnished ranch house with a manicured front lawn. But at Brooklyn College male and female students alike learned that women could enjoy an intellectual life and manage a professional career. Remembering all the powerful women professors from whom I had taken courses, I realized again at that graduation luncheon how liberating, how exhilarating, the years at Brooklyn College had been for me. And for so many others.

Like its tuition-free counterparts—City College and Hunter College in Manhattan and Queens College in Queens—Brooklyn College had been conceived amid a very different public discourse about educa-tion than the one we know now. On 4 March 1933, just two years before the ground-breaking for a new, permanent campus for the col-lege,[2] President Franklin Delano Roosevelt had been forced to declare a four-day bank "holiday." Even so, when New York mayor Fiorello La-Guardia spoke at the ground-breaking ceremonies for the new Brook-lyn College campus in October of 1935, he referred neither to eco-nomic depression nor to cultural decline. Instead, this campus was being constructed amid a deliberative public conversation that en-trusted the nation's future prosperity to the education of its young. Even in the throes of the catastrophic Great Depression, New York-ers—with grants and low-interest loans from the federal government—had chosen to invest in a college education for the children of immi-grants and the working poor. The president of the Brooklyn Board of Aldermen told those assembled for the ground-breaking that he fore-saw in the "free city colleges . . . a splendid educational system which will make better citizens" ("Brooklyn College Started" 27). Two years later, when the campus officially opened its doors to students, another speaker told a throng of 7,000 that the role of this college was one of "complementing democracy. Our democracy is based on an educated citizenry who dare to doubt, to ask questions, to think independently" (qtd. in Horowitz 43). The public conversation was one of opportunity, courage, personal growth and social responsibility.[3]

So sustaining was that conversation that, without apology or equivocation, William S. Boylan, the college's first president, boasted in a *New York Times* article of how "beautiful" this new campus would be. In 1935, with the nation still in the grip of economic depression, Boylan apparently felt no need to defend the fact that "a beautiful college in the heart of a large city is nearing realization." Appealing to civic pride, he detailed the architectural style ("Georgian in spirit, touched by a feeling of Greek revival") and described "a spacious campus with shaded walks." Even if this was "an institution devoted to the free higher education of the citizens of New York," and even if most of the citizens who attended would come from immigrant families and families of modest means, nonetheless Boylan saw it as a mark of merit that "as much attention has been paid to appearance as to utility." Engaged as he was in a public conversation that honored the value of accessible higher education in a democracy, Boylan could assume that the majority of his readers would want the new college to have "a body befitting its spirit" (Boylan 15).

ii.

Unfortunately, except as a piece of nostalgia, the public conversation about higher education that built my alma mater no longer has resonance. Other conversations have replaced it. Since the 1980s, the conversation *on campus* has been about declining resources and the need to protect quality education, while *off campus* the conversation has focused on rising costs. In more recent years, the second conversation has drowned out the first. Weekly magazines and the network news all announce the staggering tuition fees of a few elite private institutions as though these represented some kind of national norm. There is little mention of the fact that the vast majority of students at expensive colleges and universities receive financial aid from their schools. And there is even less mention of the fact that only 8 percent of undergraduates pay more than $12,000 a year in tuition and that over 60 percent of all undergraduates at four-year colleges and universities pay less than $3,000 a year in tuition. The best-kept secret of all is that at public universities, the average tuition nationwide in 1997 was $3,363 for state residents and $9,495 for nonresidents. At the University of Arizona, for example, during the 1996–97 academic year, Arizona residents were charged $2,009 in tuition, and nonresidents paid $8,378. And, again, many of these students—resident and nonresident alike—received loans and scholarship assistance from the university. At Brooklyn College today, 90 percent of the students receive some form of financial aid.

Still, even with aid, for many students, the costs of higher education are burdensome. Those from families too poor to afford the luxury of debt cannot take on even low interest education loans and are forced to work at least part time throughout their undergraduate years. And because of family necessities, too many students try to work full time while carrying a full academic courseload.

The general response to the hard realities of qualified students who cannot afford to enroll in a four-year college or university has not included any groundswell of support for a national need-based scholarship program or even significant tax credits for families with children in school. And there certainly has been no voice for the tuition-free education that enabled my father, the son of impoverished immigrants, to attend City College in New York and that enabled me, after my father's early death, to attend Brooklyn College. Instead, the din of conversation in the public media has tended to allow the private elite schools to cater to those students who can afford them while insisting that a college education for the rest of us be purchased at a much lower price. To get to that lower price, we are told, dormitories at public institutions should be spartan, with few amenities; libraries should be pared of frills like comfortable reading rooms and expensive journal subscriptions; and support for athletic programs, playing fields, and extracurricular activities should be cut severely. And, to limit instructional costs, media pundits argue for a significant decrease in the size of the faculty, insisting that the remaining professors teach four or five courses each semester and eschew research or creative work. Wherever possible, moreover, live faculty are to be replaced by computer programs and videotaped lectures. In short, education for the children of those who are not affluent, according to sources like *U.S. News and World Report,* is to be absolutely "bare-bones," with no resemblance to Boylan's image of a campus that combines both beauty and utility (see Lemann 47).

What those who carry on this side of the conversation won't admit is that they themselves would never want to attend such a school; nor would they choose to send their children there. Indeed, those who argue for a stripped-down, bare-bones education for the masses are rarely those who share the financial constraints of the masses.

When faculty on campus hear this side of the conversation, they cringe. Faculty know that efforts to downsize and drastically increase teaching loads only end up shortchanging those students who most need personalized attention and individual tutoring. A faculty limited in size is also a faculty limited in the subject areas it can cover. Students are thus shortchanged again, confined to ever more circumscribed choices of courses and majors. And to reduce faculty hiring at this particular moment inevitably means curtailing the professional opportunities of available women and minority Ph.D.s. In the face of an exploding student population that includes increasing numbers of minorities, a downsized faculty offers fewer guides and role models for undergraduates who need a sense of their own possibilities. These students will not share my experience of having discovered in college women who, by their own example, opened up new worlds for me. Finally, to divorce faculty research and creative work from the teaching enterprise, most educators agree, deprives the majority of students from sharing in the risk-taking, critical thinking that makes new knowledge possible. Students privileged to attend colleges and universities with research and creative faculty will continue to participate, first hand, in the myriad engagements of intellectual and artistic discovery; but all the rest, the overwhelming majority of students, will encounter only received wisdom.

Worst of all, faculty recognize this side of the conversation as a scenario for turning the pursuit of knowledge at public institutions into something cramped, uninspiring, and uncelebrated. And the best of us know that, under conditions like these, we would not have entered the professoriate in the first place. To borrow a phrase from Lesley Stahl, let's "get real." When it is done well, college and university teaching is one of the most demanding jobs in the world, requiring professors to think hard about perplexing problems, to keep up with and to contribute new knowledge to their fields, as well as to act as guides, mentors, intellectual gadflies, and sometimes as friends or surrogate parents for their students. Given the multiple responsibilities laid upon us, most of us do our jobs for relatively modest remuneration. In 1997, the average first-year salary of a graduate of the New York University law school—a three-year degree—was $85,000. Most of my full professor colleagues in the fine arts, social sciences, and humanities disciplines, with a Ph.D. that took at least six years to complete and a lifetime of dedicated teaching and sustained research, will consider themselves lucky to *retire* at such a salary.

However immediately compelling, neither media-hyped quick fixes for the rising costs of higher education nor anxiety-laden faculty responses—in other words, neither side of the current conversation—moves us into the next century. Hence my purpose in this book has been to try to shift the conversation from the fruitless and ultimately frustrating discourse of decline and defeat and, in its place, offer another set of questions altogether. As I observed earlier, a 1930s-style conversation about the necessity of free higher education as a tool for educating citizens in a democracy may enjoy only residual resonance at the end of the 1990s. But whether we like it or not, the twenty-first century will force us to reexamine how higher education can help to sustain a democracy when its citizenry is becoming more and more ethnically, culturally, and racially diverse with every passing year. The twenty-first century will also find us asking how colleges and universities can better educate citizens to protect a democracy with a strong Bill of Rights, a tradition of civil liberties, and a relatively recent commitment to women's equality and to civil rights for all—a democracy, however, that must survive in a global economy where such values are not universally shared. And in lieu of sustaining higher education as essentially a tool for "complementing democracy," the urgency in the year 2000 will be to determine how higher education can help to eliminate the increasingly destructive extremes of wealth and poverty that threaten democracy at its very core.

If I have succeeded in my aims, then the conversation about failing K–12 public schools, underprepared college freshmen, and minority student drop-out rates will situate those issues in the context of decaying inner cities, joblessness, and inequitable school-funding formulas. The conversation about K–12 student achievement will begin and end not with an attack on unresponsive teachers or an appeal for national standards but with an appreciation of cognitive diversity, the need for quality affordable childcare and after-school programs, and the upgraded training and remuneration of teachers at all levels. When the conversation focuses exclusively on higher education, hasty recommendations for the abolition of tenure will be supplanted by a considered discussion of how best to protect academic freedom for the increasingly diversified communities of scholars now earning Ph.D.s and entering the professoriate. The design of campus physical facilities in the next century will encompass a conversation about emerging technologies, of course, but also a conversation about changing family structures and the appropriate responses of higher education to those new realities. And in place of a discourse of decline, I have tried to remind readers that we are now the heirs of the peace dividend that followed upon the end of the Cold War as well as the beneficiaries of the healthy tax revenues of a newly robust economy that has marked the Clinton presidency. If we will put off further tax cuts for the rich, we can begin the reinvestment in higher education that will allow colleges and universities to accommodate increasing numbers of students from a radically different demographic base and, at the same time, retool for the interdisciplinarity and global focus that will be required in the twenty-first century. In sum, I have tried to offer a language of schooling that honors difference, diversity, risk-taking, imagination, and social responsibility. And I have tried to be scrupulously honest in offering an account of change that acknowledges its difficulty, its ambiguity, its inevitable blunders, but also its necessity, exhilaration, and promise.

With her pronounced Yiddish inflection, my grandmother used to tell me that a good conversation was one in which everybody talked. But a great conversation was one in which some participants also listened. In putting together this book, I have tried to listen hard to students and colleagues and put their voices, as well as my own, into these chapters. Now I can only hope that someone else is also listening.

Appendix 1. University of Arizona College of Humanities Promotion and Tenure Procedures

The specific qualifications required for tenure and/or promotion are discussed in full in the departmental promotion and tenure documents and in the College of Humanities (COH) Promotion and Tenure "Criteria" document. What follows here pertains only to the "Procedures" to be followed in conducting tenure and/or promotion reviews.

Immediately upon assuming their duties, all newly-hired tenured or tenure-eligible faculty members, regardless of rank, will receive from their respective department heads copies of three sets of promotion and tenure materials:

    1. The promotion and tenure guidelines adopted by their respective departments.

    2. The COH Promotion and Tenure "Criteria Document," together with the COH Promotion and Tenure "Procedures Document," and the COH Promotion and Tenure "Timetable."

    3. All relevant University promotion and tenure documents.

Department heads will also provide copies of these promotion and tenure documents, where appropriate, to all candidates for hire into tenured or tenurable positions.

College of Humanities Promotion and Tenure Procedures

I. Appointment of Committees.

The procedures to be followed in the College of Humanities (COH) for the constitution of promotion and tenure committees must conform to those regulations which, by regental authority, are binding upon the University as a whole. We therefore note the following governing paragraphs from the *University Handbook for Appointed Personnel (UHAP)*, First Edition, 1988 (3.11.01):

"Standing Committees

Provided there are sufficient faculty members in a department to warrant such a committee, each college and department shall have a standing committee on faculty status to advise the Dean and Department Head before recommendations are forwarded to higher administrative levels concerning all faculty personnel matters. Each committee shall be composed of at least three tenured members of the faculty.

In promotion to tenure matters, the committees shall be so constituted that recommendations shall be made only by faculty members holding rank superior to the rank of the candidate being considered, except in the case of full professors where the committee members shall each be a full professor. Normally standing committees shall meet without the administrator whom they advise."

A. The College of Humanities Promotion and Tenure Committee (a.k.a., "the Dean's Committee").

1. Each year the Dean will appoint a COH Promotion and Tenure Committee and will name its Chairperson. The committee will be charged to act in the best interest of the College of Humanities as a whole.

2. The Dean will make appointments to the COH Promotion and Tenure Committee in such a way as to ensure compliance with the equitable gender and minority representation requirements of Federal and State antidiscrimination laws and with ABOR and University policies and rules against discrimination. No one who is otherwise qualified shall be barred from service on promotion and tenure committees on the basis of religion, race, color, national origin, physical disability, or sexual orientation.

3. The committee will consist of no fewer than six members. Four of those members will be from four different departments of the College of Humanities; two will be from departments or programs in other faculties or colleges. Appointments will be for one or two years.

4. The Dean will appoint to this committee only faculty members who have met the current criteria by which the candidates under consideration are being judged. Members of the committee from units other than COH shall be those who have met the current criteria for promotion to Full or Associate Professor in their respective fields. In accordance with the Provost's guidelines, Associate Professors may serve when there is no candidate for promotion to the rank of Full Professor.

5. The committee will be presented with a detailed statement of the University's affirmative action policies and guidelines, which will be explained by a representative of the Affirmative Action Office. Also, it will be explained to the whole committee at their first meeting that, should there arise in the course of deliberation any questions regarding race, gender or other sorts of bias, then, at the request of one or more members, the committee will consult with a representative of the University's Affirmative Action Office for advice and guidance in such matters.

6. In any given year, it is likely that the committee will include members from departments that are presenting candidates. It is therefore stipulated that a committee

member may not participate in discussions concerning candidates from his or her own department, that he or she must leave the room during such discussions, and that he or she must abstain from voting on those cases.

7. The membership of this committee will be considered public information, and the Dean will announce the names of its members at the beginning of each academic year.

8. Faculty under review for possible promotion and tenure are to have no direct or indirect contact with the committee or its members regarding their own cases.

9. At each stage in the review process every candidate is to be promptly informed of the recommendations (including any minority reports) made regarding her or his tenure and/or promotion, in order that her or his response may go forward to the next level with the recommendation. Therefore, before the Dean's recommendation concerning a candidate is sent to the Provost, the candidate will be furnished with a complete and verbatim copy of that same recommendation. The candidate will also be provided at this time with a copy of the COH committee's report to the Dean, which shall include a record of the committee's numerical vote. However, the votes of particular members of the committee, as well as their individual judgments and comments, shall be kept confidential. Moreover, any quotations from external reviewers included in the Dean's recommendation or the committee's report shall be referred to as having been made by "Reviewer A," "Reviewer B," "Reviewer C," etc. Each candidate will indicate that she or he has received and read these documents by signing a copy of each and returning it to the Dean's office, along with any comment or reply she or he may wish to make. At this point the file will be forwarded to the next level.

B. Departmental Promotion and Tenure Committees.

Membership on Standing or *ad hoc* departmental promotion and tenure committees is by appointment. In each department, it is the Department Head who appoints the members of that department's promotion and tenure committee, after thorough consultation with the department faculty. However, a Department Head's discretion in this matter is subject to the following constraints.

1. In accordance with UHAP regulations, a Standing departmental promotion and tenure committee "shall be composed of at least three tenured faculty members."

2. Department Heads will make their appointments to the promotion and tenure committees in such a way as to ensure compliance with University affirmative action and non-discrimination guidelines and policy. To this end, whenever feasible and appropriate, Department Heads may appoint to their committees tenured faculty from other departments and programs who are qualified to evaluate the candidates' work. No one who is otherwise qualified shall be barred from service on promotion and tenure committees on the basis of religion, race, color, national origin, physical disability, or sexual orientation.

3. Whenever possible, the departmental promotion and tenure committee will include at least one member with expertise in the candidate's particular field. The

committee should also include as many members as possible conversant with the candidate's general area of specialization.

4. The committee will be presented with a detailed statement of the University's affirmative action policies and guidelines, which will be explained by a representative of the Affirmative Action Office. Also, it will be explained to the whole committee at their first meeting that, should there arise in the course of deliberation any questions regarding race, gender or other sorts of bias, then, at the request of one or more members, the committee will consult with a representative of the University's Affirmative Action Office for advice and guidance in such matters.

5. Each candidate, in consultation with the head, will compile a list of five University of Arizona faculty members with the rank and expertise necessary to evaluate the candidate. The list may include former or present members of the departmental standing promotion and tenure committee. The Department Head will select from this list two persons who, if they are not already members of the standing promotion committee, will join it as *ad hoc* members to participate in discussion of, and to vote upon, that particular candidate's case. Appointment of such additional, *ad hoc* members is also subject to the qualifications listed immediately above (B.1, B.2, & B.3).

6. Whenever the department's workload so demands, a Department Head may appoint more than one promotion and tenure committee.

7. Members of the promotion and tenure committee are not permitted to discuss the candidate's evaluation with her/him, unless the committee as a whole should formally request such a discussion. Any such request on the part of a committee must be communicated to the candidate through the Department Head. Likewise, any questions the candidate may have regarding the committee's procedures must also be directed to the Department Head.

8. At each stage in the review process every candidate is to be informed, promptly, of the recommendations (including any minority reports) made regarding her or his tenure and/or promotion, in order that her or his response may go forward to the next level with the recommendation. Therefore, before the Department Head's recommendation concerning a candidate is sent to the Dean, the candidate too will be furnished with a complete and verbatim copy of that same recommendation. The candidate will also be provided at this time with a copy of the departmental committee's report to the Department Head, which shall include a record of the committee's numerical vote. However, the votes of particular members of the committee, as well as their individual judgments and comments, shall be kept confidential. Moreover, any remarks from external reviewers quoted in the Department Head's recommendation or in the departmental committee's report shall be referred to as having been made by "Reviewer A," "Reviewer B," "Reviewer C," etc. Each candidate will indicate that she or he has received and read these documents by signing a copy of each and returning it to the Department Head, along with any comment or reply she or he may wish to make. At this point the file will be forwarded to the next level.

II. Preparing the Promotion and Tenure File.

(Note: The following procedures are to be understood as subordinate to and governed by the procedures outlined in the document issued every spring by the Provost's Office (hereinafter referred to as the current Provost's Guidelines), which deals with continuing status and promotion process and preparation of dossiers. This document, which must be studied carefully by all involved in the promotion and tenure process, is subject to change. Changes that it may undergo in the future may necessitate changes in COH procedures and thus may require alteration of the directions given below.)

A. Identification and Notification of Candidates.

By March 1 of each year Department Heads will write to all members of their departments who are eligible for tenure and/or promotion, inviting candidates for mandatory or optional review to submit their candidacies to the Department Head and the Chairperson of the departmental promotion and tenure committee. (For dates of all subsequent steps, see the most recent COH Promotion and Tenure Timetable.)

B. Proper Format for the Preparation of Dossiers.

1. Dossiers must be prepared using the outline form (headings and subheadings) from the most recent version of *"Provost's Guidelines for Preparing Promotion and Tenure Cases"* issued each spring by the Provost.

2. All published or forthcoming works listed in a dossier must be cited according to the complete citation form, i.e., all citations must include title, publisher, place and date of publication, and page numbers.

3. In the event that a candidate for promotion and tenure presents published or soon-to-be-published materials which cannot be given adequate critical evaluation because they are written in a language insufficiently known to members of the departmental or the COH committee, the chairperson of either committee may request that the candidate prepare an English translation of selected portions of the materials (or a précis of them) that would permit the committee to make an informed evaluation. In certain cases it may be deemed necessary to invite a consultant, fluent in the language in question, to participate in the committee's discussions (but not to vote).

C. Referees and Letters of Evaluation.

1. Each candidate may submit up to ten names of potential reviewers from outside the UA, but in so doing must take care to nominate only those persons whose objectivity will not be put in question (for example, by previous close association with the candidate as a research collaborator, co-editor, or dissertation adviser).

2. To the list of possible reviewers nominated by the candidate the Department Head will add the names of other persons of his or her own choosing who are knowledgeable in the candidate's field.

3. The full list of potential reviewers—i.e., the list of all those whom the candidate has suggested together with all others whom the head is considering—will be discussed with the candidate, who will be given the opportunity to present compelling and legitimate reasons for removing any person(s) from the list. A list of all potential reviewers to whom the candidate has objected will be kept as a part of the official promotion and tenure file.

4. The final decision as to which persons will serve as reviewers will be made by the Department Head, in consultation with the departmental promotion and tenure committee—this in accordance with the current Povost's Guidelines, which specify that "candidates may suggest names, but the Department Head or review committee should select the individuals to be contacted." It is understood, however, that in any case in which a candidate has presented compelling reasons for removing a particular person from the list of potential reviewers, the Department Head will respect the candidate's wishes and not solicit a reference from that person.

5. Some (but no more than half) of those finally selected to serve as reviewers will be from the candidate's list of nominees.

6. The names of all reviewers finally chosen, including those suggested by the candidate, will be kept confidential. At no point in the process will the candidate contact, either directly or indirectly, external reviewers or potential reviewers regarding the tenure and/or promotion review. If contacted by a reviewer, the candidate shall refrain from responding to questions about the promotion and tenure case and, instead, shall direct the reviewer to the Department Head or the Chairperson of the departmental promotion and tenure committee for any required information or directions.

7. By the date established in the current COH Timetable, the Department Head will write a standard letter to all outside reviewers requesting an evaluation of the candidate. (A sample letter is usually provided in the current Provost's Guidelines.) Referees will be assured that their letters of reference will be held in strictest confidentiality, within the limits of applicable law, ABOR policy, and University regulations. The letters to all reviewers must be substantively identical.

8. At least three of the letters of reference included in any promotion and tenure file must be recent.

9. In order to ensure the confidentiality of the reviewers, once their letters have been received, the Department Head shall label them "A," "B," "C," etc., and prepare a separate list of the reviewers identifying them as "A," "B," "C," etc. All subsequent references to external reviewers in written documents shall refer to them as "Reviewer A," "Reviewer B," "Reviewer C," etc. Reviewers' letters, with their original signatures, shall remain part of the candidates' files.

10. In the Department Head's letter to the Dean, the Department Head shall call attention to letters that are not in accordance with Federal and State antidiscrimination laws, or with ABOR and University policies and rules against discrimination.

11. For further information on outside reviewers, consult the current version of the Provost's Guidelines.

D. Collection of Supporting Documents.

1. It is the responsibility of the candidate to provide a copy, offprint, or preprint of each work published or accepted for publication. Each manuscript accepted for publication but not yet actually published must be accompanied by a letter from the publisher, journal editor, or other responsible person indicating its acceptance.

2. A candidate's teaching record must be documented, not merely asserted. It is the responsibility of the Department Head and the candidate to provide an evaluation of teaching and advising, as directed in the current Provost's Guidelines.

3. Proof of professional honors or recognition and proof of professional service, both within and without the University, is the responsibility of the candidate. He or she should submit all pertinent documentation when citing such honors, awards, or service—e.g., letters of appointment to committees; letters of recognition from local, regional, national organizations; etc.

4. In any case in which a professional honor or award is cited, the candidate should also provide some information or documentation about the award or honor.

5. The candidate should discuss with the Department Head submission of any other documents that may be deemed pertinent to promotion or tenure action.

6. Significant new materials may be added to the candidate packet during the review process in accordance with the procedures described in the current Provost's Guidelines.

7. The Department Head shall ensure that the candidate's file remain intact and the identical file as was reviewed at the department level be forwarded intact to the Dean's level.

III. Procedures for Evaluation of Research,
Teaching, and Service.

A. Evaluation of Research.

1. As noted above, the candidate must provide copies of all her or his published and soon to be published works. The candidate should also provide copies of any published reviews of those works which he or she wishes the committees to consider.

2. It is possible that an external reviewer's initial letter will prompt further questions on the part of the Department Head or the departmental committee. In such cases the Department Head may request a second letter of reference from the reviewer, asking him or her to provide clarification of points in the initial letter or requesting additional information. All such follow-up requests, and all responses to them, must be in writing. Referees will again be assured that all such correspondence will be held in the strictest confidentiality within the limits of applicable law.

3. The departmental committee will summarize the content of all available reviews of the candidate's publications.

4. The departmental committee will evaluate anthologies, books, and journals in

which the candidate's works have appeared or will appear, and will summarize their relative standing in the candidate's field.

5. The departmental committee will summarize and evaluate invited and volunteered conference papers, talks, poetry readings, performances, etc. that the candidate has given, while also assessing the relative importance of the meetings (conferences, colloquia, etc.) at which the contributions were made.

6. The departmental committee will summarize the relative importance to the department and institution of the candidate's scholarly and creative production. If the candidate is said to have national or international standing, this claim must be substantiated.

7. In addition to judging the quality of the candidate's individual contributions, the departmental committee will also assess the coherence, quality, development, and potential value of the candidate's overall research program and will assess the relevance to that general program of all individual research products.

8. Scholarly editing, where it can be shown to require sustained research and original or critical activity, may be offered as another example of scholarly activity. In most instances, however, journal editing or similar activity will be understood as "professional service."

B. Evaluation of Teaching.

A full statement of what information to provide on teaching, and what not to provide, is contained in the current Provost's Guidelines. The following procedural points are for use by the candidate, the Department Head, and the promotion and tenure committees, in implementing those guidelines.

1. The committees will evaluate local, regional, national awards or recognition the candidate may have won for teaching, and determine their importance.

2. The departmental committee will appoint qualified individuals to provide peer review of the candidate's teaching. This may include actual classroom visits arranged in consultation with the candidate.

3. The head will provide summary statements of the results of teaching evaluations conducted since the candidate's last formal promotion evaluation, or for at least the three years preceding the year of the current review. The departmental committee will evaluate and comment on the candidate's teaching effectiveness.

4. The departmental committee will include any other pertinent information concerning the quality of the candidate's teaching.

C. Evaluation of Service.

The committees will evaluate and summarize all evidence provided by the candidate concerning service to the department, university, region, and/or profession and will carefully weigh all claims made about the significance of such service.

IV. Supplementary Procedures to Be Followed in Considering the Tenure
and/or Promotion of Faculty Engaged in Interdisciplinary Programs.

Participation in the activities of interdisciplinary programs may comprise an ongoing and integral part of a faculty member's professional activities. To the extent
that this is so, these efforts should be recognized, alongside other relevant activities, in the evaluation procedures for promotion and tenure.

If the candidate's formal workload includes a significant portion within graduate
and/or undergraduate interdisciplinary programs, then it shall be evaluated according to the procedures outlined below, consistent with current Graduate College
procedures. Moreover, if the candidate, in consultation with the Department Head,
considers his or her informal or "overload" participation in teaching, research, or
service within the framework of an interdisciplinary program to constitute a significant portion of his or her workload, the Head of the home department shall
seek a written evaluation of the candidate's performance from the Director of the
interdisciplinary program, according to the procedures outlined below. These procedures are to be followed in addition to—not in place of—all the other procedures
prescribed above.

1. The candidate will be asked to include, as part of her or his promotion and tenure
dossier, a detailed statement of all teaching, research, and service activities that she
or he has undertaken as a participant in the relevant interdisciplinary program.

2. The Head of the candidate's home department shall request from the Director or
Chairperson of the relevant interdisciplinary program an evaluation of the degree
and quality of the candidate's contributions to the interdisciplinary program.

3. This evaluation will be written by the Director or Chairperson of the IDP in
consultation with an *ad hoc* committee comprising three tenured faculty of appropriate rank. The evaluation document will be sent to the Head of the candidate's
home department for inclusion in the candidate's promotion and tenure dossier.

4. Ordinarily, membership on such an *ad hoc* committee will be drawn from the
interdisciplinary program's Executive Council and will include the Director or
Chairperson of the interdisciplinary program. However, in the case of a candidate
being considered for promotion to Full Professor in an interdisciplinary program
the Director or Chairperson of which is not a full professor, that Director or Chairperson will join the *ad hoc* committee as a non-voting member (that is to say, he or
she will participate in the discussion of the candidate's case but will not vote), and
an additional Full Professor shall be added to the committee.

5. In cases in which the *ad hoc* committee mechanism appears unnecessary or re-
dundant (e.g., when the candidate's involvement in the interdisciplinary program's
activities is minimal, or when there is a large overlap between the membership of
the home department's promotion and tenure committee and the interdisciplinary
program's *ad hoc* committee), one or more tenured members of the interdisciplinary
program's Executive Council may be invited by the Head of the home department
to serve as *pro tempore* and *ad hoc* voting members of the home department's promotion and tenure committee.

6. In the case of a member of a graduate interdisciplinary program, additional input may be solicited from the University's Director of Graduate Interdepartmental Programs whenever this is deemed appropriate by the candidate, by the Head of the home department, or by the Director or Chairperson of the interdisciplinary program.

7. Once documentation of a candidate's interdisciplinary program activities has been incorporated into the candidate's dossier it will be considered—at all stages of review and by all reviewers—as integral to the evaluation of the candidate.

V. Appeals.

Should a candidate feel that procedures have not been followed at the departmental committee level, a written appeal may be directed to the Department Head. Should a candidate feel that procedures have not been followed at the Department Head or COH Promotion and Tenure Committee levels, a written appeal may be directed to the Dean.

VI. Deferred Teaching Assignments and
Delays of the "Tenure Clock."

We call attention to the *Provost's Guidelines* of June 29, 1989 regarding "stopping the tenure clock" (attached). COH is seeking ways further to enhance candidates' ability to delay the "tenure clock." A proposal to this effect was drafted in 1992 by the Planning and Policy Advisory Committee (see the underscored matter, below), but it was not accepted by Central Administration because general University policy in this area has not yet been formulated. The following are therefore recommended:

1. That candidates consult regularly with their Department Heads regarding the current status of proposals and procedures to delay the "tenure clock."

2. That the COH Planning and Policy Advisory Committee, together with the COH Department Heads and Program Directors, the University Affirmative Action Office, and the Committee on the Status of Women consider the possibility of including, in a future version of the *"COH Promotion and Tenure Procedures"* document, a procedure like the following:

In addition to, or in lieu of, the Provost's provisions for stopping the "tenure clock" (outlined in the attached June 29, 1989 "Provost's Memorandum on the Promotion and Tenure Process"), the College of Humanities offers the following further options:

A faculty member who has urgent "family care responsibilities," or who can offer other appropriate reasons, may request of her or his Department Head, and of the Dean, a semester of deferred teaching assignment at full salary.

At the time such a request is made the faculty member may also request, again of both the Department Head and the Dean, a commensurate delay of the "tenure clock."

All such arrangements will be made upon the written and legally binding under-standing (signed by the faculty member, his or her Department Head, and the Dean) that the faculty member has a contractual obligation to reimburse the de-partment in one of the following ways:

1. By teaching, without pay, one summer session course in each of two consecutive summers; or

2. By teaching, without extra compensation, a one-course "overload" in each of any two semesters within the four semesters following the semester of the deferment; or

3. By some other negotiated combination of additional teaching and/or advising duties to be fulfilled within a specified time after the semester of the deferment.

Such deferred teaching assignments are not automatically granted, but every effort will be made to accommodate those with clear and pressing "family care responsi-bilities" or other appropriate reasons.

NOTE: Throughout this document, the terms "publication," "publisher," and "pub-lished" shall be understood to refer both to work available in printed form (books, articles, etc.) and to work available in electronic media (computer programs, soft-ware, etc.).

Appendix 2. Summary Checklist of Selected Family-Friendly Initiatives and Programs

Begin campus dialogue that studies the diversity of family structures now emerging. Use this dialogue as the basis for reviewing all benefits policies so that they embrace care of both the young and the old and recognize nontraditional family arrangements, including (but not limited to) nonmarried domestic partners and co-operative domestic units.

Institute comprehensive data-gathering to assess current and future family-related needs; and determine realistic cost projections for any anticipated new benefits or services.

Maintain a resource and referral service for all child and senior care needs; and provide comprehensive information on services available both on- and off-campus.

Provide low-cost on- or near-campus housing for married students and their families; and design campus dormitories to accommodate students who are single parents with young children.

Establish an on-campus shelter for battered women and children. The shelter should sponsor on-campus education and counselling programs for abusers and their victims; and the shelter should work with other campus units—like a School of Social Work or a College of Law—to educate the campus regarding the prevalence and prevention of domestic violence, battering, and abuse.

All female faculty and staff should be eligible for a minimum of twelve weeks paid leave for birth or infant adoption (i.e., maternity leave). Additionally, all faculty and staff—male and female alike—should be eligible for a designated period of paid family care leave at full salary as well as adjusted workload assignments at full or half salary for care of newborns, a newly adopted child, or a foster care placement, and for other family emergencies. Men should be assiduously encouraged to take advantage of these benefits.

Junior faculty who take family-related leaves should also be eligible for commensurate delays in the tenure clock.

Faculty and staff should be offered flexible work options, including flex-time, part-time, and flex-year schedules for staff; and up to two tenure clock delays, as well as half-time and shared tenure-track appointments for faculty.

When scheduling department or committee meetings, the needs of those who must pick up a small child from school, be home to prepare dinner, or relieve a home health care provider should be considered and respected.

Without any reduction in pay, up to four times a year, employees should be able to attend their children's school functions during working hours.

Subsidize and support the use of a combination of on-campus and off-campus child care facilities, staffed by qualified and well-trained personnel. Whether these facilities are operated solely by the school or operated in partnership with private providers, facilities should be available to students, staff, and faculty, with subsidies and/or fees based on ability to pay; and parental oversight, supervision, and participation must be assured. Such child care centers should be open extended hours, on weekends, and during the summers, and they should be able to accommodate requests for occasional "drop-in" care.

In addition to child care centers, schools should establish a subsidized Sick Child Program, providing trained (and licensed) home health care professionals who will come to the home to care for a temporarily sick child when the parents (students or employees) must be on campus. Such services would cover occasional and minor illnesses only. The daily or hourly fee paid by the parent would be modest. In states where such services are not currently available for senior citizens, the school should expand the program to include occasional care for an ailing senior in a student, staff, or faculty household.

Enhance facilities and outreach programs for senior citizens. These might include fee-based lifelong learning programs, expanded Elderhostel offerings, specialized degree programs, and "wellness" programs coordinated through a medical school or college of nursing.

Investigate opportunities for combining child care and elder care services in professionally supervised settings. Consider surrogate grandparent programs as one means for involving senior citizens in the care of young children within supervised facilities.

Expand current financial arrangements that set aside monies for low-cost or no-interest college tuition loans for the children of faculty and staff by involving additional schools in tuition-exchange agreements.

Explore the development of a comprehensive benefits and family services program that offers a menu of variable options to employees; design the program so as to allow individuals to change their benefits/services options as circumstances demand.

Encourage local businesses and national corporations to support special scholarship funds earmarked for part-time working students and to grant tuition vouchers to employees seeking to upgrade their skills through a college or university degree program.

Review financial aid distribution formulas and work both locally and nationally to expand scholarship opportunities for older, part-time undergraduates.

Expand interactive distance-learning services, especially with a view toward developing selected high quality off-campus degree programs that involve substantial interaction with faculty mentors.

Offer part-time students greater flexibility in course scheduling; and develop on-campus specialized degree programs for working parents who can enroll only for weekend and evening classes.

Seek partnerships with the private business sector, government agencies, and private foundations for developing and funding appropriate family-friendly initiatives.

Establish private fundraising endowments that can generate revenues to support family-friendly services like child care and elder care centers.

As part of the national education agenda, senior administrators in academe must lobby the president and Congress to forgo the empty rhetoric of "traditional family values" and, in its place, develop realistic support programs for the changing American family.

Protect the rights and privileges of those who will never utilize family care benefits or policies and reward these individuals' cooperation in family-sensitive workplace activities.

Notes

A Personal Preface

1 Salary compression refers to the stagnation of a faculty member's salary follow-ing years of inadequate salary increases—or no increases at all. Compression is most glaring when entry-level salaries have continued to rise, thereby ap-proaching the salary levels of those who have been in rank for some years. The problem is compounded when salary increases are across-the-board percentage increases, since those already earning higher salaries benefit most.

2 In Arizona, for example, new campus buildings are sometimes financed by pri-vate donations or, more often, the university takes on debt by selling revenue bonds on which, over the years, it pays interest. Raises for faculty, as for all state employees, are allocated by the state legislature and taken from annual state revenues. These forms of money are not interchangeable, and, by law, revenue bonding can only be used for limited building projects.

1. Facing the Future: An Introduction

1 New classroom approaches to teaching the work of Lady Mary Wroth have been influenced by Naomi Miller's *Changing the Subject: Mary Wroth and Figu-rations of Gender in Early Modern England* (1996) and *Reading Mary Wroth: Representing Alternatives in Early Modern England* (1991).

2 These new insights into Henry James owe a debt to Marcia Jacobson's *Henry James and the Mass Market* (1983).

3 See Stanley Fish's collected essays in *There's No Such Thing as Free Speech . . . and It's a Good Thing, Too* (1994) and Lawrence W. Levine's *The Opening of the American Mind* (1996).

2. "60 Minutes" at the University of Arizona: The Polemic against Tenure

1 On 27 February 1995, the day after the "60 Minutes" program aired, I spoke with Professor Lehrer by telephone, and he shared his memories of the original interview with me. This quote was taken from my notes of that conversation.

2 According to "Growth in Number of Doctoral Recipients Led by Women," since

1987 the steady growth in the number of doctorates awarded in the United States has been fueled "by the increase in foreign nationals studying" here, especially in science and engineering fields ("Growth," 5). As a result, this large pool of international graduate students necessarily provides some of the most talented candidates for lab and teaching assistantship positions. Since Americans training for careers in science and engineering will thus become part of an internationalized workplace, the opportunity to begin preparing for that future during college should surely be counted an asset.

3   All quotes from Keith Lehrer's tape cassette are identified as such within the text and carry no further citation. My own handwritten transcription of the tape is the immediate source for the quotes, which were reviewed by both Lehrer and Stahl.

4   Before formal termination procedures were to be enacted, the faculty member chose to retire.

5   The analysis of the drop in public funding for colleges and universities was performed by Ernst Benjamin of the American Association of University Professors and is summarized by John K. Wilson in "The Academy Speaks Back" (29). Benjamin's analysis is confirmed by a study of state spending trends from the Nelson A. Rockefeller Institute of Government that reveals, among other things, that state spending for higher education continues to decline: whereas state expenditures for prisons and welfare increased between 1990 and 1994, "the percentage for higher education decreased from 14% to 12.5%" (see Lindenberger 3).

6   A good example of the way in which research funding supports undergraduate education is the $5 million addition to the Kuiper Space Sciences Building at the University of Arizona. Built in 1989 with research dollars from NASA, the high-tech addition features classrooms with computers and VCRs and is generally regarded as one of the best teaching facilities on campus; it is used, among other things, for the introductory-level courses in lunar and planetary sciences (see Christie 1).

7   That the cut in the NEH budget was not motivated by financial concerns is made clear by the fact that in December 1995 a Republican Congress voted to appropriate a new military spending budget of $260 billion—a full $7 billion more than the Pentagon had requested.

8   In the summer of 1996, the Japanese government "adopted a plan proposed by the Science and Technology Council to increase government spending on research by 12.4 per cent a year in each of the next five years." The bulk of the money will support research and improve facilities "at national universities and research institutes" (Findlay-Kineko A35).

9   For an overview of organized right-wing attempts to influence policy, research, and teaching in higher education, see John K. Wilson, *The Myth of Political Correctness* (1995); Jeffrey Williams, ed., *P.C. Wars: Politics and Theory in the Academy* (1995); and Michael Berubé and Cary Nelson, eds., *Higher Education under Fire: Politics, Economics, and the Crisis of the Humanities* (1995). The most detailed and comprehensive analysis of how the right has organized its many resources in order to impact all aspects of the academy is to be found in Ellen Messer-Davidow's articles "Manufacturing the Attack on Liberalized

Higher Education" (1993) and "Who (Ac)Counts and How" (1994) and in her *Disciplining Feminism: Episodes in the Discursive Production of Social Change.*

10 See chapter 3 for an explanation. Note also that the gender gap has been widening. In 1982, "27 percent of all faculty [were] women, although women obtain[ed] 35 percent of all PhDs—an 8 percent gap." By 1994, women were "31 percent of all faculty," even though, by now, they "earn[ed] 47 percent of all PhDs—a 16 percent gap" ("Women Faculty" 2).

11 The abolition of affirmative action admissions procedures in California and Texas had an immediate impact on law school admissions, an impact that is ominously predictive of future trends in all areas of admissions. According to a 2 June 1997 report in *Time* magazine, "The best law schools in both states— recently ordered not to consider the race of their applicants—said the number of blacks and Hispanics enrolling for next year had fallen to levels not seen in decades. At the University of Texas, which has produced more minority lawyers than any other school in the country—and where, typically, 30 to 40 blacks enter each year—only 11 blacks were accepted and none had enrolled; the number of Hispanics dropped from more than 50 to 14. In California the schools at both Berkeley and UCLA saw black admissions drop 80%, while the number of Hispanic students fell 50% and 32% respectively" (Gwynne 48).

12 Adopted by voters in 1996 but still being contested in the courts as this book goes to press, California's Proposition 209 includes the following as its chief provision: "The state shall not discriminate against, or grant preferential treatment to, any individual or group on the basis of race, sex, color, ethnicity, or national origin in the operation of public employment, public education, or public contracting." The proposition provides exemptions for policies and programs required under federal law.

13 By forcing schools to reorganize or close down academic programs, budget cuts and hiring freezes have had disparate impacts on women and minorities. Analyzing "academic freedom cases investigated by the American Association of University Professors . . . between 1980 and 1990," Sheila Slaughter concluded that "reorganization and retrenchment cases revealed a pattern of preference in firing. . . . Professors were most frequently cut in fields that had as students the greatest number of new entries to higher education—women and minorities." Similarly, "in the reorganization and reallocation cases, the fields in which women were most likely to concentrate as students were usually the fields that experienced the heaviest cuts" (Slaughter, "Retrenchment in the 1980s," 73, 96). Slaughter's sample was almost evenly divided between public and private institutions.

14 Part-timers add to the workload of full-time faculty. According to Slaughter, "because part-time faculty were usually hired on a per-course basis, full-time faculty had to give more time to advising students, planning the curriculum, and supervising part-timers. Every time ratios of part- to full-time faculty increased, full-time faculty workload increased." This two-tier labor design also caused inevitable frictions. Slaughter notes that "the full-time tier had benefits and a degree of job security and was at one and the same time supported and threatened by part-timers, who made full-timers' workload possible even as they increased that workload and constituted a reserve labor pool, implicitly

challenging the continued security of full-time jobs" (Slaughter, "Retrenchment in the 1980s," 268).

15 These remarks are quoted, by permission, from Keith Lehrer's letter to me, dated 25 August 1995.

16 I discuss this experience in Kolodny, "I Dreamt Again That I Was Drowning."

17 For a discussion of the model promotion and tenure procedures developed by faculty in the College of Humanities at the University of Arizona, see chapter 3.

3. Raising Standards While Lowering Anxieties: Rethinking the Promotion and Tenure Process

1 A 1990 survey by the Carnegie Foundation, published in *Change* magazine, also reveals that women "are the most conscientious members of the campus community" when it comes to "contributing to the processes of governance on campus" (Carnegie Foundation 39).

2 To avoid this kind of damaging tokenism, the College of Humanities sought to make *all* committees gender-balanced and inclusive of significant minority representation. Until we had employed sufficient numbers of new faculty to make this a reasonable goal, however, we were in danger of severely overburdening the women and minority faculty already in place. As a result, as dean, I authorized department heads to reduce the teaching loads of women and minority faculty carrying unusual service burdens. In this regard, a feminist dean can make a difference, and no one suffered unduly from our efforts at balance and diversity. Happily, at the end of two years of active and successful recruitment, no department or program within the humanities any longer needed repeatedly to call upon the services of the same few women and/or minority faculty.

3 This pattern can often be predicted from disparities in the treatment of men and women in the initial recruitment process, as when male candidates are asked to deliver a research paper while women candidates are asked to "guest teach" an introductory-level class. Antidiscrimination laws prohibit this kind of gender-inflected treatment, of course, but some departments persist in it unthinkingly.

4 See Banner et al., especially 4–6.

5 My own experience at the University of New Hampshire twenty years ago was remarkably similar. See Kolodny, "I Dreamt Again That I Was Drowning."

4. Paying the Price of Antifeminist Intellectual Harassment

1 For a chilling examination of the networks of right-wing organizations currently impacting our campuses, see Messer-Davidow, "Manufacturing the Attack on Liberalized Higher Education."

2 For the personal and emotional costs of this kind of litigation, see Kolodny, "I Dreamt Again That I Was Drowning."

3 This is also a recurrent theme in Warren Bennis's anatomy of the corporate sector, *Why Leaders Can't Lead* (1989).

4 Private telephone conversation with Emily Toth, January 1994.

5 A useful analysis of the concept of "surplus visibility" within an academic set-

ting is offered by Daphne Patai, "Minority Status and the Stigma of 'Surplus Visibility.'"

6 A residential program that offers "intensive training in educational administration," the Summer Institute at Bryn Mawr is organized by HERS, Mid-America, University of Denver, Park Hill Campus, 7150 Mountview Blvd., Denver, CO 80220.

5. Creating the Family-Friendly Campus

1 As of November 1994, according to a campus newspaper article titled "Employees Can Obtain Child-Care Assistance," the University of Arizona only provided students and employees with a Resource and Referral Service, designed to help people in "locating and selecting child-care arrangements"; a financial subsidy for child care costs was not available until 1996. The university also offered the Sick Child Program, "designed to support the working parent who has a mildly ill child unable to attend school or child care." Under this program, "a trained provider will come to the employee's home and stay with the child while the employee is at work. . . . Parents are charged $1 and hour and the UA picks up the remaining charges" ("Employees Can" 8). Even with these services, however, as an *Arizona Daily Wildcat* article of 2 September 1994 made clear, an on-campus child care center still remained "on UA parents' wish list" (Mayhew 3).

2 For example, in 1994 "the central administration office for the California State University system" began developing "a project intended to create a degree program in business administration by combining courses taught on various campuses and delivering them electronically" (DeLoughry A36). When in place, such a program could be delivered to any of the participating campuses and, as well, to appropriate off-campus sites in order to enable distance learning.

3 At the University of Arizona, according to Kimberly Kayler, a flex-year arrangement requires the agreement of "the employee and his or her supervisor. . . . Eligible employees can take from one to four pay periods off each year, usually during the slowest time period for their department. Although this registers as unpaid-vacation time, the reduced annual compensation is distributed over the entire fiscal year so that employees still receive the normal number of paychecks during that time off" (Kayler 1).

4 Copies of a report about Stanford's experience, "Domestic Partner Benefits: A Case Study," are available from the College and University Personnel Association, 1233 20th Street, N.W., Suite 301, Washington, D.C. 20036; (202) 778-0392. The cost is $15 for CUPA members, $20 for all others (see "In Box" A19).

7. Setting an Agenda for Change

1 According to Robert L. Jacobson's article in the 4 August 1993 *Chronicle of Higher Education*, "Some 30 million American adults have such trouble with literacy tasks—reading, writing, arithmetic, and everyday problem-solving— that they cannot function effectively in society. And in what experts call a national crisis, the great majority of those who need help aren't getting it" (A16). See also Sharon Darling, "Illiteracy."

2   In passing this requirement, the Arizona Department of Education failed to specify what constitutes a *foreign* language. English may be the second language for some Native American students from the reservations and for students who come from largely Spanish-speaking enclaves. As yet, the Department of Education has not come to terms with the fact that English may have to be taught as a "foreign" or second language to some; nor has the department clearly made provisions for teaching Native American languages as the second language. Once the language requirement begins to be implemented statewide, however, these issues will have to be addressed.

3   Currently, over forty faculty participate in the SLAT program, representing departments in the College of Humanities, the College of Social and Behavioral Sciences, and the College of Education. All language programs at the University of Arizona are represented, including the Program in American Sign Language and a variety of American Indian languages.

4   Currently, the Program in Comparative Cultural and Literary Studies offers the Ph.D. and several sections of a popular undergraduate course that fulfills general education requirements. An undergraduate minor is being planned. Because the CCLS graduate program builds on courses already available in existing departments; and because a number of CCLS courses have been designed to serve the intellectual interests of students in other humanities departments and programs—as well as the interests of its own Ph.D.s—CCLS's comparativist approaches can be fully integrated into a number of Ph.D. programs for full credit.

5   Women and minority faculty repeatedly "borrowed" for search committees were, of course, in danger of becoming exhausted by these service duties, and their writing and research projects might be jeopardized, thus hurting their own career progress. To prevent this, I authorized department heads to reduce the teaching assignments of these faculty members. As a result, no one suffered unduly from our determination to diversify the makeup of search committees. Indeed, there was a positive effect: the loss of faculty teaching time, combined with some faculty members' discomfort at the concept of "borrowing," led some units to intensify their efforts to seek out qualified women and minority candidates. As a result, after only two years, the composition of the faculty had changed so substantially that no unit *needed* to borrow from any other; several departments continued the practice voluntarily, however, because it added a new intellectual perspective to the search process.

6   If the team concept is really to take hold, mechanisms must also be developed so that individuals other than administrators can define a problem and recommend a team to address it. In this way, potential problems may be recognized *before* they become large and serious.

7   The financial pressures on many of today's college students cannot be overstated. The 9–16 August 1993 issue of the *Nation* quotes a report from the Center on Budget and Policy Priorities that cites May 1992 census data showing "that the proportion of full-time year-round workers who are paid wages too low to lift a family of four out of poverty has grown sharply in recent years. In 1979, some 12.1 percent of full-time year-round workers were paid wages this low. In 1990, some 18 percent were" (Hitchens 164). When the bright, talented,

and eager children of these growing numbers of "working poor" families look at a college education, they will discover that President Clinton's national service plan, AmeriCorps, provides too meager a support system for their financial urgencies, that local and federal scholarship resources are insufficient for the numbers of students in need, and that their families can ill afford to suffer the loss of their children's modest part-time wages for a consecutive four-year period. Moreover, few students from this background are willing to take on staggering debts. As a result, their higher education record will probably reflect movement from a community college to a four-year institution, with many breaks and several part-time semesters. Some talented students simply will never be able to complete their degrees. The best solution, of course, is to develop a national need-based scholarship program for all qualified students. This is the most effective response; but the current mood of the Congress does not augur well for such an eminently intelligent course of action.

8. Failing the Future; or, How to Commit National Suicide at the End of the Twentieth Century

1 Enrollment increases are already beginning. A 1995 *New York Times* article reports that "kindergarten enrollment rose 7.2 percent from 1988 to 1993, from 3.357 million to 3.597 million, according to the National Center for Education Statistics, a research arm of the Department of Education. Preschool enrollment over the same period was up 14 percent, from 2.621 million to 2.984 million" (Gabriel 15).

2 Although the recommendations of the Japanese National Personnel Authority are directly applicable only to national schools, these recommended salary structures tend also to be closely followed by most public elementary and secondary schools, which, as in the United States, are locally controlled (see Barro 8).

3 Some aspects of the Japanese formula do not translate. As Hawley observed in 1986, in addition to base salary and other incentives, Japanese "teachers receive various allowances depending on where they live, the number of their dependents, whether they commute, the cost of their housing and other conditions. So," concluded Hawley, "a beginning teacher in a heavily populated city with dependent spouse and two children, who commuted from the suburbs[,] could earn an additional thirty percent of the average base salary" (Hawley 2–3). The American civil rights principle of equal pay for equal work renders certain aspects of the Japanese salary system illegal—as in the case, for example, of differential pay scales pegged to the number of dependents. Other aspects of the Japanese system simply do not coincide with American realities—such as that system's assumption of a single (male) earner with dependent spouse.

4 According to Snyder and Hoffman, p. 429, in 1990–91, the Japanese spent 8.8 percent of their total public expenditures on primary and secondary schools but only 1.1 percent on higher education. That same year, the United States expended 10.2 percent of total public expenditures on K–12 education, and another 3.6 percent of total public expenditures on postsecondary education.

5 The majority of the students at Erasmus Hall High School today are of African-American and African-Caribbean descent. As part of an ongoing $95 million

restoration, the school has been administratively restructured into three distinct schools, each with its own principal: the High School for Science and Mathematics, the High School for Humanities, and the High School for Business and Technology. In 1997, after years of neglect, the swimming pool was renovated, complete with new tiles, decorations, and eight competition diving boards. The Campus Student Choir has replaced the music groups that I knew. And in a stunning demonstration of support, in 1987, over 1,100 former Erasmians attended a bicentennial dinner.

6   As Matthew Cooper, a contributing editor at the *Washington Monthly* and a national correspondent for *Newsweek* points out: "A balanced budget is not an end in itself but a means to an end—faster growth. If the country can grow briskly while running a small budget deficit, then it's not a major problem" (Cooper 17). As this book goes to press, all economic indicators show a strong economy and continued growth. The dire consequences of the budget deficit are being exaggerated for political ends.

7   While minority enrollments in higher education continue to increase, graduation rates do not. In 1994, the latest year for which degree-completion information is available as this book goes to press, "black students made up 10.7 per cent of the undergraduate population at four-year institutions, but earned only 7.2 per cent of all bachelor's degrees. Hispanic students were 7.9 per cent of the undergraduate population that year, but they earned only 4.3 per cent of the bachelor's degrees" (Gose A38).

A Closing Refrain

1   In 1955, just three years before I entered Brooklyn College, the school's president estimated that "roughly one-third of our student body earns all or most of its living expenses—and sometimes those of other members of the family." He then estimated that "perhaps another third of our students" are involved "in part-time employment of one type or another" (qtd. in Coulton xii).

2   Prior to the opening of a permanent campus in the Flatbush-Midwood district in 1937, Brooklyn College was housed in rented office space in downtown Brooklyn.

3   To be sure, the public conversation had its dissenters. Writing in the *Brooklyn Magazine* of April 1935, journalist William Kennelly opined that "[a] free college education does not make better citizens nor is it a license for success in life.... It is part of the scheme of reaching for too high a social standing which can only result in chaos" (qtd. in Horowitz 33). Wealthy New York real estate developer Stewart Browne protested that "[a]ll these ideas about educating the masses are so much nonsense" and advocated abolishing the free municipal colleges; even in the midst of an economic depression, he complained that he couldn't find a housemaid "because all your Hunter College girls are too proud to do housework" (qtd. in Horowitz 41). Clearly, the fact that tuition-free higher education was providing a gateway into the middle class for the children of recent immigrants was disturbing to some observers.

Works Cited

Altbach, Philip G. "The Pros and Cons of Hiring 'Taxicab' Professors." *Chronicle of Higher Education,* 6 January 1995, B3.

Alter, Jonathan. "Busting the Big Blob." *Newsweek,* 8 April 1996, 40.

Altfeld, Clifford B. "The State of the State's Education." *Desert Leaf,* March 1996, 3.

Arch, The. Ed. Richard Schlefer. Brooklyn, N.Y.: Senior Class of Erasmus Hall High School, 1958.

Arenson, Karen W. "Alumni Generosity Has a Catch." *New York Times,* 19 March 1995, sec. 4: 5.

———. "Harvard President's Medical Leave Highlights the Pressures of Life in a University." *New York Times,* 4 December 1994, 22.

Aronowitz, Stanley and William DiFazio. *The Jobless Future: Sci-Tech and the Dogma of Work.* Minneapolis: University of Minnesota Press, 1994.

Atwood, Margaret. *Second Words: Selected Critical Prose.* Boston: Beacon Press, 1984.

"Baby Makes Three." *U.S. News and World Report,* 27 December 1993/3 January 1994, 106.

Banner, Lois, Eileen Boris, Mary Kelley, Annette Kolodny, Cecelia Tichi, and Lillian Schlissel. *Personal Lives and Professional Careers: The Uneasy Balance.* With a commentary by Joyce Antler. College Park, Md.: Report of the Women's Committee of the American Studies Association, 1988.

Bar-Haim, Gabriel and John M. Wilkes. "A Cognitive Interpretation of the Marginality and Underrepresentation of Women in Science." *Journal of Higher Education* 60, no. 4 (July/August 1989): 371–87.

Barro, Stephen M. *A Comparison of Teachers' Salaries in Japan and the United States.* Washington, D.C.: U.S. Department of Education, Office of Educational Research and Improvement, September 1986.

Bennis, Warren. *Why Leaders Can't Lead: The Unconscious Conspiracy Continues.* San Francisco: Jossey-Bass, 1989.

Berliner, David C. and Bruce J. Biddle. "Making Molehills Out of Molehills: Reply to Lawrence Stedman's Review of *The Manufactured Crisis.*" *Education Policy Analysis Archives* 4, no. 3 (26 February 1996). Online: Internet.

———. *The Manufactured Crisis: Myths, Fraud, and the Attack on America's Public Schools.* New York: Addison-Wesley, 1995.

Bernstein, Alison and Jacklyn Cock. "A Troubling Picture of Gender Equality." *Chronicle of Higher Education,* 15 June 1994, B1–B3.

Berubé, Michael and Cary Nelson, eds. *Higher Education under Fire: Politics, Economics, and the Crisis of the Humanities.* New York: Routledge, 1995.

Blackburn, Robert T. and Janet H. Lawrence. *Faculty at Work: Motivation, Expectation, Satisfaction.* Baltimore: Johns Hopkins University Press, 1995.

Blackwell, Patricia. "New Child Care Voucher Program Assists UA Employees." *Lo Que Pasa,* 7 December 1995, 1–2.

Blum, Debra E. "Medical Professor, U. of Iowa Face Aftermath of Sexual-Harassment Case." *Chronicle of Higher Education,* 13 March 1991, A15–16.

———. "Old Issues Unresolved: Environment Still Hostile to Women in Academe, New Evidence Indicates." *Chronicle of Higher Education,* 9 October 1991, A1, A20.

Boylan, William A. "A New Brooklyn College Is Rising." *New York Times,* 8 December 1935, sec. 6: 15.

Bradsher, Keith. "Do Income Gaps Retard Growth? More on the Wealth of Nations." *New York Times,* 20 August 1995, sec. 4: 6.

"Brooklyn College Started by Mayor." *New York Times,* 3 December 1935, 27.

Brown, Ronald H., David J. Barram, and Everett M. Ehrlich. "Master's and Doctorate Degrees Earned, by Field: 1971–1991." In *Statistical Abstract of the United States 1994,* 190. Washington, D.C.: Bureau of the Census, September 1994.

Burd, Stephen. "Ready to Cry Foul: Defiant Conservative Relishes the NEH Fights to Come." *Chronicle of Higher Education,* 29 June 1994, A25.

Burd, Stephen, Patrick Healy, Kit Lively, and Christopher Shea. "Low-Income Students Say College Options Are Limited by the Actions of Lawmakers and Campus Officials." *Chronicle of Higher Education,* 14 June 1996, A10–A12.

Cage, Mary Crystal. "New Fla. University to Offer Professors Alternative to Tenure." *Chronicle of Higher Education,* 2 June 1995, A15.

Callan, Patrick M. "Government and Higher Education." In *Higher Education in America, 1980–2000,* ed. Arthur Levine, 3–38. Baltimore: Johns Hopkins University Press, 1993.

Carnegie Foundation for the Advancement of Teaching. "Women Faculty Excel as Campus Citizens." *Change,* September/October 1990, 39–43.

Cheney, Lynne V. "Scholars and Society." *ACLS Newsletter,* summer 1988, 5–7.

"Chilly Climate for Graduate Women, A." *About Women on Campus* 2, no. 4 (fall 1993): 2.

Christie, Shayne D. "Foundation Ranks UA 14th for Research in U.S." *Arizona Daily Wildcat,* 5 December 1996, 1, 7.

Clinton, Hillary Rodham. *It Takes a Village and Other Lessons Children Teach Us.* New York: Simon and Schuster, 1996.

Coiner, Constance. "Silent Parenting in the Academy." In *Listening to Silences: New Essays in Feminist Criticism,* ed. Elaine Hedges and Shelley Fisher Fishkin, 197–224. New York: Oxford University Press, 1994.

"Comparative Cultural and Literary Studies." In *University of Arizona Record: General Catalog 93-94, 94-95,* 174. Tucson: University of Arizona, April 1993.

Condition of Education, 1995, The. Washington, D.C.: U.S. Department of Education, National Center for Education Statistics, 1995.

Cooper, Matthew. "Debt before Dishonor." *New York Times Book Review,* 27 April 1997, 17.

Coulton, Thomas Evans. *A City College in Action: Struggle and Achievement at Brooklyn College, 1930-1955.* New York: Harper and Brothers, 1955.

Cremin, Lawrence A. *Popular Education and its Discontents.* New York: Harper Collins, 1990.

Darling, Sharon. "Illiteracy: An Everyday Problem for Millions." *Appalachia: Journal of the Appalachian Regional Commission* 18, nos. 1-2 (1984): 21-28.

"Data Bit: Women Still Work More at Home Than Men." *About Women on Campus* 4, no. 2 (spring 1995): 4.

DeLoughry, Thomas J. "Pushing the Envelope: California State U. Seeks to Use Technology to Improve Teaching and Serve More Students." *Chronicle of Higher Education,* 19 October 1994, A36-A38.

DePalma, Anthony. "Rare in Ivy League: Women Who Work as Full Professors." *New York Times,* 24 January 1993, 1, 11.

"Diagnosis: Harassment." *Newsweek,* 26 November 1990, 62.

"Domestic Partner Benefits Increasing." *About Women on Campus* 4, no. 4 (fall 1995): 3.

"Earned Degrees Conferred by U.S. Institutions, 1992-93." *Chronicle of Higher Education,* 9 June 1995, A37.

"Education Vital Signs 1995." *Executive Educator* 17, no. 12 (December 1995): A1-A31.

"Employees Can Obtain Child-Care Assistance." *Lo Que Pasa,* 7 November 1994, 8.

"Fast Facts." *Monthly Forum on Women in Higher Education,* December 1995, 10.

Feemster, Ron. "College Goes to the Student." *New York Times,* 7 August 1994, sec. 4A: 28-29.

Findlay-Kineko, Beverly. "Japan Plans Major Increases in Its Spending on Research." *Chronicle of Higher Education,* 9 August 1996, A35-A36.

Finkel, Susan Kolker and Steven G. Olswang. "Child Rearing as a Career Impediment to Women Assistant Professors." *Review of Higher Education* 19, no. 2 (1996): 123-39.

Fish, Stanley. *There's No Such Thing as Free Speech . . . and It's a Good Thing, Too.* New York: Oxford University Press, 1994.

"Florida Invests in Women as Leaders." *Women in Higher Education* 3, no. 6 (June 1994): 2.

Foreign Language Essential Skills. Phoenix, Ariz.: Arizona Department of Education, 1991.

Franklin, H. Bruce. "The Real Issues of My Case." *Change,* 4 June 1972, 31-39.

Fredette, Amy and Kimberly Miller. "Tenure." *Arizona Summer Wildcat,* 14 June 1995, 1, 6-7.

Friedman, Thomas L. "Japan Inc. Revisited." *New York Times,* 25 February 1996, sec. 4: 15.

"Future: Women Get More Degrees Than Men Except at Doctoral Level, The." *About Women on Campus* 6, no. 2 (spring 1997): 7.

Gabriel, Trip. "A Generation's Heritage: After the Boom, a Boomlet." *New York Times*, 12 February 1995, 1, 15.

"Get Real." *60 Minutes*, 26 February 1995, 1, 9–15. Transcript produced for CBS News by Burelle's Information Services, Box 7, Livingston, NJ 07039.

"Getting a Terminal Degree Need Not Be Terminal." *Women in Higher Education* 4, no. 5 (May 1995): 6–7.

Ginis, Kerri. "Program Helps Student-Parents Subsidize Child-Care Costs." *Arizona Daily Wildcat*, 27 March 1996, 6.

Glickstein, Howard A. "Inequalities in Educational Financing." *Teachers College Record* 96, no. 4 (summer 1995): 722–28.

Gold, Andrew. "Return of the Alumni." *Campus* 5, no. 1 (fall 1993): 2.

Gose, Ben. "Minority Enrollments Rose in 1995, a Study Finds." *Chronicle of Higher Education*, 23 May 1997, A38–A40.

Graubard, Stephen R. "The Research University: Notes toward a New History." In *The Research University in a Time of Discontent*, ed. Jonathan R. Cole, Elinor G. Barber, and Stephen R. Graubard, 361–90. Baltimore: Johns Hopkins University Press, 1994.

Greene, Gayle. "Looking at History." In *Changing Subjects: The Making of Feminist Literary Criticism*, ed. Gayle Greene and Coppelia Kahn, 4–27. New York: Routledge, 1993.

"Growth in Number of Doctoral Recipients Led by Women." *About Women on Campus* 4, no. 2 (spring 1995): 5.

Guernsey, Lisa. "Tuition Costs Outpace Incomes, Report Says." *Chronicle of Higher Education*, 6 September 1996, A59.

Gwynne, S. C. "Back to the Future: Forced to Scuttle Affirmative Action, Law Schools See Minority Enrollment Plummet to 1963 Levels." *Time*, 2 June 1997, 48.

Hancock, LynNell and Yahlin Chang. "The Power of the Purse." *Newsweek*, 15 May 1995, 58–59.

Hartmann, Adam. "UA Debating Child Care." *Arizona Daily Wildcat*, 11 February 1994, 1, 4.

Hawley, Willis D. *The Education of Japanese Teachers: Lessons for the United States?* ERIC Report #ED280830, January 1986. Nashville, Tenn.: Peabody College, Vanderbilt University.

Haycock, Kati. "Thinking Differently about School Reform." *Change*, January/February 1996, 13–18.

Head, Simon. "The New, Ruthless Economy." *New York Review of Books*, 29 February 1996, 47–52.

Healy, Patrick. "Arizona's Public Universities Curb Some Affirmative-Action Efforts." *Chronicle of Higher Education*, 6 September 1996, A58.

———. "N.Y. Governor Proposes Cuts for CUNY, SUNY." *Chronicle of Higher Education*, 24 January 1997, A22.

Heller, Scott. "President Rudenstine's Leave Stuns Harvard." *Chronicle of Higher Education*, 7 December 1994, A18.

Hitchens, Christopher. "Minority Report." *The Nation*, 9–16 August 1993, 164.

Honan, William H. "New Pressures on the University." *New York Times*, 9 January 1994, sec. 4A: 16–18.

Horowitz, Murray M. *Brooklyn College: The First Half-Century.* New York: Brooklyn College Press, 1981.

Huber, Bettina J. "Women in the Modern Languages, 1970–1990." In *Profession 90,* ed. Phyllis Franklin, 58–73. New York: MLA, 1990.

"HUD Helping Yale to Be a Better Neighbor." *Yale Alumni Magazine,* November 1995, 23.

"In Box." *Chronicle of Higher Education,* 21 September 1994, A19.

Jacobson, Marcia. *Henry James and the Mass Market.* University, Ala.: University of Alabama Press, 1983.

Jacobson, Robert L. "Computers' Role in Fight for Adult Literacy May Be Stymied by Professional Problems." *Chronicle of Higher Education,* 4 August 1993, A16.

Jacoby, Barbara. "Bringing Community Service into the Curriculum." *Chronicle of Higher Education,* 17 August 1994, B2.

Jamieson, Adrienne and Nelson W. Polsby. "The Research University as a Setting for Undergraduate Teaching." In *The Research University in a Time of Discontent,* ed. Jonathan R. Cole, Elinor G. Barber, and Stephen R. Graubard, 225–30. Baltimore: Johns Hopkins University Press, 1994.

Jones, Bonnie. "Redesigning the Ivory Tower: Opening the Drawbridge to Women with Multiple Roles." In *Cracking the Wall: Women in Higher Education Administration,* ed. Patricia Turner Mitchell, 52–68. Washington, D.C.: College and University Personnel Association, 1993.

Judson, George. "Bridging the Gap between Religion and Technology." *New York Times,* 7 January 1996, sec. 4A: 34, 42–43.

Kalikoff, Beth. "Tracking Tenure with Camera and Net." *Iris: A Journal about Women* 30 (winter 1993): 40–43.

Kaufman, Gloria, ed. *In Stitches: A Patchwork of Feminist Humor and Satire.* Bloomington: Indiana University Press, 1991.

Kayler, Kimberly. "Flex-Year Option Aids Budgets and Burnout." *Lo Que Pasa,* 29 August 1994, 1, 4.

Kennedy, Donald. "Another Century's End, Another Revolution for Higher Education." *Change,* May/June 1995, 8–15.

Keohane, Nannerl O. "The Mission of the Research University." In *The Research University in a Time of Discontent,* ed. Jonathan R. Cole, Elinor G. Barber, and Stephen R. Graubard, 153–78. Baltimore: Johns Hopkins University Press, 1994.

Kerber, Linda K. "If There Were No Humanities Endowment." *Chronicle of Higher Education,* 29 September 1995, A80.

Kinkead, Gwen. "Spock, Brazelton and Now . . . Penelope Leach." *New York Times Magazine,* 10 April 1994, 32–35.

Kolodny, Annette. "I Dreamt Again That I Was Drowning." In *Women's Writing in Exile,* ed. Mary Lynn Broe and Angela Ingram, 170–78. Chapel Hill: University of North Carolina Press, 1989.

"Kutztown Leadership Training Wins WIHE Award." *Women in Higher Education* 3, no. 3 (March 1993): 8.

Lamplot, Vern. "Regents Close PE, Statistics." *Lo Que Pasa,* 19 June 1995, 1, 8.

———. "Regents Question Need for Tenure." *Lo Que Pasa,* 3 August 1995, 1, 3.

Lazerson, Marvin. "Who Owns Higher Education? The Changing Face of Governance." *Change,* March/April 1997, 10–15.

Leatherman, Courtney. "Michigan State Offers a Refuge for Battered Women." *Chronicle of Higher Education,* 29 June 1994, A5.

Leatherman, Courtney and Denise K. Magner. "Faculty and Graduate-Student Strife over Job Issues Flares on Many Campuses." *Chronicle of Higher Education,* 29 November 1996, A12–A14.

Leibold, Janis. "Child Care Coordinator Takes Charge at UA." *Lo Que Pasa,* 22 August 1994, 3.

Lemann, Nicholas. "How Can We Cut the Costs of a College Degree?" *U.S. News and World Report,* 30 December 1996/6 January 1997, 44–47.

Lesko, P. D. Letters: "Re-examining the Role of the 'True Adjunct.'" *Chronicle of Higher Education,* 6 January 1995, B5.

Levin, Richard C. "To the Alumni and Alumnae of Yale University." Office of the President, Yale University, 23 March 1995.

Levine, Arthur. "Diversity on Campus." In *Higher Learning in America, 1980–2000,* ed. Arthur Levine, 333–43. Baltimore: Johns Hopkins University Press, 1993.

———. "Education Reform: Designing the Endgame." *Change,* 29 February 1996, 4.

Levine, Lawrence W. *The Opening of the American Mind.* Boston: Beacon Press, 1996.

Lewin, Tamar. "Workers of Both Sexes Make Trade-Offs for Family, Study Shows." *New York Times,* 29 October 1995, 14.

Lindenberger, Herbert. "The Committee on Professional Employment at Work." *MLA Newsletter* 29, no. 2 (summer 1997): 3–4.

Madrick, Jeff. "The End of Affluence." *New York Review of Books,* 21 September 1995, 13–17.

Madrid, Arturo. "Less Is Not More . . . in the Case of Education." Unpublished commencement address. Brooklyn College, New York, N.Y., 4 June 1997. Quoted by permission of the author.

Magner, Denise K. "More Black Ph.D.'s." *Chronicle of Higher Education,* 14 June 1996, A25–A26.

———. "The New Generation: Study Shows Proportions of Female and Minority Professors Are Growing." *Chronicle of Higher Education,* 2 February 1996, A17–A18.

Mayhew, Sarah. "Child Care on UA Parents' Wish List." *Arizona Daily Wildcat,* 2 September 1994, 3.

Meier, Deborah. *The Power of Their Ideas: Lessons for America from a Small School in Harlem.* Boston: Beacon Press, 1995.

Messer-Davidow, Ellen. *Disciplining Feminism: Episodes in the Discursive Production of Social Change.* Durham, N.C.: Duke University Press, 1999.

———. "Manufacturing the Attack on Liberalized Higher Education." *Social Text* 36 (Fall 1993): 40–80.

———. "Who (Ac)Counts and How." *MMLA* 27, no. 1 (spring 1994): 26–41.

Miller, Judith E. and Ronald D. Cheetham. "Teaching Freshmen to Think—Active Learning in Introductory Biology." *BioScience* 40, no. 5 (May 1990): 388–91.

Miller, Naomi. *Changing the Subject: Mary Wroth and Figurations of Gender in Early Modern England.* Lexington, Ky.: University Press of Kentucky, 1996.

————. *Reading Mary Wroth: Representing Alternatives in Early Modern England.* Knoxville, Tenn.: University of Tennessee Press, 1991.

Mitchell, Patricia Turner. "Introduction." In *Cracking the Wall: Women in Higher Education Administration,* ed. Patricia Turner Mitchell, x–xi. Washington, D.C.: College and University Personnel Association, 1993.

Mooney, Carolyn J. "Dismissal 'for Cause' Can Be a Lengthy, Bitter Process." *Chronicle of Higher Education,* 7 December 1994, A17, A19–A20.

Nicklin, Julie L. " 'Completely Overhaul' Teacher-Education Programs by 2006 or Shut Them Down, a Blue-Ribbon Commission Demands." *Chronicle of Higher Education,* 20 September 1996, A12.

Noble, Barbara Presley. "Women Pay More for Success." *New York Times,* 4 July 1993, 25.

Orr, David W. "Educating for the Environment: Higher Education's Challenge of the Next Century." *Change,* May/June 1995, 43–46.

Pacheco, Manuel T. "Dear Colleague." Office of the President, University of Arizona, 3 March 1995, 1–3.

Park, Denise C. "Research on Aging Deserves Top Priority." *Chronicle of Higher Education,* 27 July 1994, A40.

Passell, Peter. "Asia's Path to More Equality and More Money for All." *New York Times,* 25 August 1996, sec. 4: 5.

Patai, Daphne. "Minority Status and the Stigma of 'Surplus Visibility.' " *Chronicle of Higher Education,* 30 October 1991, A52.

Paul, Annie Murphy. "At Home Abroad." *Yale Alumni Magazine,* February 1997, 38–43.

Poch, Robert K. *Academic Freedom in American Higher Education: Rights, Responsibilities, and Limitations.* ASHE-ERIC Higher Education Report no. 4. Washington, D.C.: George Washington University, School of Education and Human Development, 1993.

"Promotion and Tenure Criteria." College of Humanities, University of Arizona. Rev. May 1992.

"Quick Response to 60 Minutes." Office of the President, University of Arizona. n.d. 1–3.

Ratliff, Charles. "Did CBS Dupe Profs?" *Arizona Daily Wildcat,* 1 March 1995, 1, 6.

Reaching the Vision: Women in Arizona's Universities in the Year 2000. Phoenix, Ariz.: Summary Report of the Arizona Board of Regents' Commission on the Status of Women, 1991.

Rohter, Larry. "Women Gain Degrees, but Not Tenure." *New York Times,* 4 January 1987, sec. 4: 9.

Rosser, Sue V. *Female-Friendly Science: Applying Women's Studies Methods and Theories to Attract Students.* New York: Pergamon Press, 1990.

Ruether, Rosemary Radford. *Liberation Theology: Human Hope Confronts Christian History and American Power.* New York: Paulist Press, 1972.

Sandler, Bernice Resnick. *Women Faculty at Work in the Classroom, or, Why It Still Hurts to Be a Woman in Labor.* Washington, D.C.: Center for Women Policy Studies, 1993.

Schaberg, Jane. "The (A) Contribution of Feminist Scholarship to Historical Jesus

Research." Unpublished paper delivered to the Canadian Society of Biblical Studies, 1993 Historical Jesus Seminar, The Learneds, Ottawa, June 1993.

Schneider, Alison. "Graduate Students on 30 Campuses Rally for Unions and Better Wages." *Chronicle of Higher Education*, 7 March 1997, A13–A14.

———. "Proportion of Minority Professors Inches Up to About 10%." *Chronicle of Higher Education*, 20 June 1997, A12–A13.

Scott, Joan Wallach. "Defending the Tradition of Shared Governance." *Chronicle of Higher Education*, 9 August 1996, B1–B3.

Shea, Christopher. "Community College Will Schedule Its Classes 24 Hours a Day." *Chronicle of Higher Education*, 26 October 1994, A44.

Slaughter, Sheila. "Academic Freedom at the End of the Century: Professional Labor, Gender, and Professionalization." In *Higher Education in American Society*, ed. Philip G. Altbach, Robert O. Berdahl, and Patricia J. Gumport, 3d ed., 73–100. Amherst, N.Y.: Prometheus Books, 1994.

———. "Retrenchment in the 1980s: The Politics of Prestige and Gender." *Journal of Higher Education* 64, no. 3 (May/June 1993): 250–82.

Smith, Karen L. "Collaborative and Interactive Writing for Increasing Communication Skills." *Hispania* 73 (1993): 77–87.

Smith, Karen L. and Barbara Hoffman Maginnis. "Computer Conferencing." In *Encyclopedia of Computer Science and Technology*, ed. Allen Kent and James G. Williams, vol. 26, suppl. 11, 101–20. New York: Marcel Dekker, 1992.

Snyder, Thomas D. and Charlene M. Hoffman. *Digest of Education Statistics 1994*. Washington, D.C.: U.S. Department of Education, Office of Educational Research and Improvement, 1994.

Stack, Carol B. "The Kindred of Viola Jackson: Residence and Family Organization of an Urban Black American Family." In *A Heritage of Her Own: Toward a New Social History of American Women*, ed. Nancy F. Cott and Elizabeth H. Pleck, 542–54. New York: Simon and Schuster/Touchstone, 1979.

"State of the Children." *The Nation*, 17 June 1996, 7.

Sterngold, James. "The Budget Knife Boomerangs Home." *New York Times*, 30 July 1995, sec. 4: 3.

"Students without Desks." *New York Times*, 5 February 1995, sec. 4: 16.

"Surprise!: Survey Shows Most Faculty Are White Males." *About Women on Campus* 4, no. 2 (spring 1995): 3.

Thurow, Lester C. "Companies Merge; Families Break Up." *New York Times*, 3 September 1995, sec. 4: 11.

Tobias, Sheila. "They're Not Dumb. They're Different." *Change*, July/August 1990, 11–30.

———. *They're Not Dumb, They're Different: Stalking the Second Tier*. Tucson, Ariz.: Research Corporation, 1990.

Tomasky, Michael. "Waltzing with Sweeney: Is the Academic Left Ready to Join the AFL-CIO?" *Lingua Franca*, February 1997, 40–47.

Wagner, Jane. *The Search for Signs of Intelligent Life*. New York: Harper and Row, 1986.

Weiner, Emily. "Reflections of an On-Line Graduate." *New York Times*, 4 August 1996, sec. 4A: 42.

"Who Got Doctorates from U.S. Universities." *Chronicle of Higher Education*, 8 December 1995, A18.

Will, George F. "Liberal Fads Bad for Kids' Prose." *Arizona Daily Star*, 3 July 1995, A13.

Williams, Jeffrey, ed. *P.C. Wars: Politics and Theory in the Academy.* New York: Routledge, 1995.

Wilson, John K. "The Academy Speaks Back." *Democratic Culture* 4, no. 1 (spring 1995): 29–30.

———. *The Myth of Political Correctness.* Durham, N.C.: Duke University Press, 1995.

Wilson, Robin. "A Report Praises 29 Colleges for 'Family Friendly' Policies." *Chronicle of Higher Education*, 11 October 1996, A13–A15.

———. "A Scholar's Conclusion about Mary Stirs Ire." *Chronicle of Higher Education*, 6 October 1993, A7.

———. "Colleges Help Professors Balance Work and Family." *Chronicle of Higher Education*, 17 November 1995, A24.

———. "Hiring of Black Scholars Stalls at Some Major Universities." *Chronicle of Higher Education*, 2 June 1995, A16.

"Women Faculty—This is Progress?" *About Women on Campus* 4, no. 4 (fall 1995): 1–2.

Index

Page references followed by "q" refer to quoted material, while page references followed by "n." or "nn." refer to material in endnotes.

Annette Kolodny was Dean of the College of Humanities
at the University of Arizona from 1988 to 1993. She is
currently Professor of Comparative Cultural and Literary
Studies at the University of Arizona in Tucson. Before
becoming Dean, Kolodny taught at Yale University, the
University of British Columbia, the University of New
Hampshire, the University of Maryland, and Rensselaer
Polytechnic Institute. She is the author of numerous
articles and two groundbreaking studies, *The Lay of the
Land: Metaphor as Experience and History in American
Life and Letters* and *The Land before Her: Fantasy and
Experience of the American Frontiers, 1630–1860*, which
helped to establish the field of feminist literary studies.

Library of Congress Cataloging-in-Publication Data
Kolodny, Annette.
Failing the future: a dean looks at higher education
in the twenty-first century / Annette Kolodny.
Includes bibliographical references and index.
ISBN 0-8223-2186-6 (cloth: alk. paper)
1. Education, Higher—Aims and objectives—United States.
2. Education, Higher—Social aspects—United States.
3. Education, Higher—United States—Administration.
I. Title.
LA227.4.K65   1998   378.73—dc21   97-37781 CIP